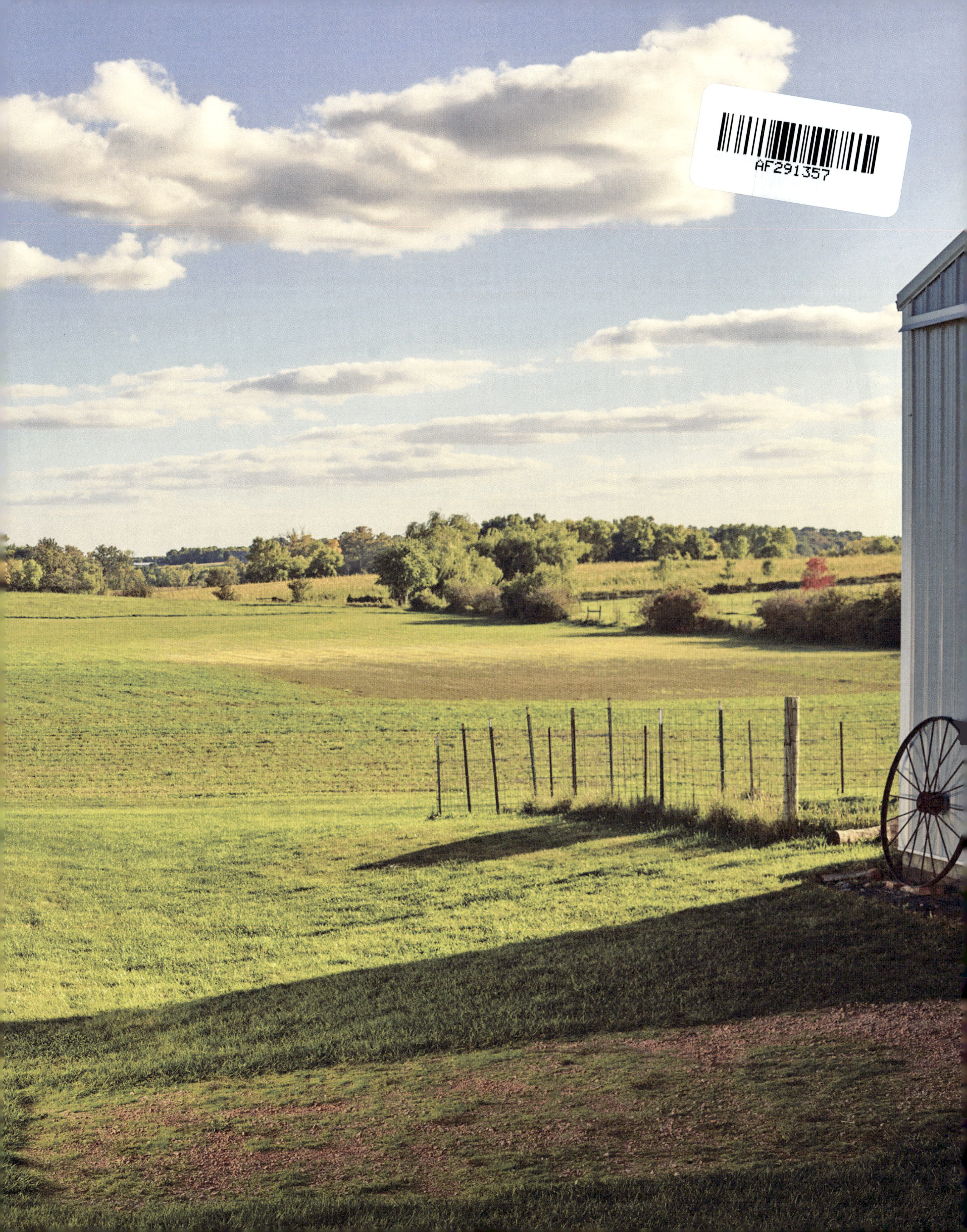
AF291357

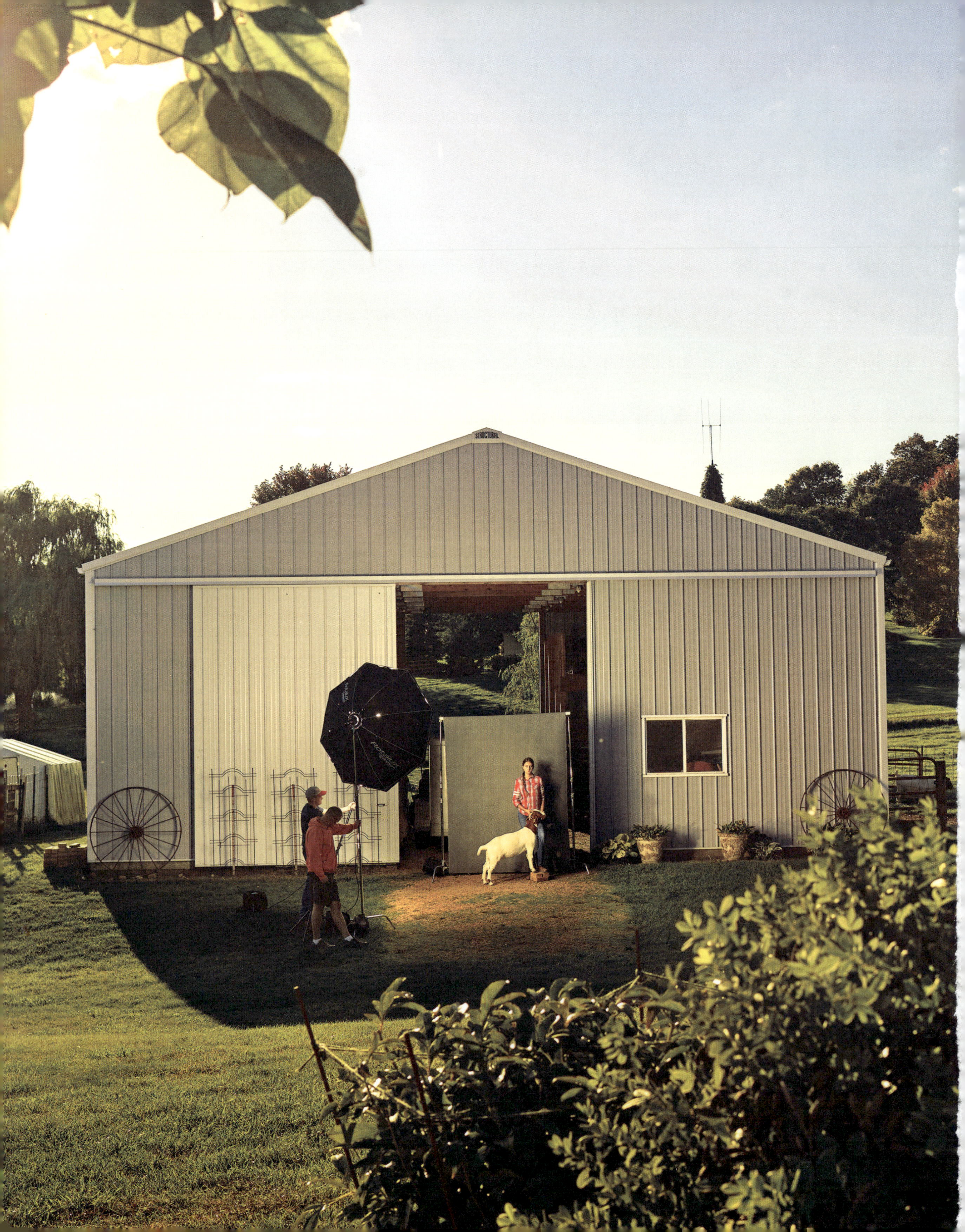

THE UNCHOSEN ONES

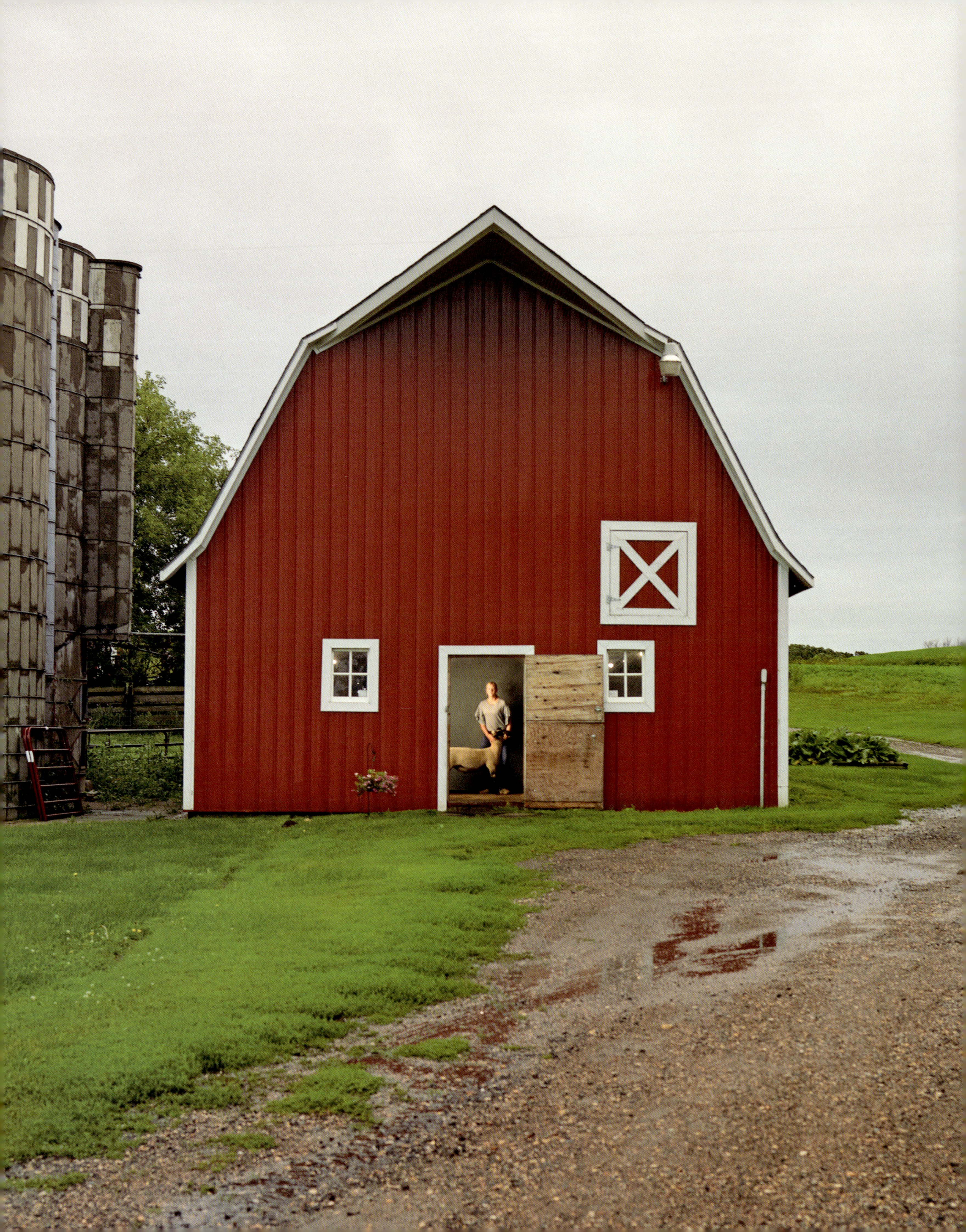

PHOTOGRAPHS BY R. J. KERN
ESSAY BY ALISON NORDSTRÖM

THE UNCHOSEN ONES

PORTRAITS OF AN AMERICAN PASTORAL

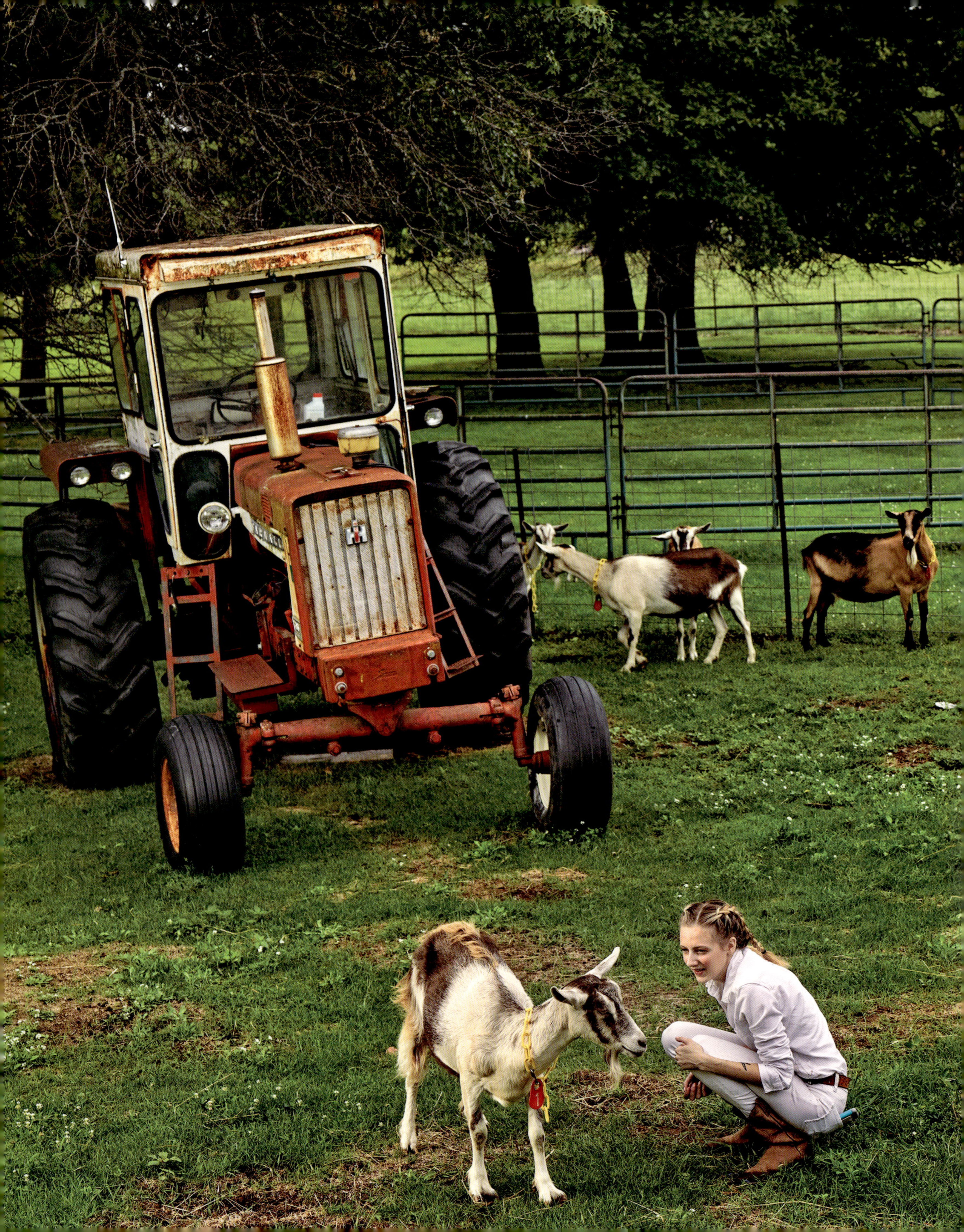

CONTENTS

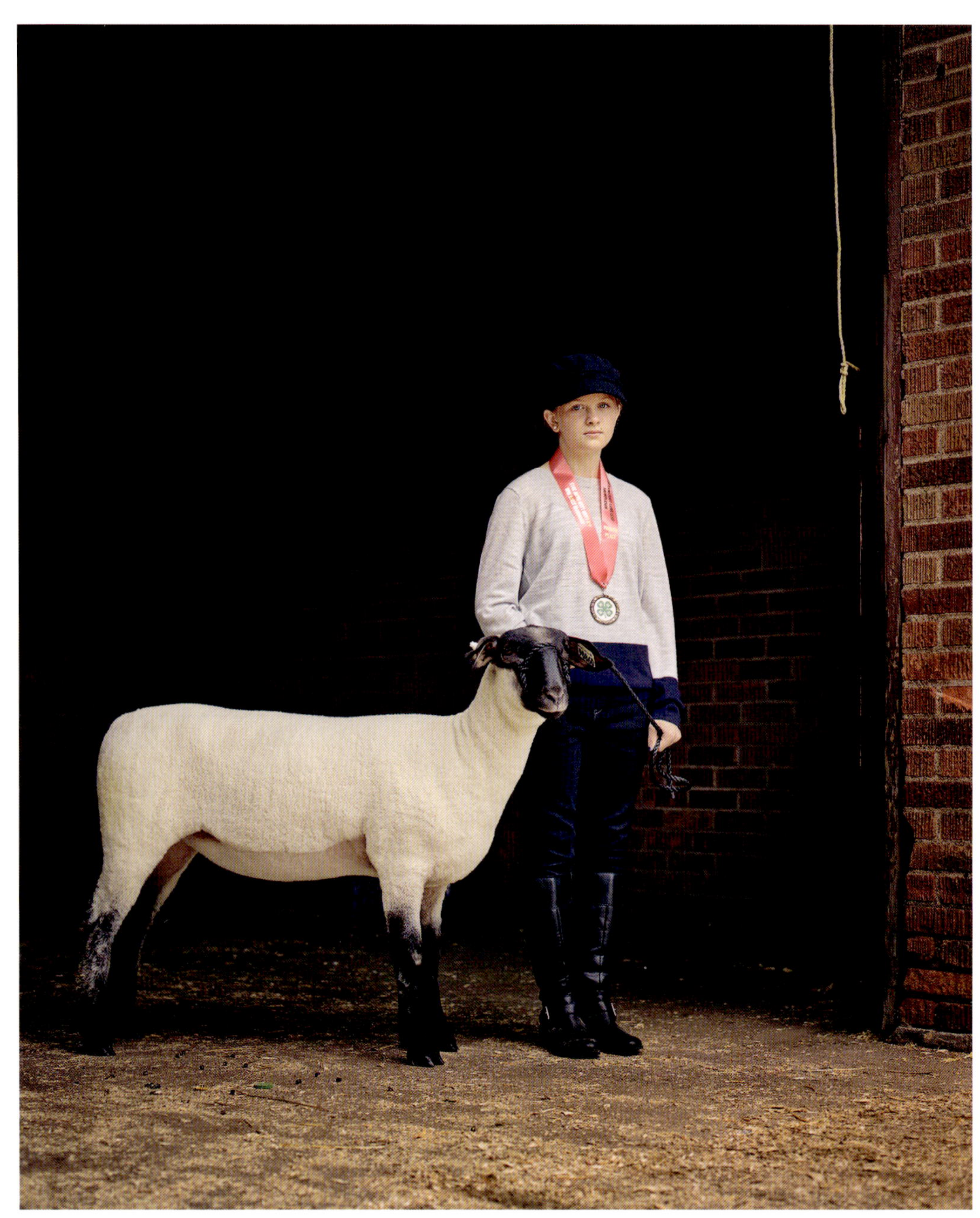

Josilin and Tantor, 2015

GREENER PASTURES

R. J. Kern

The Unchosen Ones began with a visit to a quintessentially American event, the state fair. I was in Minnesota, where I live, which still has a strong community of small family farms. My longstanding interest in animals and their connection to humans drew me to the 2015 Minnesota State Fair. For my previous project, *Divine Animals: The Bovidae*, I photographed goats and sheep in lush landscapes throughout Western Europe. I knew I wanted to continue photographing domesticated animals, but my ideas about a new series were still inchoate. As I was canvassing the fair looking for inspiration, I took in all the carefully tended-to animals and their owners, often young children. After the 4-H Lamb Lead show, I met the fourth-place finishers, Josilin, and her sheep, Tantor. I could see Josilin was disappointed, yet she held her head high. Her determination inspired me, and I made a portrait of them. Photographing the pair spurred me to think about my own childhood and its run-of-the-mill disappointments. I had a supportive family and a fulfilling childhood, yet I still vividly remember being picked last for the basketball team and not earning a ribbon at the local science fair, even though I had tried my best. As I grew older, I knew well the feeling of not being chosen—for a job, or for love. But not being chosen for something can have a valuable upside: it can create empathy. Empathy connects people and forges bonds. Later that year, I included the portrait in a Minnesota State Arts Board grant application, and that act would shape my artistic journey.

I continued to think about Josilin's resilience and wondered if I could make a series of portraits of the kids who didn't win first place, who weren't chosen despite all their hard work. In 2016, I photographed ten county fairs in Minnesota. County fairs are a little like beauty pageants for animals. The way humans have selectively bred goats and sheep has shaped the course of their evolution, and these fairs judge what are considered to be desirable qualities in farm animals. I wanted to somehow capture the competitiveness in maintaining or improving livestock lineage. In the movie *Talladega Nights*, Will Ferrell plays a race-car driver, who, as a boy, is counseled by his father (also a racer), "If you ain't first, you're last." That's the mindset at these fairs. Every owner wants a grand-champion animal, but most don't win. We all know what it feels like not to be chosen, whether for the prom, the basketball team, or a job. But what does it *look* like?

I watched judges line up the animals and rank them on the arena floor. The formality of the judging process contrasted with the hot, loud, smelly, messy barns. I could tell the kids were trying their best. While many of them had been practicing for months leading up to this moment, they seemed to channel their nervous energy into their stoic faces, showing confidence and poise. Often, the animals would cooperate with them, holding firm with a strong posture. Afterward, I would approach the handlers of the unchosen contestants to ask if I could create a portrait of them with their animals. The fresh manure and hay on the ground communicated the rawness of the setting (buzzing with flies!), but the studio-style backdrop lent sophistication. I asked each of the kids to imagine themselves as next year's champion. The change in their confidence was immediately reflected in their body language—shoulders pulled back, chins raised, eyes focused and serious.

I began to look for a certain typology: exemplary youth and animals from a small but geographically diverse area in Minnesota. I chose goats and sheep because they were competition animals that also fit within the constraints of the six-foot-wide backdrop I was using. The formality of the backdrop elevated the subjects and also allowed a story to emerge between the animal and the child. My strobe lights failed to flash during my initial session, so I used the diffuse, ambient light of the overcast skies. This serendipitous accident produced a soft tonality I loved: the light fell onto my dignified subject, rendering shadows as though from a painter's brush. I was drawn to this aesthetic.

Time passed and I worked on other projects, but a few years later, I revisited these kids. I was interested in how they had grown and changed, both physically and psychologically. How had not winning affected them in the long term, if at all? In 2020, I re-photographed more than fifty of the participants from 2016. I asked them what they had carried forward from their experience of losing the competition. What were their thoughts and their goals for the future? Did they see themselves making a life in agricultural America? What is changing in rural America? And, I asked myself, what is unchanged? What, if any, values are transmitted to my young subjects through breeding and caring for animals?

Their answers surprised me and contained a few unanticipated plot twists. One of them had landed in jail. Another had given birth—twice. Two had moved on to hockey. Another went on to earn a Grand Champion ribbon with the same animal the year after I photographed her and now dreams of becoming a veterinarian. As I explored these young people's doubts, fears, and frustrations, I was heartened to learn of their ability to overcome adversity and rise to a challenge, whether it was self-imposed or one that life threw at them.

In my own idealized world, I long for sweetness, something like heaven—a place filled with the innocence of childhood and the support of a strong community. A place that exists between the real and the imagined. As an outsider to daily agricultural life, I was influenced by preconceptions about that world. Working on *The Unchosen Ones* disrupted some of those notions. Living on a farm requires full-time commitment. It's not a petting zoo. There is always work to be done—a lot of it. Rivers flood. Crops rot. Animals get sick. I wanted my photographs to capture the ephemerality of youth amid the often harsh realities of rural life. Through this project I discovered a certain cultural geography of the pastoral and created a visual meditation on rural America.

Small agrarian communities in the U.S. are changing, often radically. The 360-acre family farm has grown to over 10,000 acres, which has had a huge impact on rural America, and county fairs are among the casualties. A few generations ago, every farm had livestock of various sorts and the competitions at fairs were fierce. Now, the same county fair might have only two entries for a competition.

The county fair isn't necessarily the highlight of a kid's summer the way it used to be. And yet, through their care of animals, the young people who invest their time in this endeavor express the values that have informed generations of children of the land. Although there is abundant evidence that this way of life is disappearing as kids leave the farm, the crisis of climate change and a concern for both sustainability and stewardship of the land point to a path for survival for these agricultural practices and traditions. I hope county fairs will still be around in a hundred years and that young people will still be learning the lessons that come from raising and showing animals—continuing the pastoral culture that they have inherited.

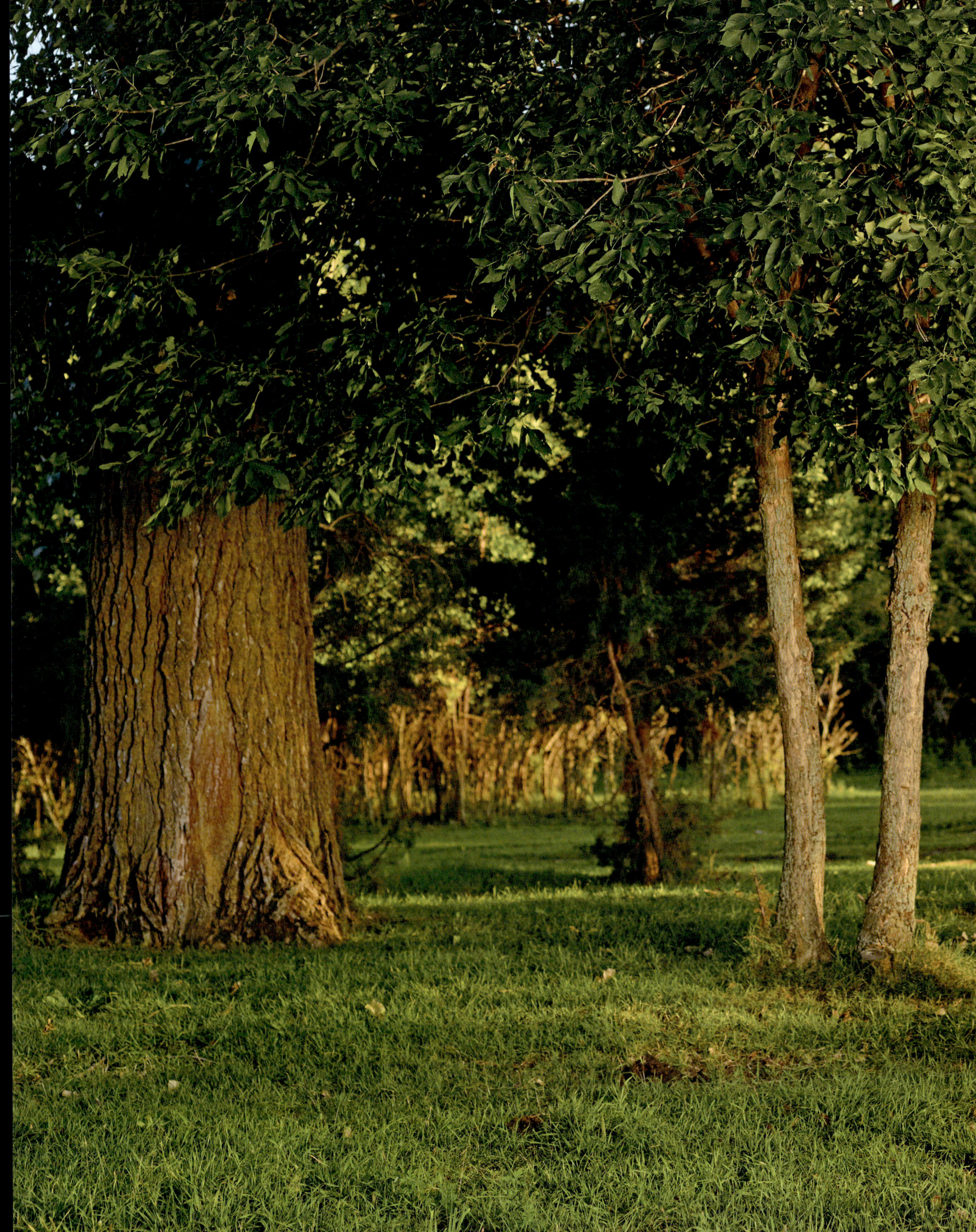

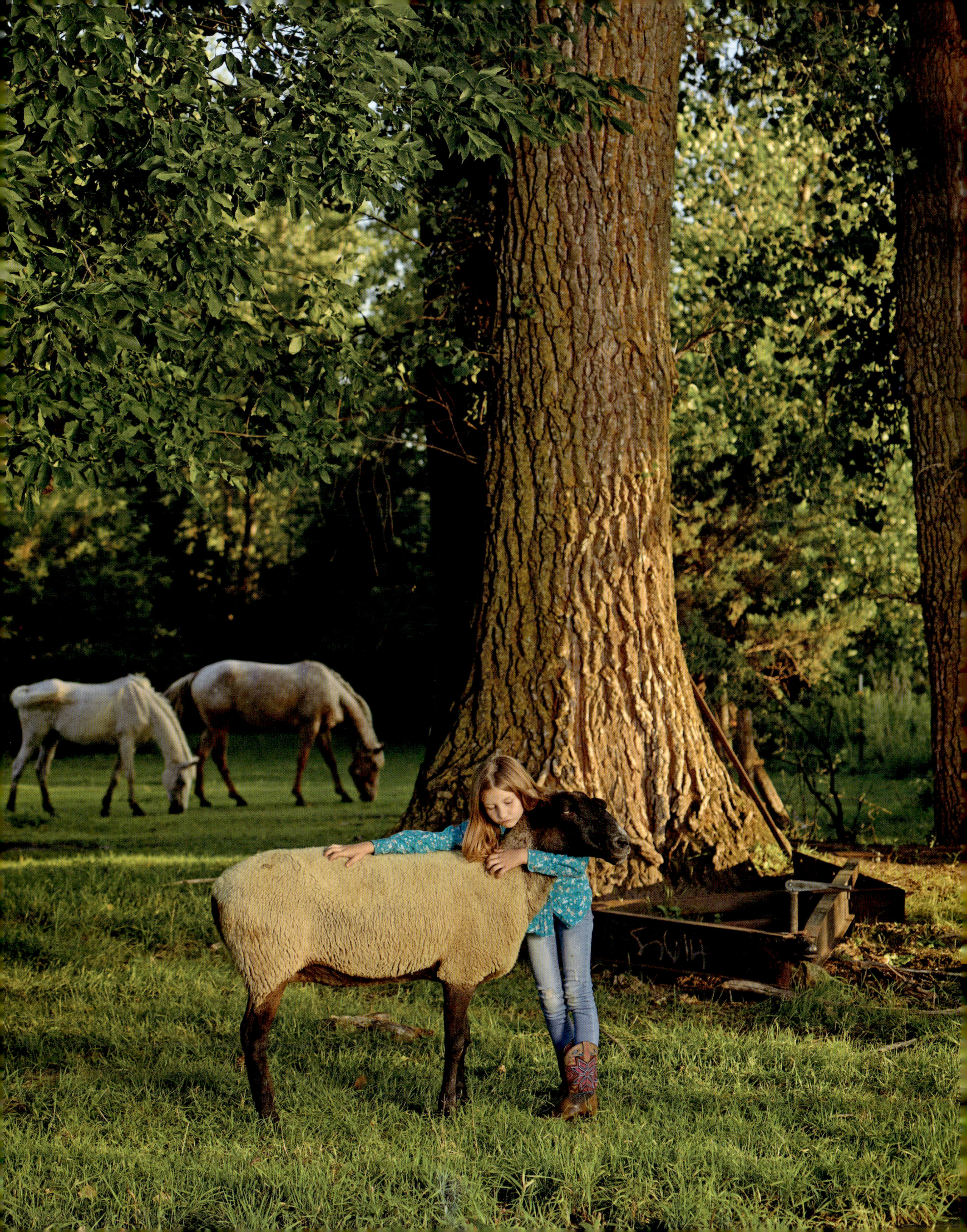

WHY PHOTOGRAPH ANIMALS?

Alison Nordström

In *The Unchosen Ones*, R.J. Kern has crafted a book of photographs that capture his knowledge of the American Midwest, his empathy for the lives of the young people who grow up there, and the multiple ways that portraiture can describe whole cultures. His photographs show how the connection between artist and subject can give rise to a powerful narrative. He began *The Unchosen Ones* as a study of children and the animals they care for, making images of competitors at Minnesota agricultural fairs. Over time, he grew to consider these young people, and their experiences of ambition and disappointment, as they themselves grew and changed—though their animals remain the markers of both rural life and coming of age. Four years later, he returned to a project that once felt finished, and in so doing, Kern has honored, humanized, and elaborated the realities of the people he has come to know.

We humans share the planet with a multitude of animals, connected by venerable, varied, and revealing relationships; we see this complexity confirmed when these connections are depicted photographically. When we photograph animals, we present and construct them in contradictory ways: they may be spectacle, entertainment, trophy, companion, commodity, enemy, pest, pet, worker, totem, symbol, or tomorrow's lunch, but they are always subjects of both the camera and the humans for whom the camera is a tool. Kern's earlier series of photographs shows us one way some humans may understand some animals—encompassing commodity, spectacle, trophy, and power, as well as responsibility—but they also show us a way of life that fuses the domestic and the mundane with, perhaps, a hint of nostalgia for a wholesome, rural America that is easy to think of as vanished in the present day. His work is about people and animals, but it is also very much about a world in which people and animals continue to coexist, and the ways a childhood experience may or may not shape a later life. It is also about photography itself, and, as such, shows us two different treatments of people and their cultures in special moments that are rarely dignified by the camera.

The first part of Kern's project resulted in a series of portraits of young people posing with the animals they had raised and groomed for entry into a best animal competition at a Minnesota county fair, with dreams of the glory of moving on to State Fair victory. No victory is shown in these images, however. These animals and their young owners were not deemed champions: they came in second or third or not at all. Here, on the sidelines of the main events, these disappointed children and their beloved animals enact a small backstory for the camera. Kern's vision transforms these fleeting moments of failure, loss, love, and hope into permanent images and a larger story. The power of these photographs, and their embodiment of youthful aspiration, make us wonder what came after the image was fixed by the camera. In some, Kern shows us idyllic natural settings where animals who have escaped the slaughter-house meander—a simple, happy ending subliminally underscored by an idealized landscape and romantic lighting. But it is his human subjects that he finds most compelling. By revisiting these children grown older, four years after his momentary encounter with them, he offers a much more complicated tale.

The first series demonstrates the value of a focused and clearly conceptualized photographic project, operating within a narrow range of time, formal considerations, and photographic tropes. Each portrait shows a child or, in a few cases, two children, standing with a sheep or a goat in front of a seamless backdrop of the portable sort often used by commercial photographers. The children—some as young as three, some teenagers, many wearing new-looking jeans and better shirts than they would usually wear for farm work—attest that this competition is a special occasion. The animals are equally well turned-out, and each is held still for the camera by a gesture that simultaneously restrains and communicates love and familiarity. The presence of the backdrop is made more significant by a composition that shows its edges and the indifferent environment around it, while the pose and awareness of the centered human subjects allude to almost every portrait ever made. We are reminded of the serious, self-important postures of the *carte-de-visite*, and of their subjects' knowing, collaborative gaze, which Roland Barthes would have characterized as affirming, "This will have been." We also make associations with the quasi-scientific studies of ethnographic types made in the nineteenth century, in which a bewildered, probably frightened, subject acquiesces to the lens and a neutral backdrop, as well as to the camera's voracious creation of evidence. In presenting us with unrelenting repetition of the intense moments experienced by these similarly posed children, Kern erases the specificity we expect from portraiture and introduces an archetype that, nevertheless, forces us to consider nuanced differences from image to image. We are struck by the emotions revealed in the human facial expressions we can study at leisure here. Some kids look stunned, others defiant. Some seem happy to be photographed. Some are elegant in their indifference. Some are stolid and accepting. Others look ready to cry.

The sequel to Kern's moving typology is more complex, both formally and in the way the images were realized. By diligently tracking down his former subjects and working with them to craft a pose that is as much their own as it is the image-maker's, Kern has produced pictures that show the children's shift in self-perception as they have matured. He also reveals much more of the worlds they inhabit. The earlier series presents almost passive subjects whose days were briefly interrupted by a stranger's invitation to stand in front of a backdrop. In the recent work, the children are active collaborators with the photographer, as Kern shares the power to shape an image. Under his guidance, these young people have chosen the props and settings that show what they value, or how they wish to see themselves, posing assertively with sports equipment, farm machinery, and, in one case, a bottle of cheap wine and a Metallica tank top. Animals may still appear, but they are as likely to be dogs or kittens as they are sheep and goats, and they are much less central to the photograph. The portable backdrop appears, but we often see much more of the environment around it; the children have literally and symbolically grown up and moved into the bigger world.

I keep returning to one particular image that may somehow serve as an explanatory bridge between the past and present bodies of work. It shows a landscape of curving meadow edged by trees, dominated by a massive eight-wheeler flatbed truck. The incongruous gray backdrop is tiny and distant within the scene, and it frames a boy, now grown so strong that he lifts his cow in his arms as he stands beside a large softbox light on a stand. This photograph of the boy is not unlike his picture of four years before, but Kern has stepped back. The presence of the tools of the studio reminds us that this image is a thoughtful construction. Rather than proposing a broad classification that smooths away aspects of individuality in favor of an emotional and even nostalgic universalism, Kern's more recent work singles out these children, now adolescents or young adults, and gives them agency in their own representation. The camera asks not "How do you feel at this moment?" but "Who do you think you have become?"

My personal experience does not include farm animals, livestock shows, or the culture of the rural Midwest, but I have no difficulty relating to this book. *The Unchosen Ones* stands as a document of these subjects, and of specific hot summer afternoons in Minnesota; I don't doubt that a hundred years from now, viewers of these photographs will marvel at their truth and greedily consume every fact and detail. This is what documentary photography is intended to do, but the best examples of it—as this work is—transcend the specificity of time and place. Kern has preserved decisive moments in photography that are also universal human moments. Youth is fleeting. Disappointment is inevitable. Kids grow up. Love endures. We carry on.

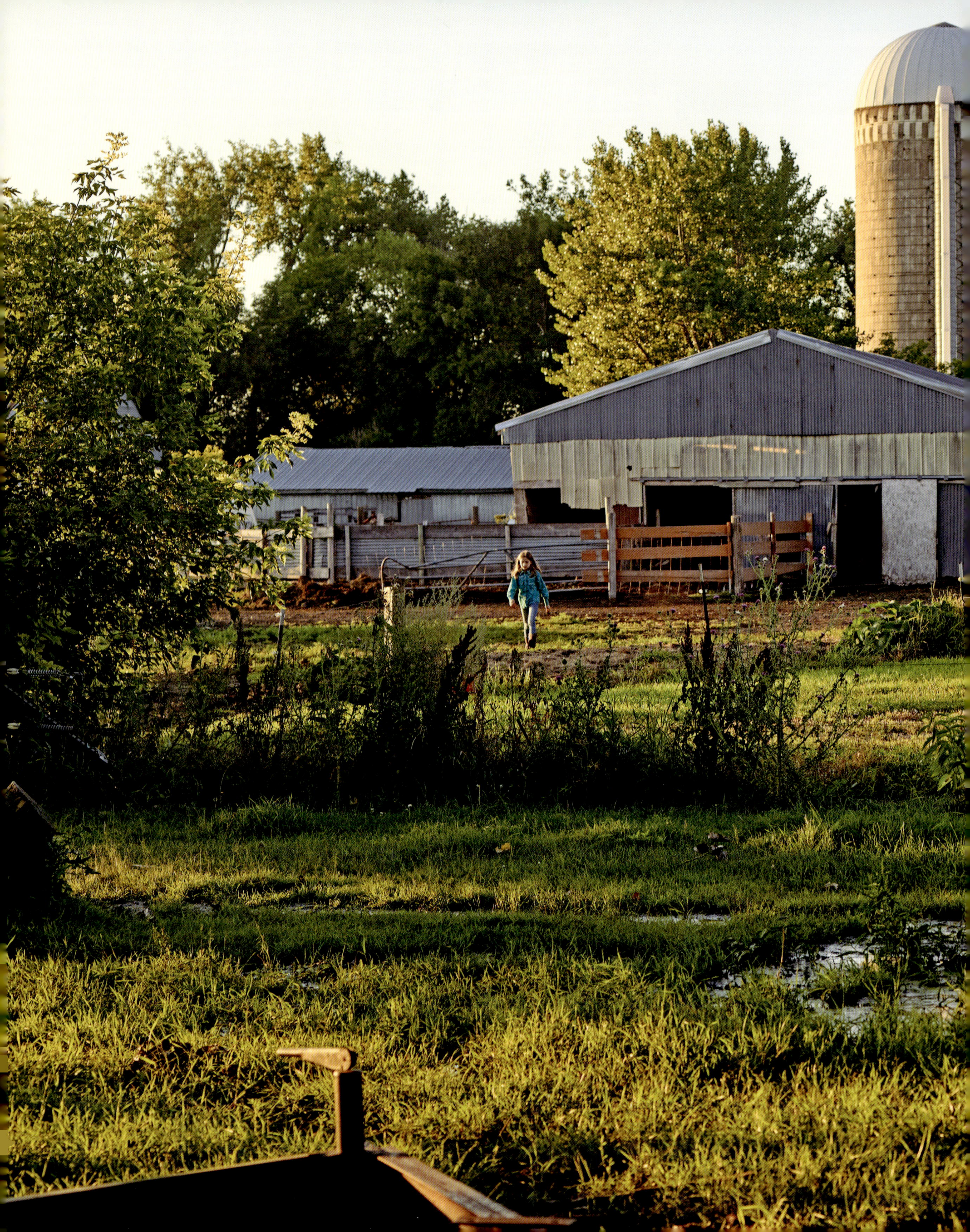

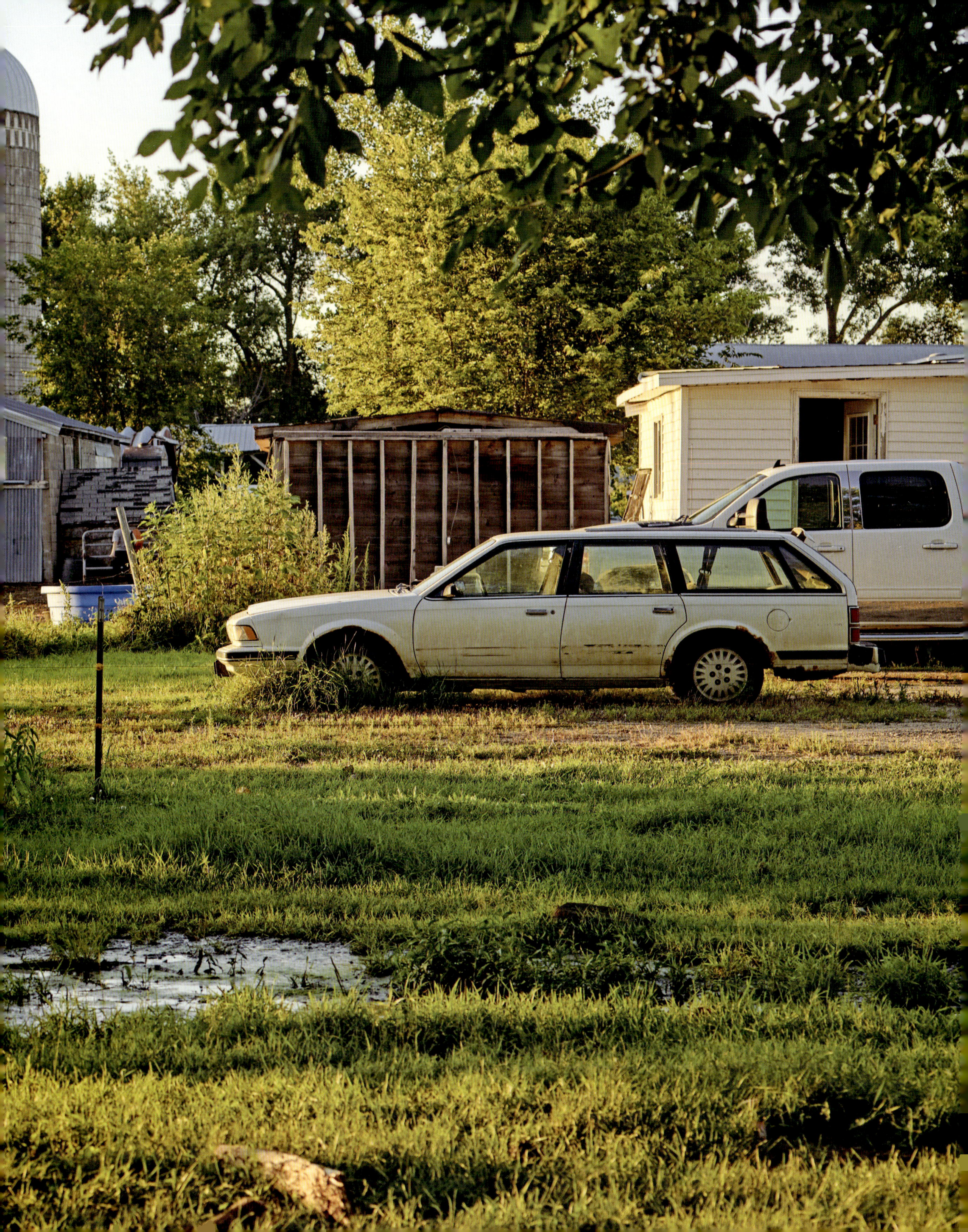

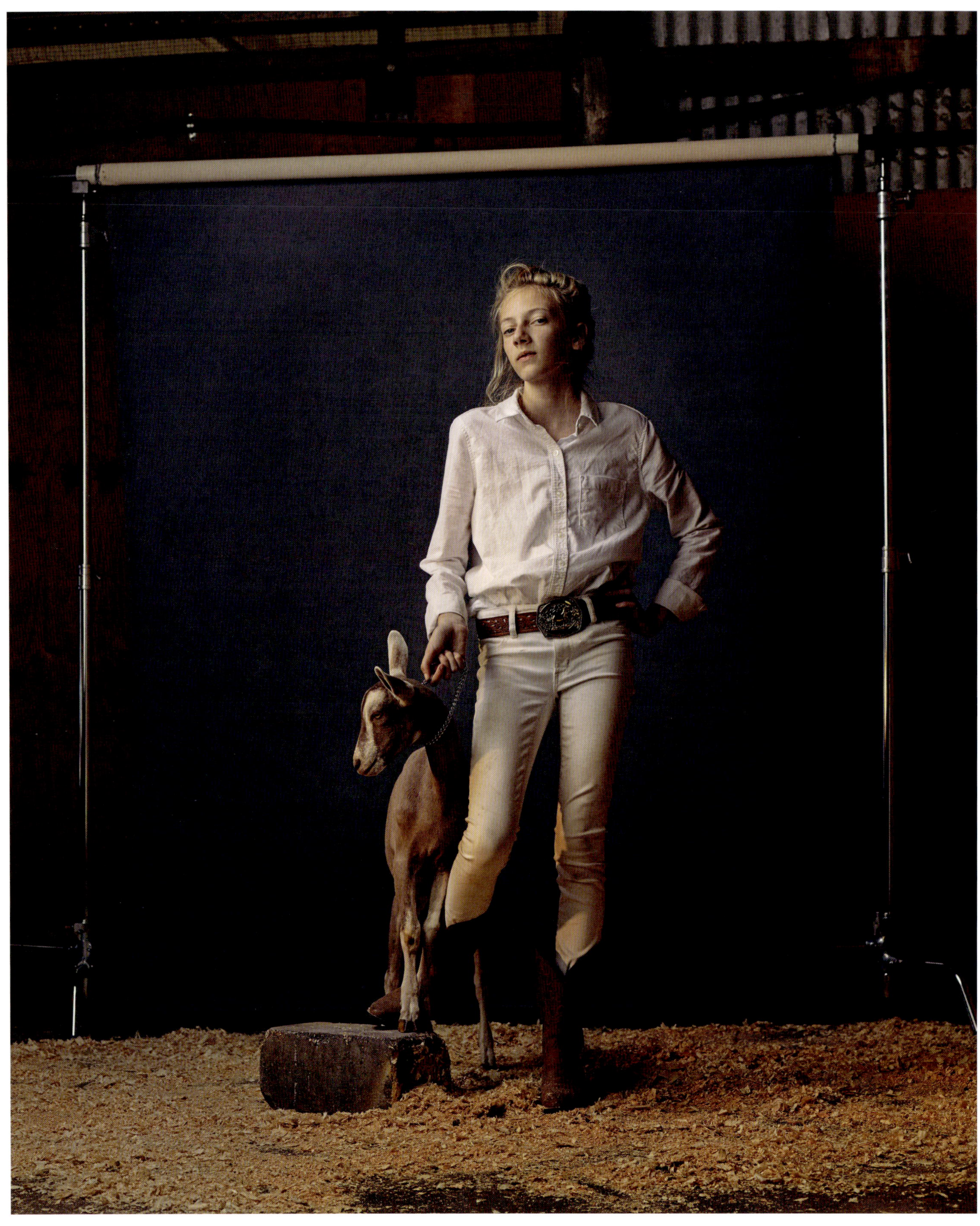

Kenzi and Hootie, 2016

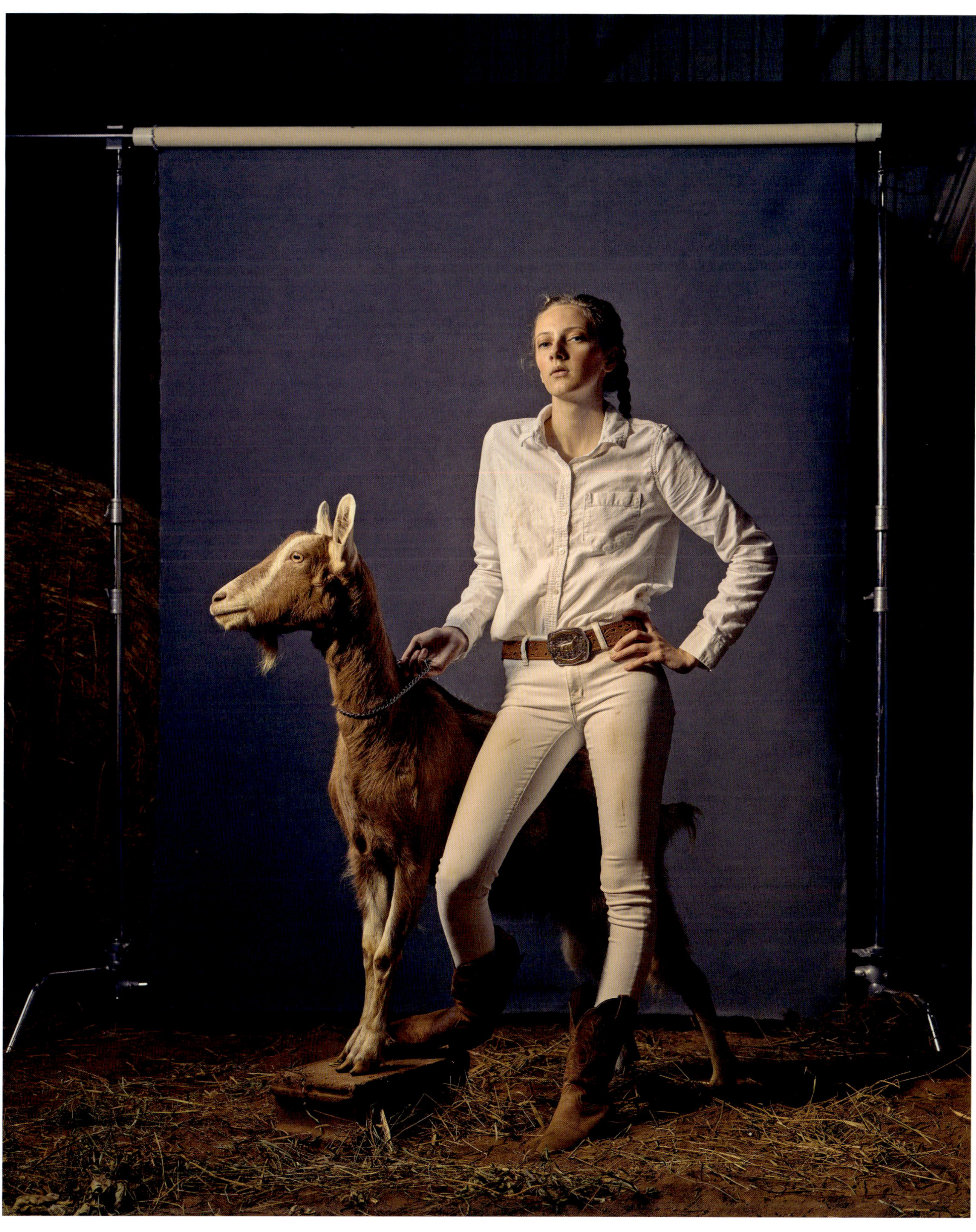

Kenzi and Hootie, 2020

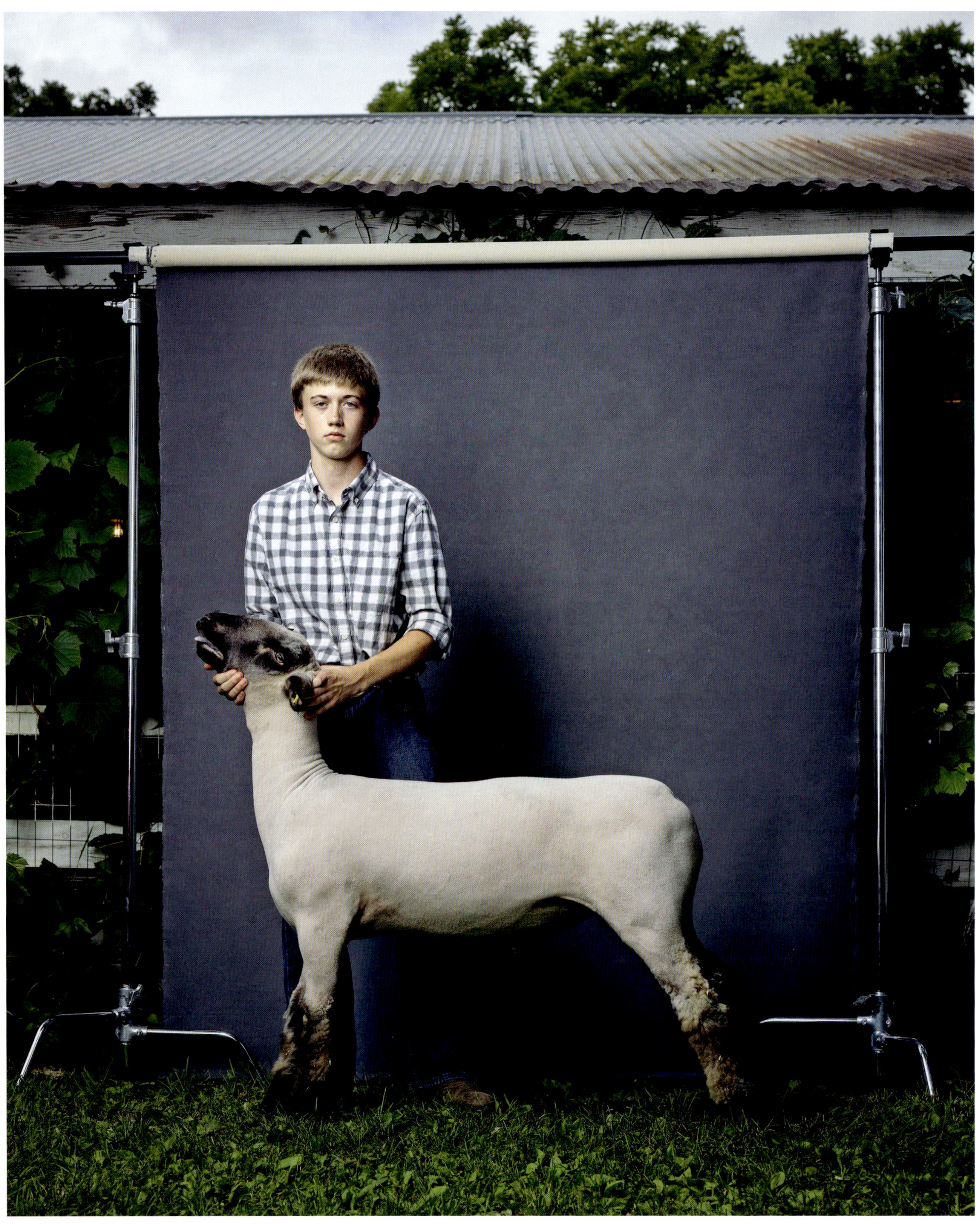

Gavin and Sheep, 2016

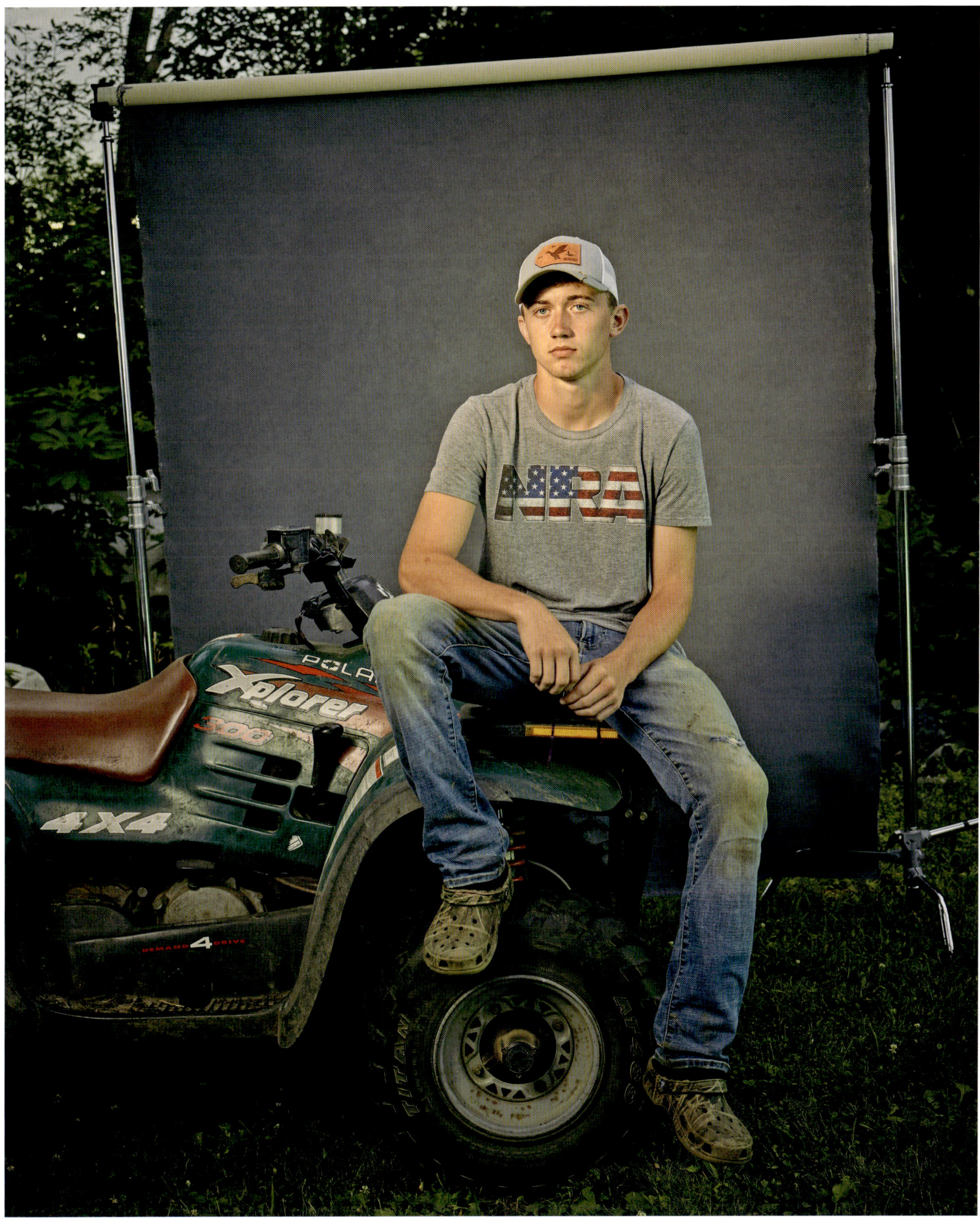

Gavin, 2020

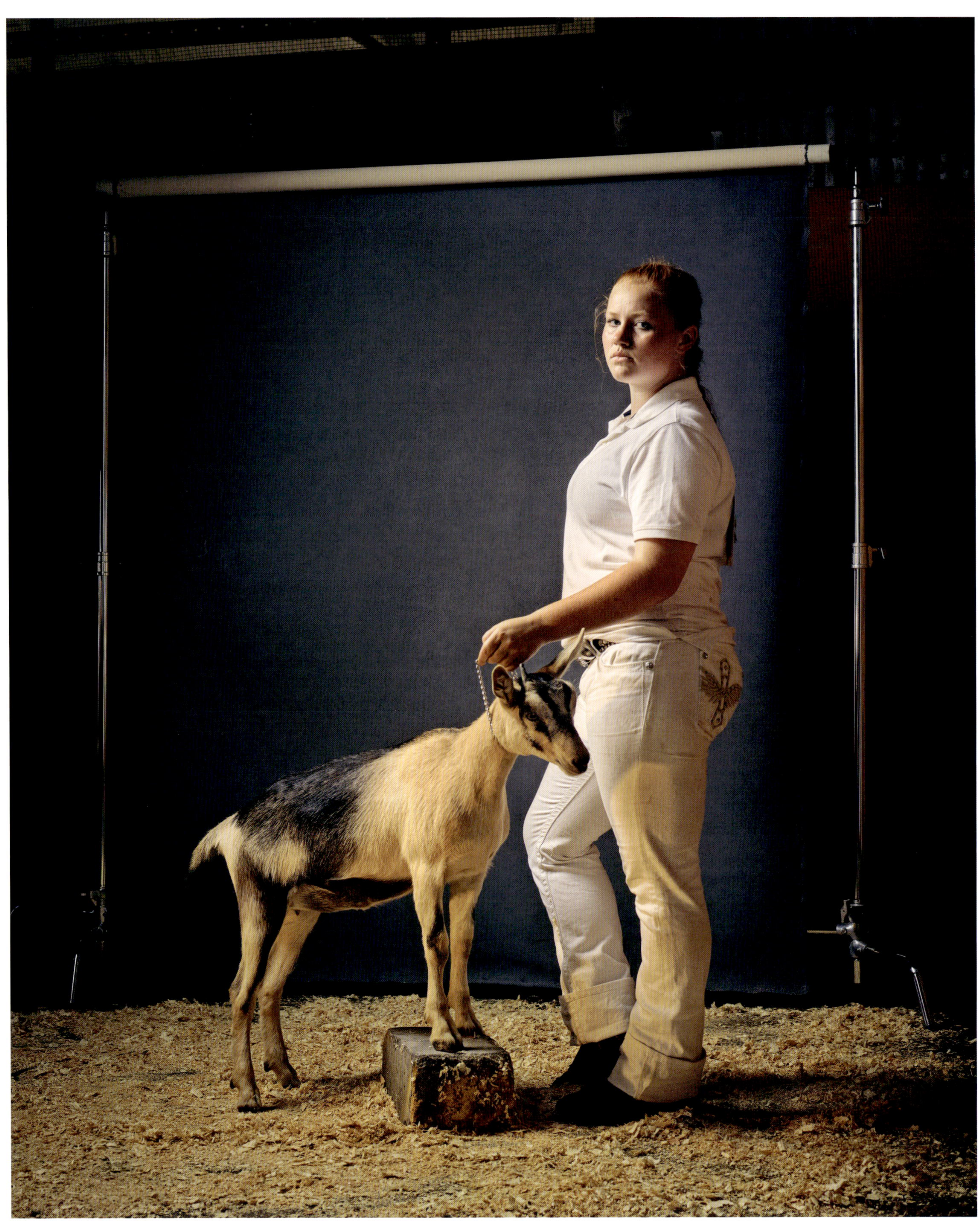

Stephanie and Honeyweiss, 2016

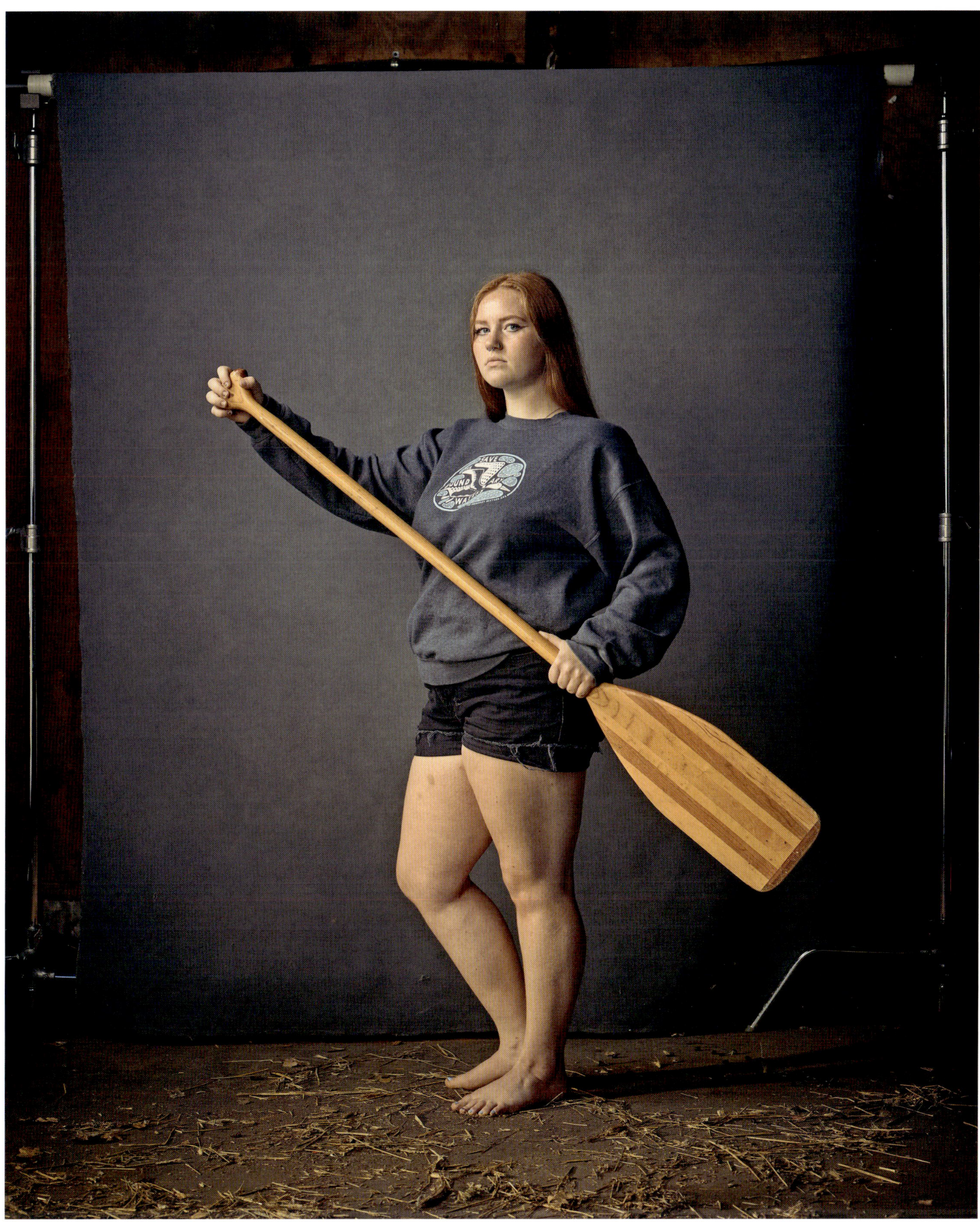

Stephanie, 2020

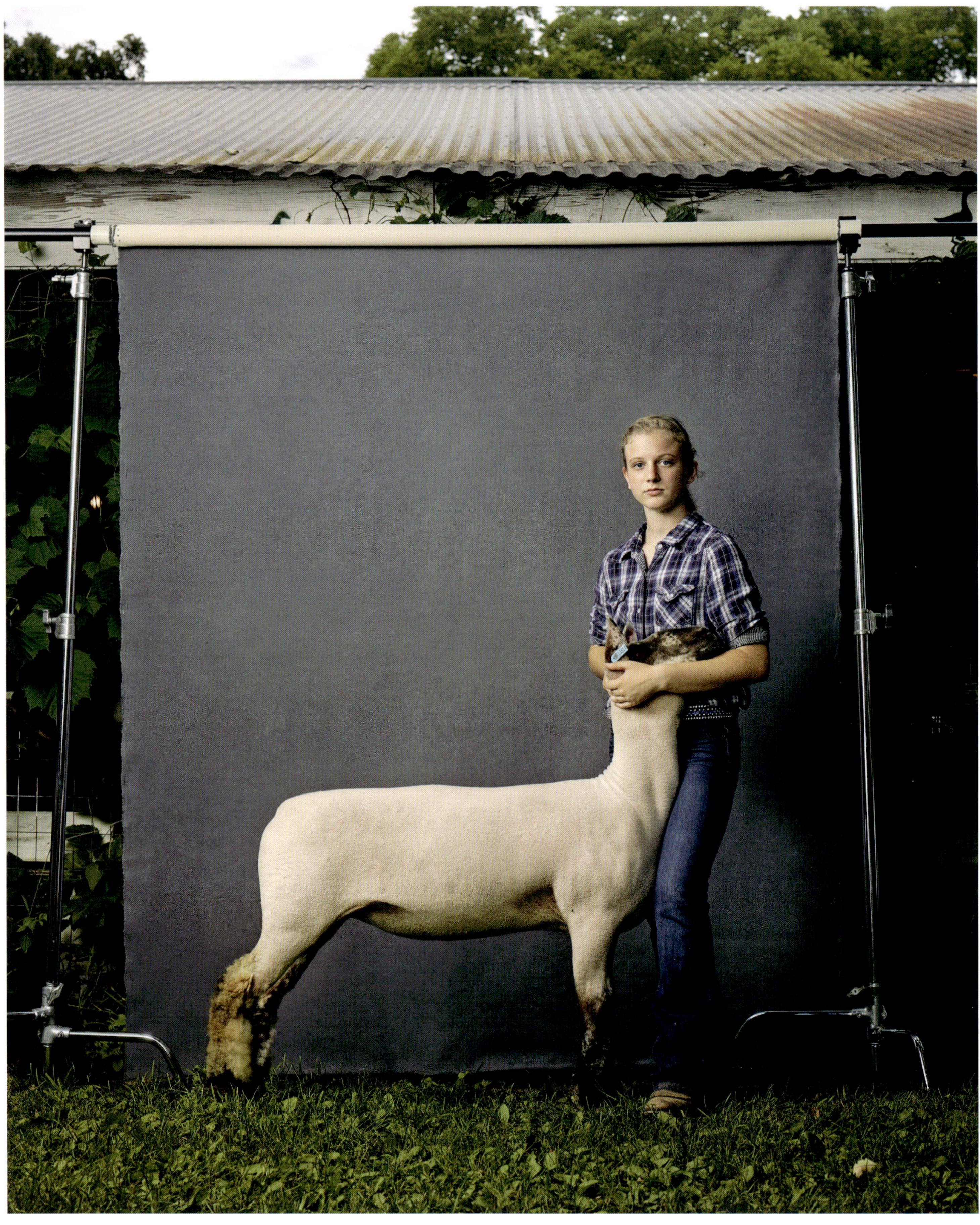

Taylor and Sheep, 2016

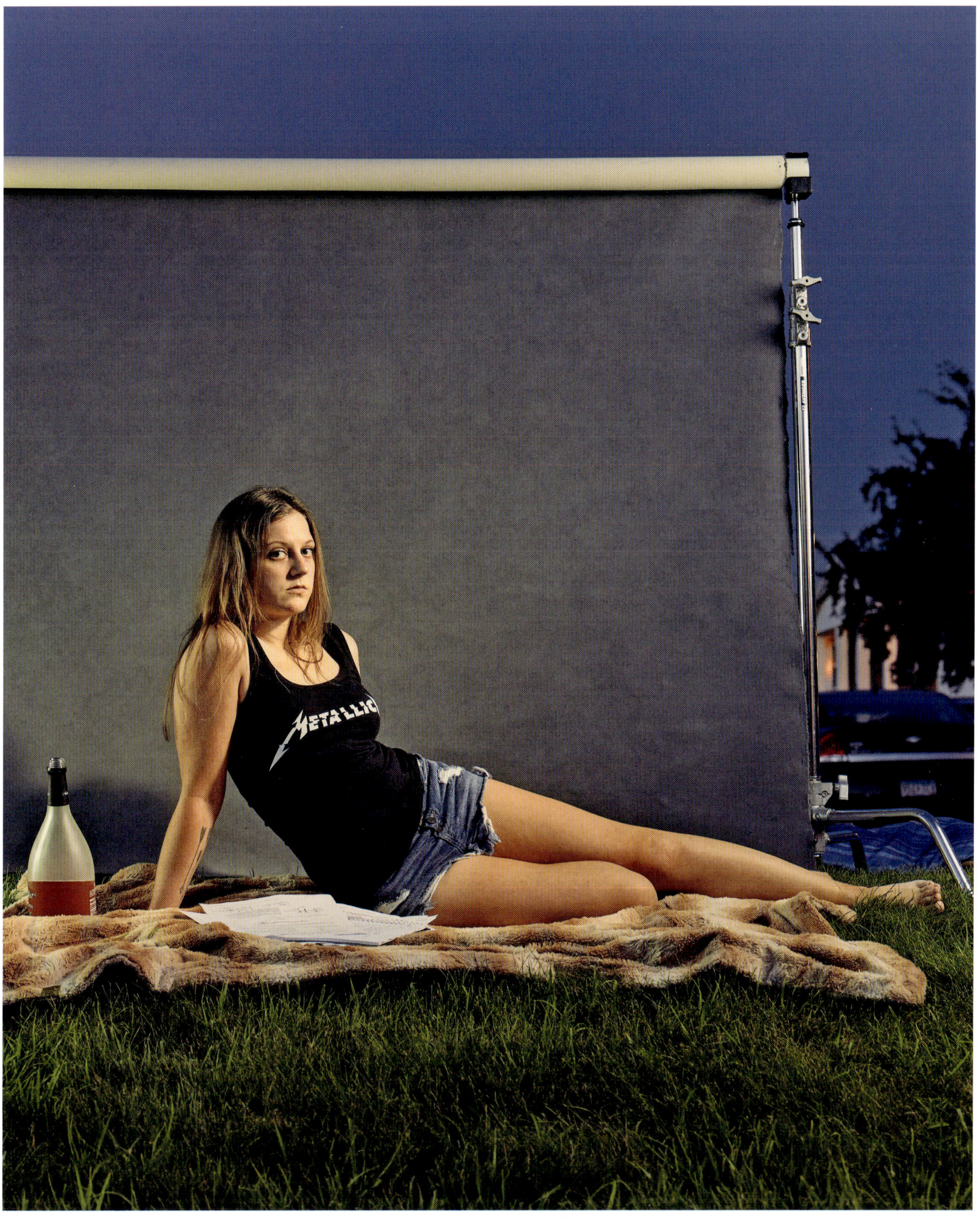

Taylor, 2020

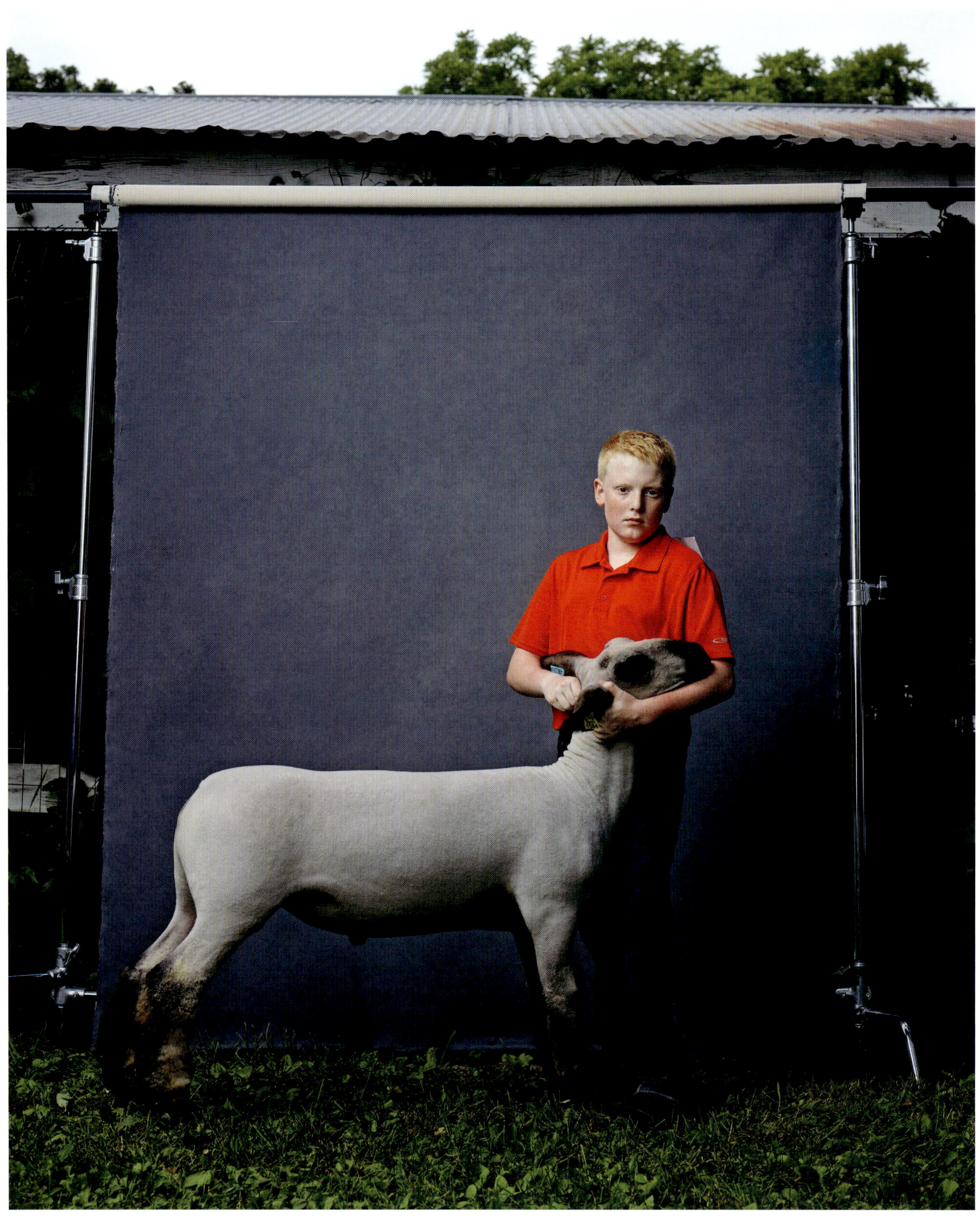

Cody and Gismo, 2016

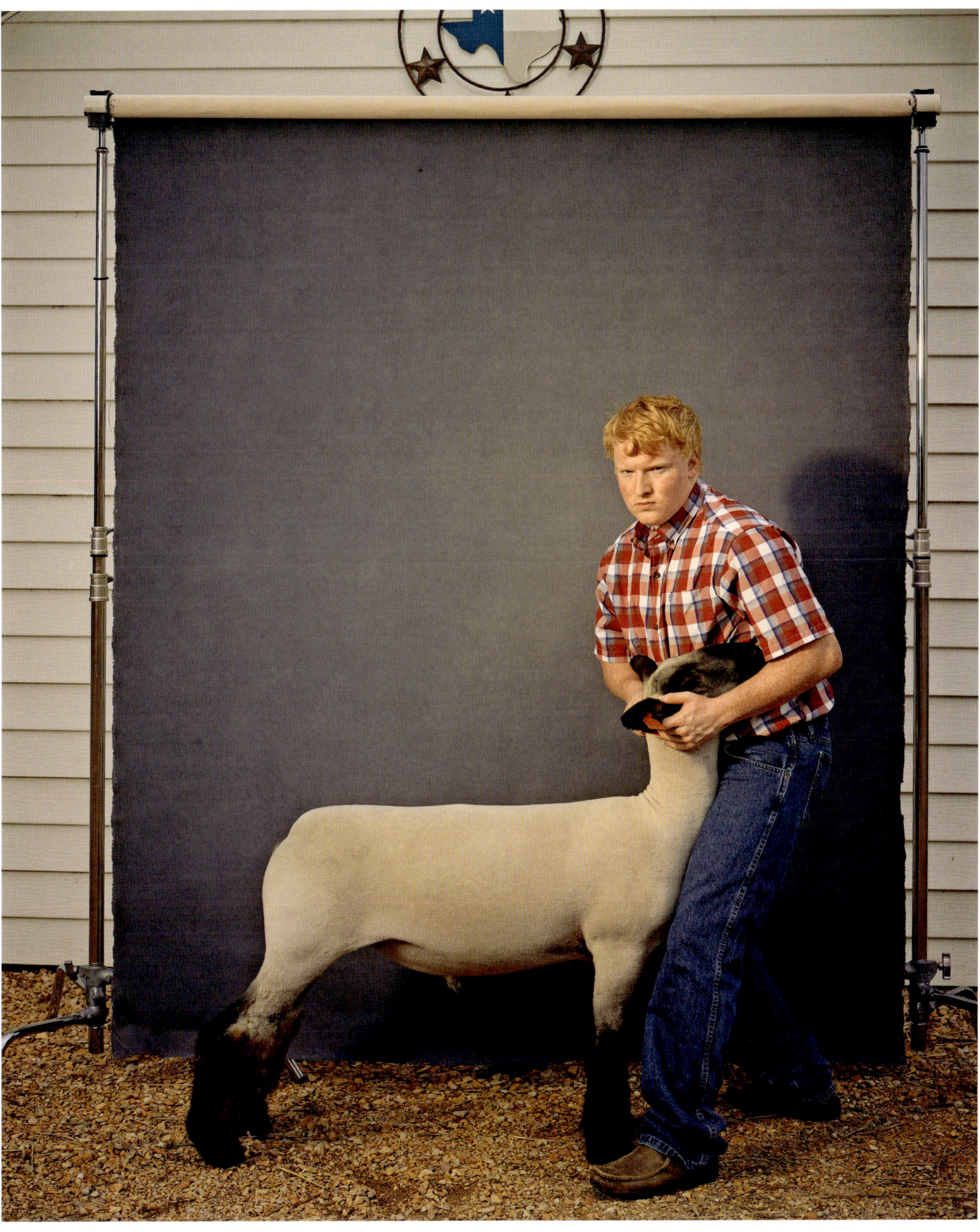

Cody and Rage, 2020

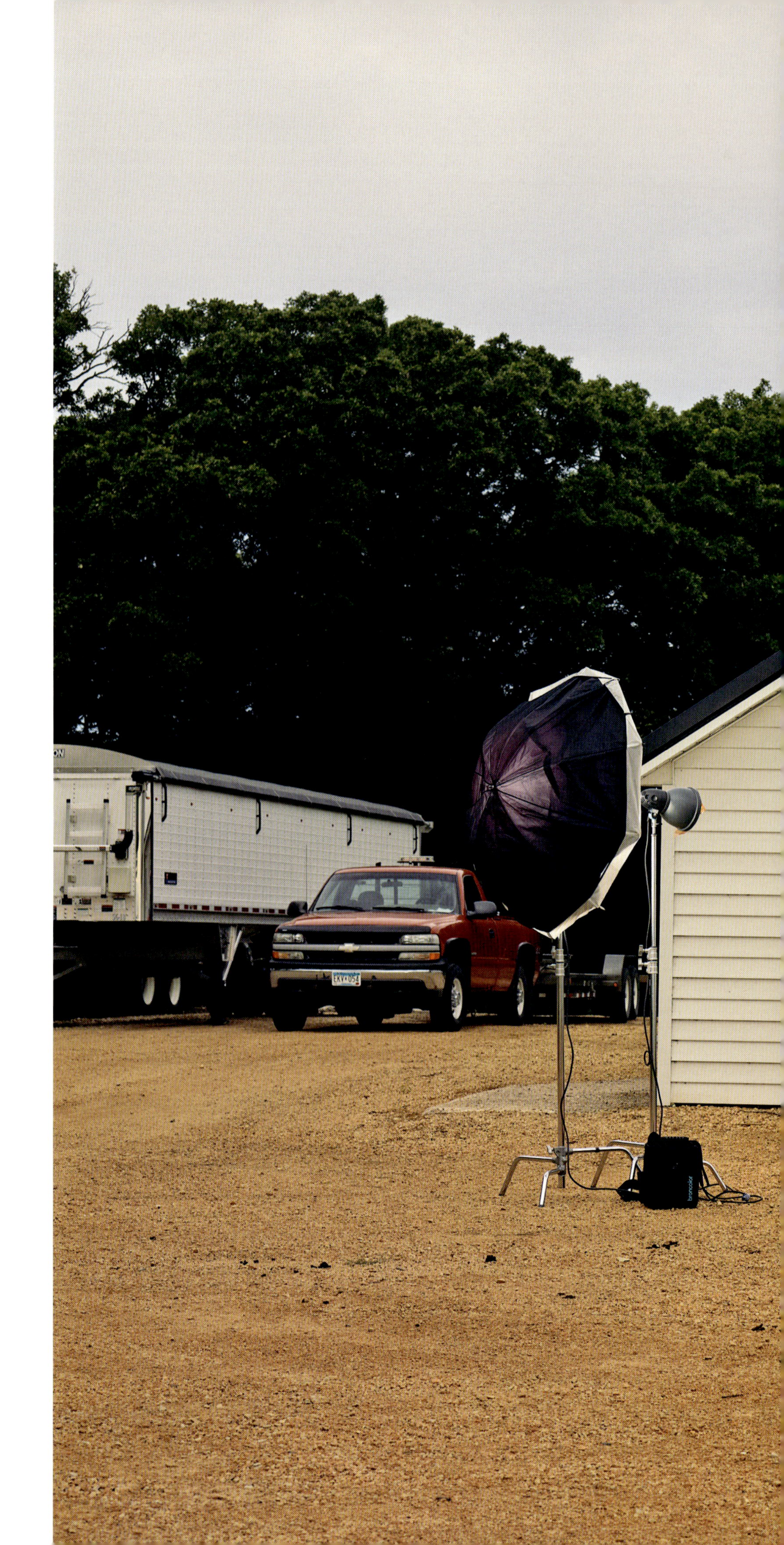

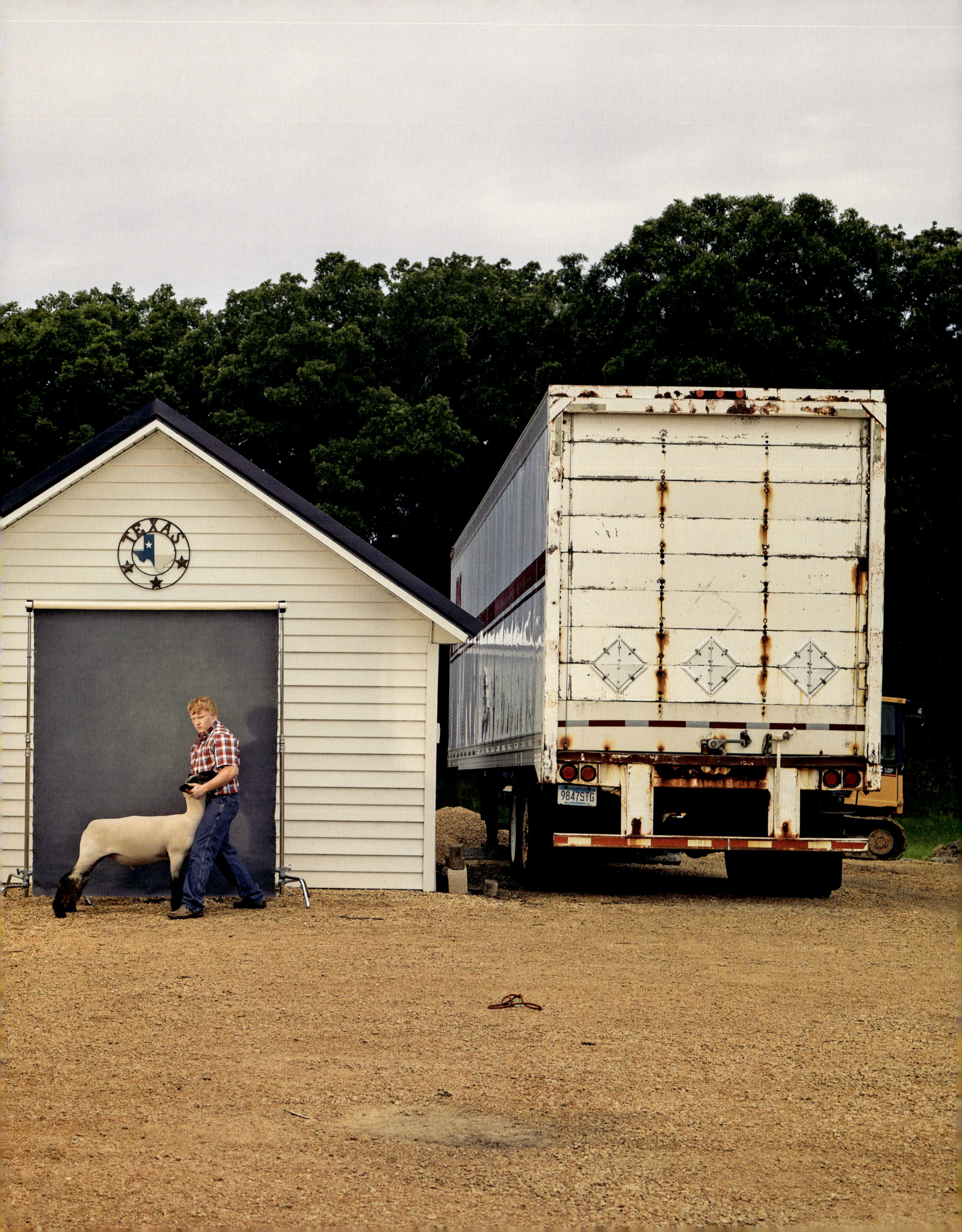
TEXAS
9847STG

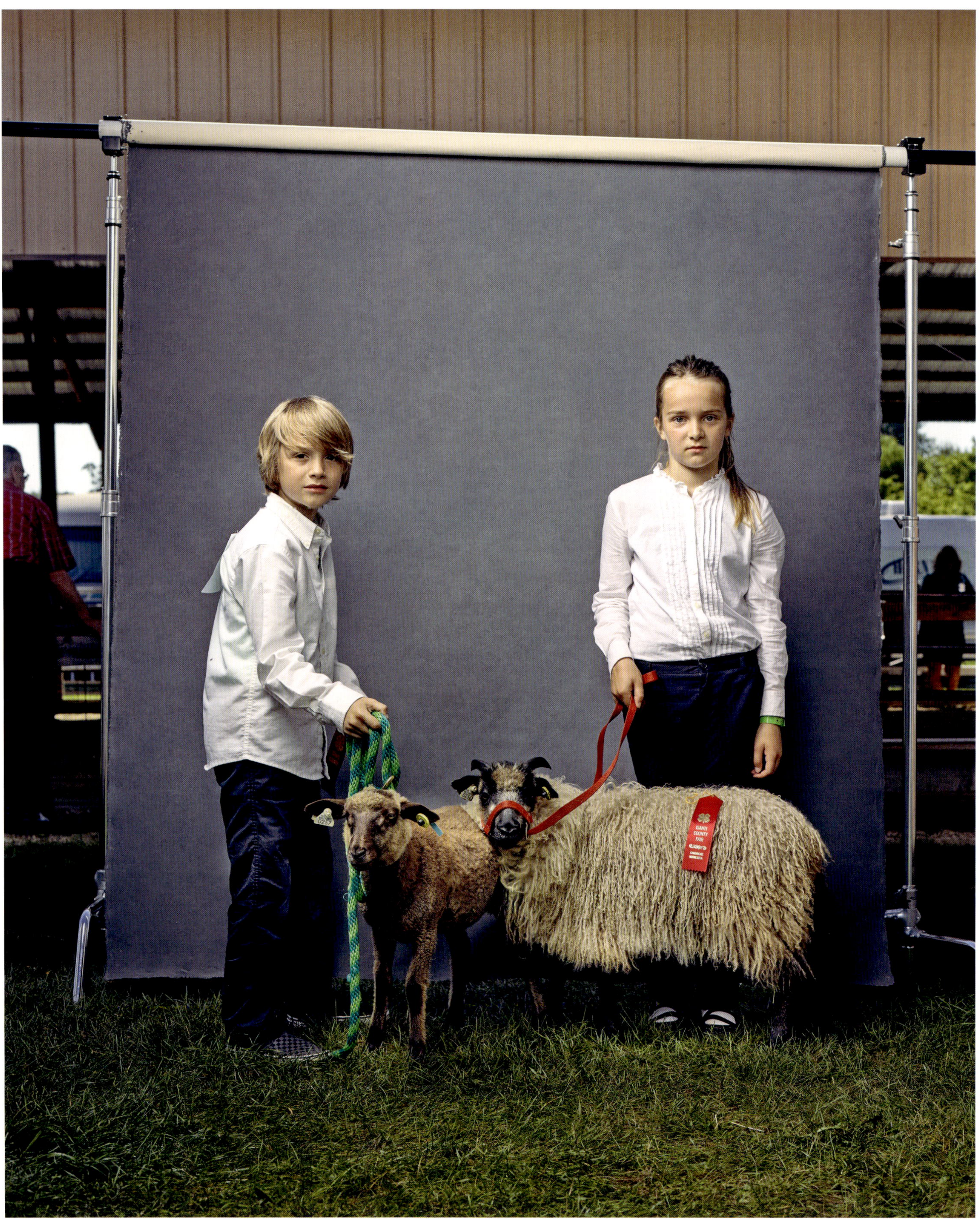

Jameson and Lola with Sophia and Lucy, 2016

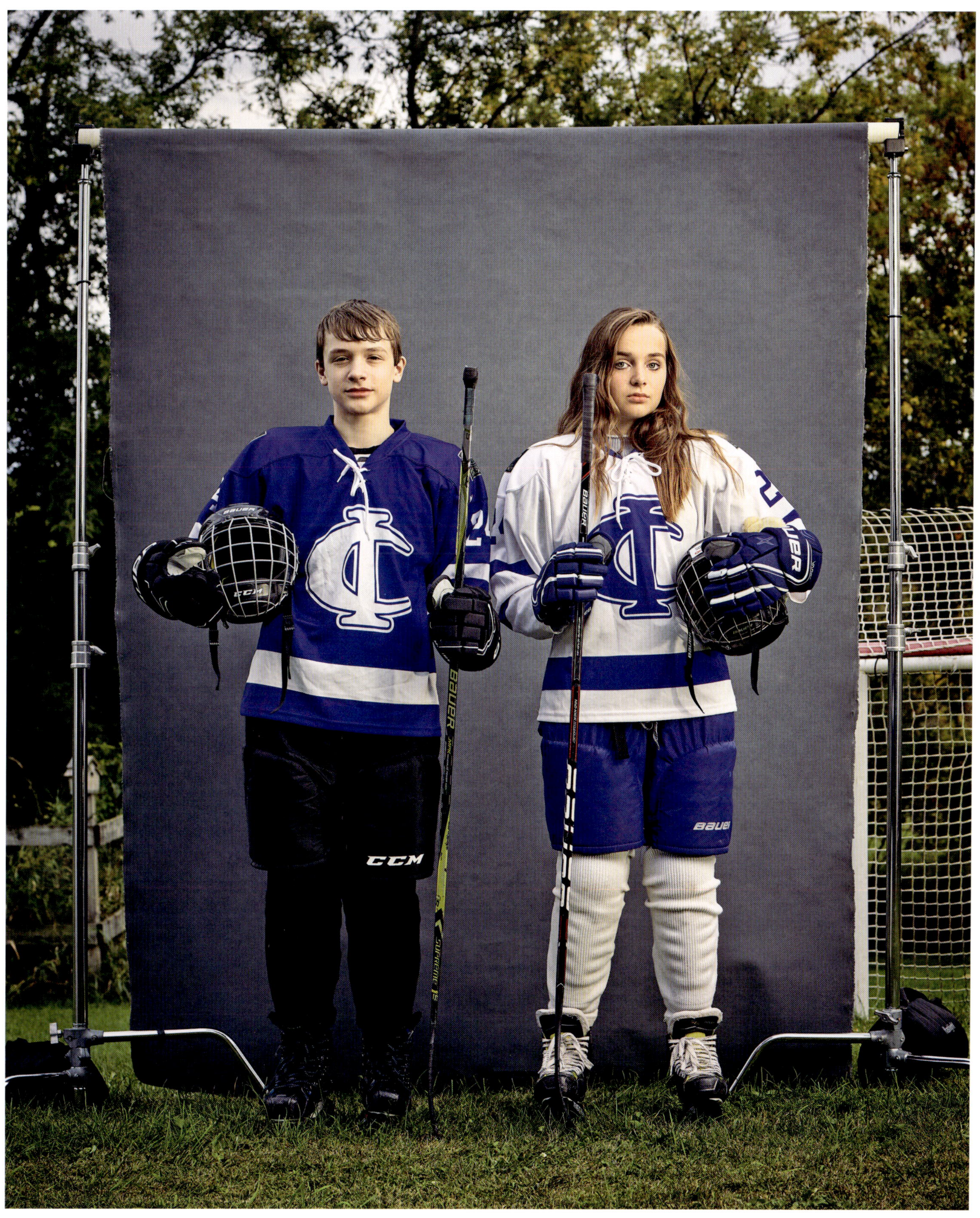

Jameson and Sophia, 2020

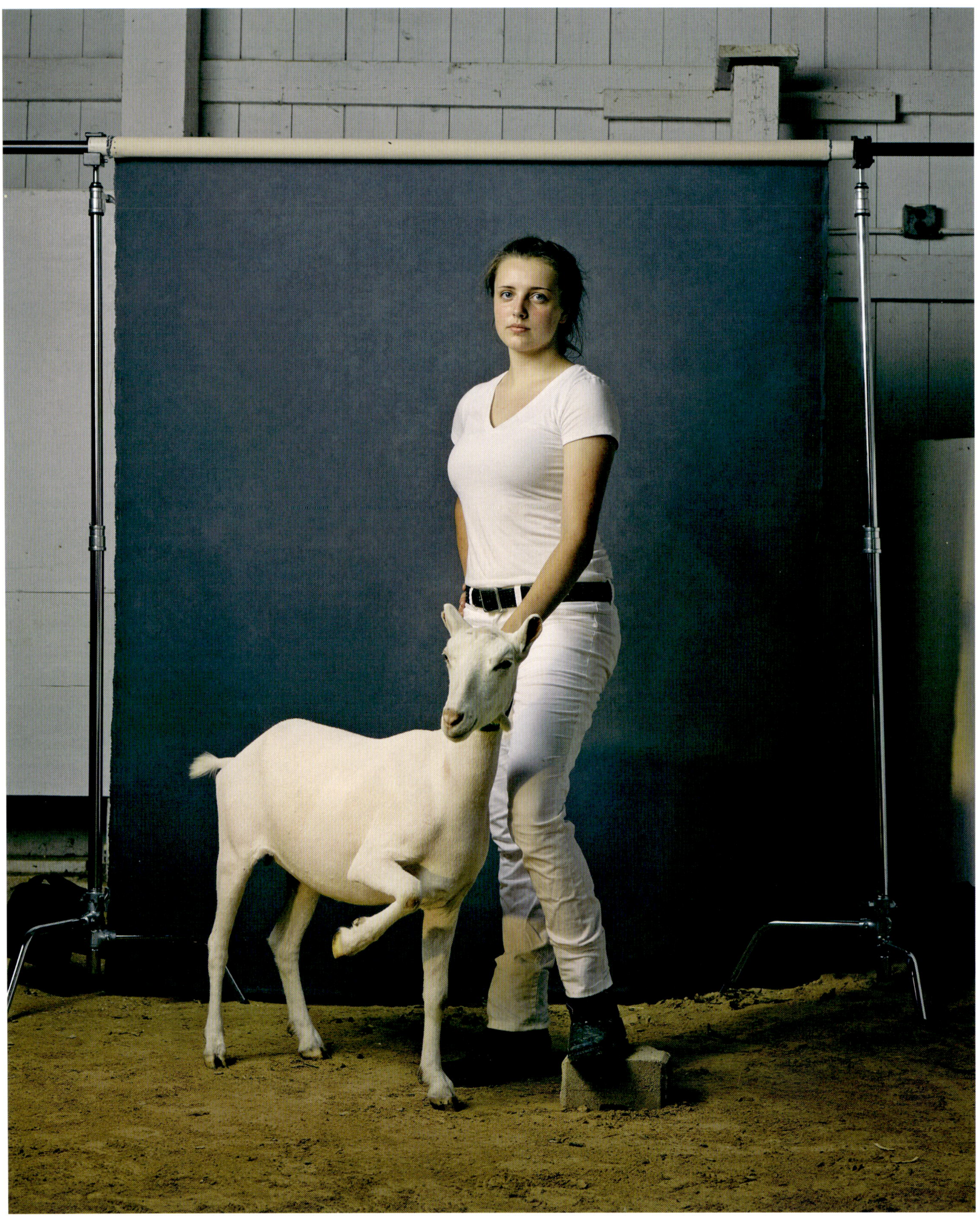

Abby and Goat, 2016

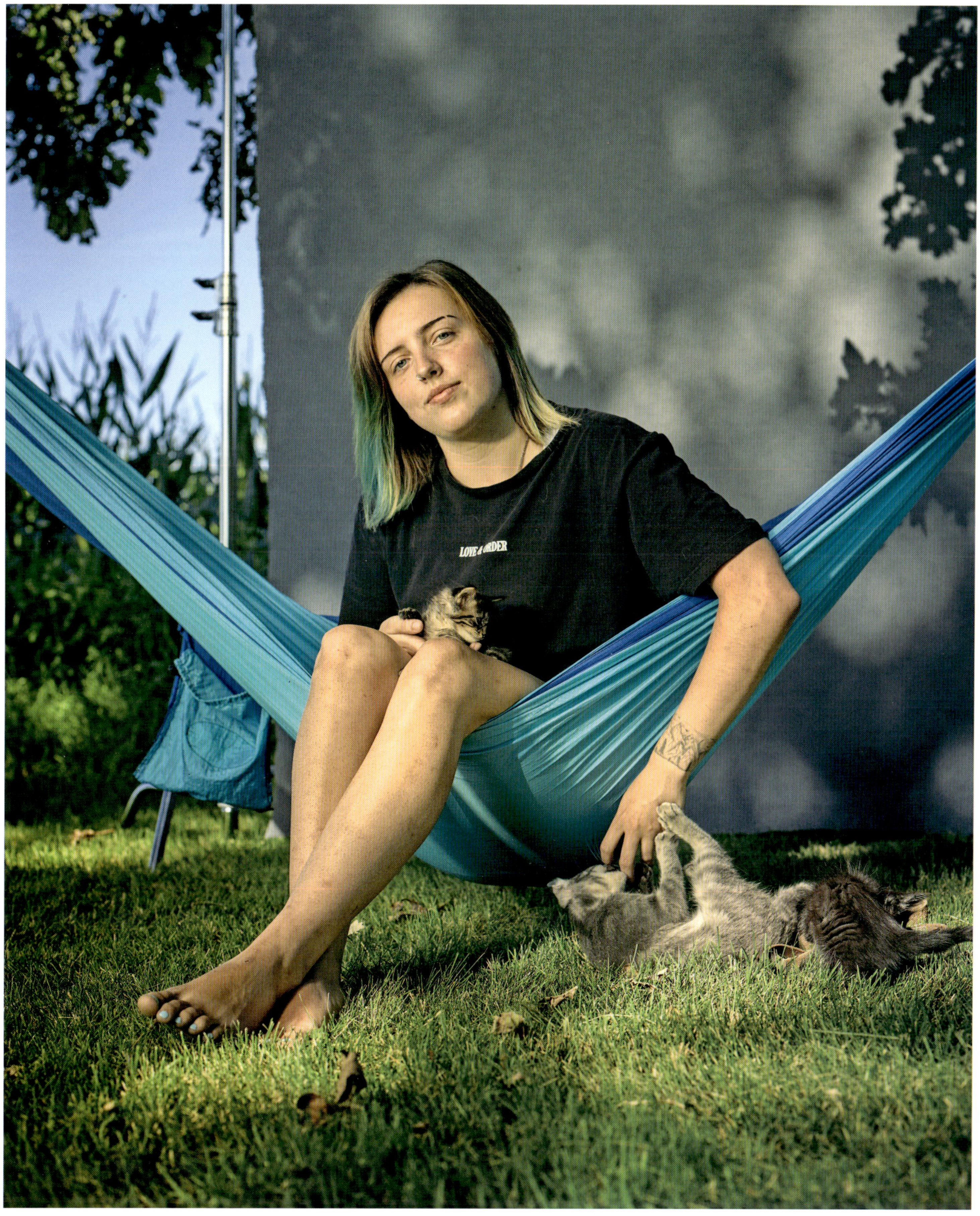

Abby, 2020

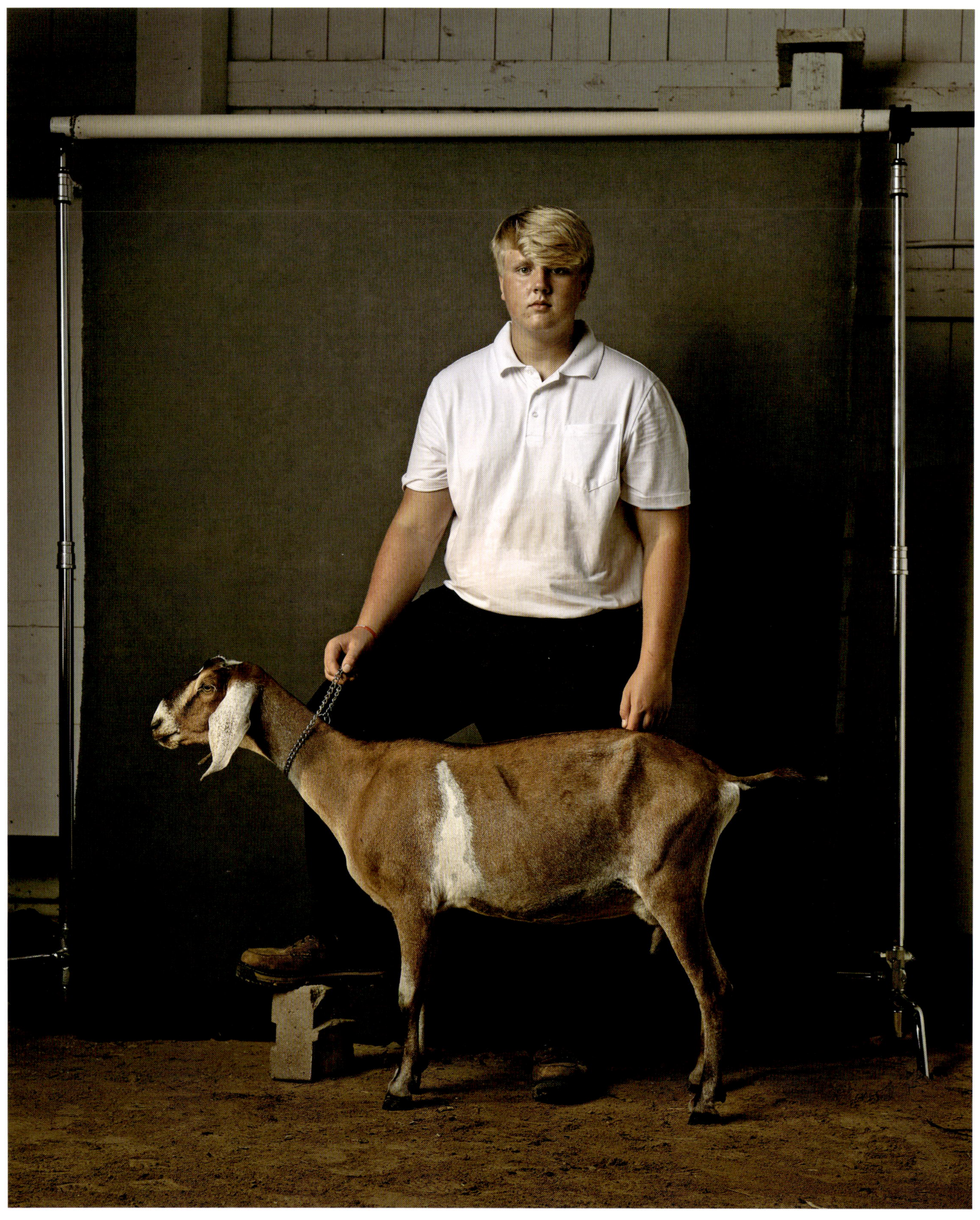

Louis and Dumb, 2016

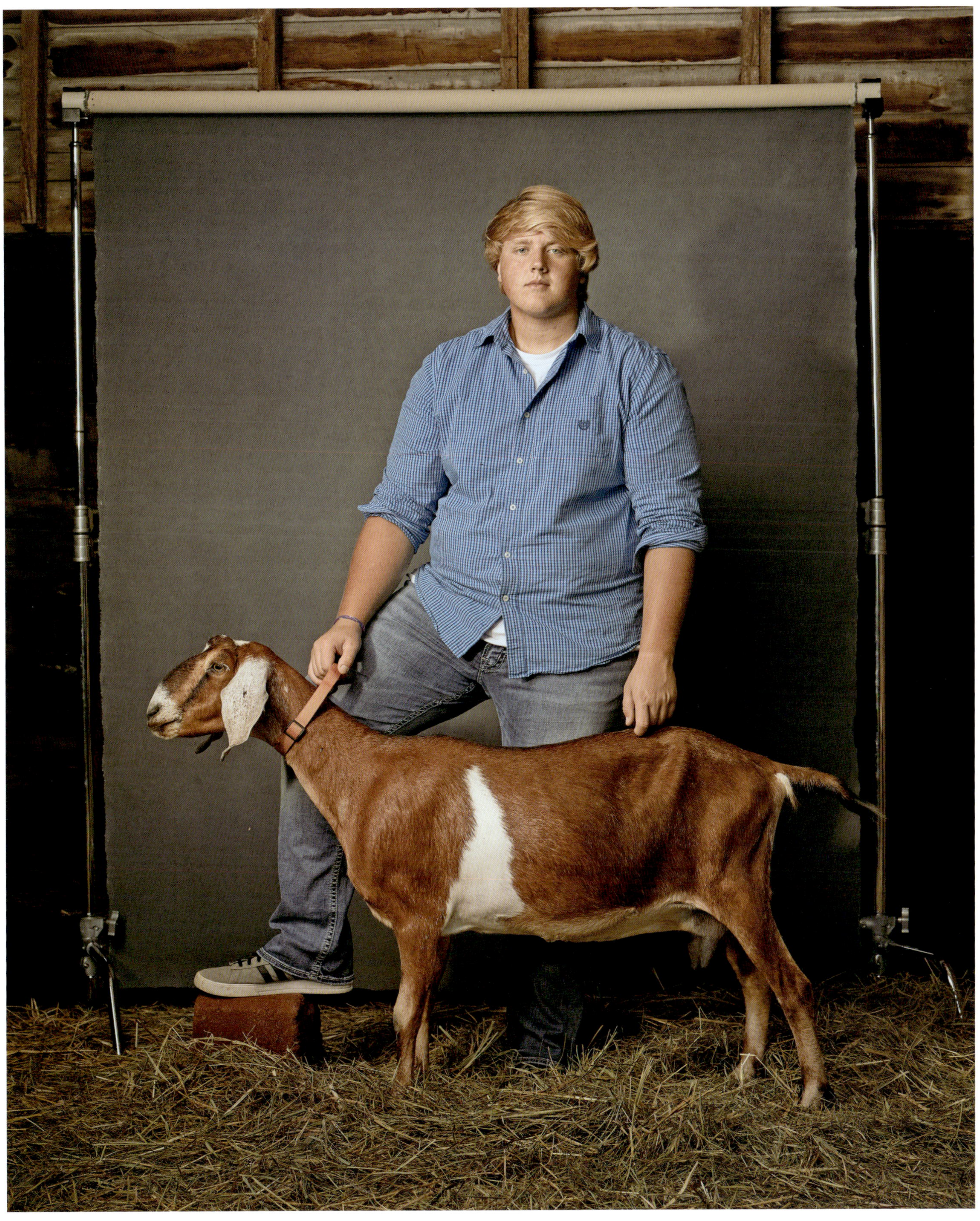

Louis and Dumb, 2020

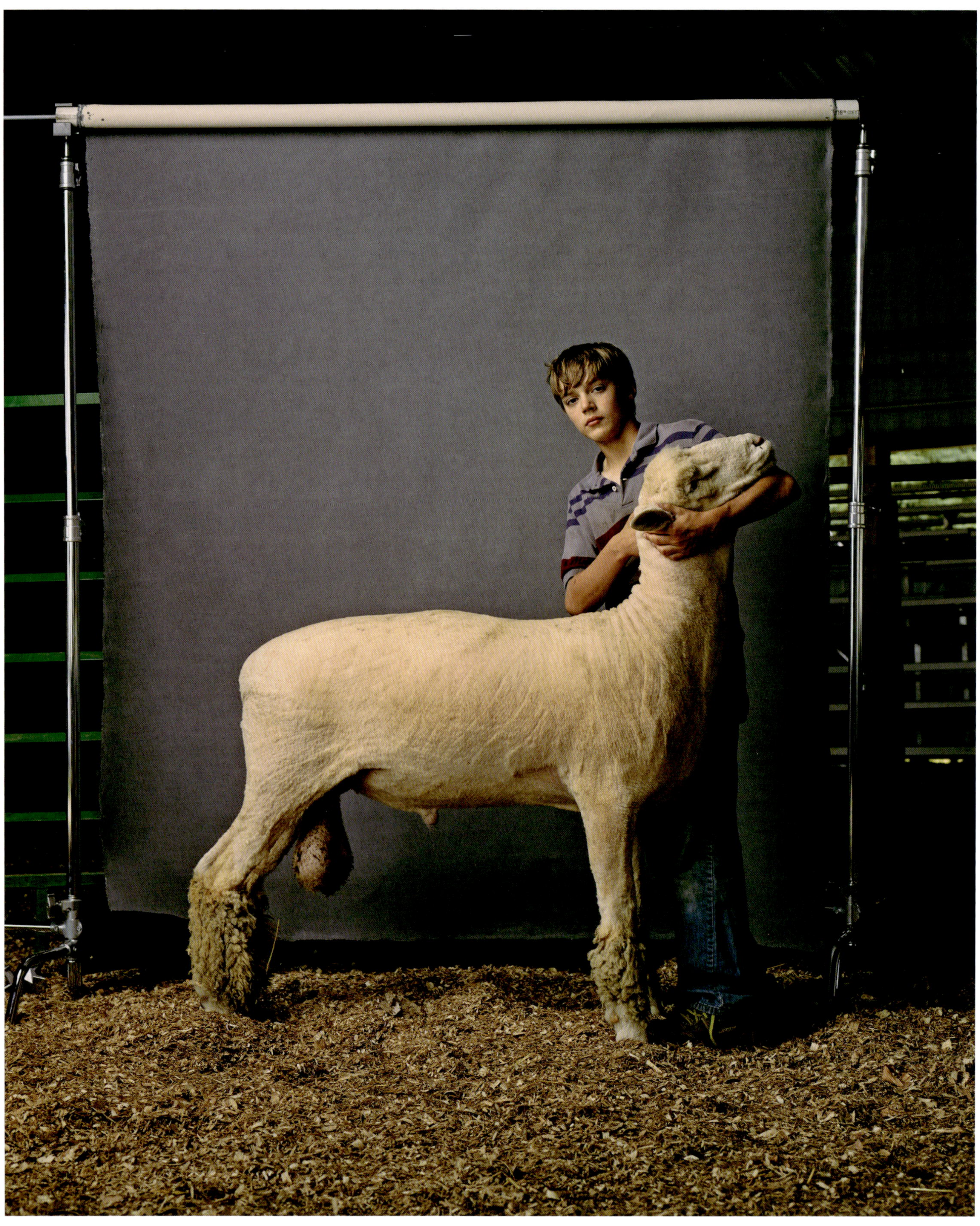

Gabe and Buster, 2016

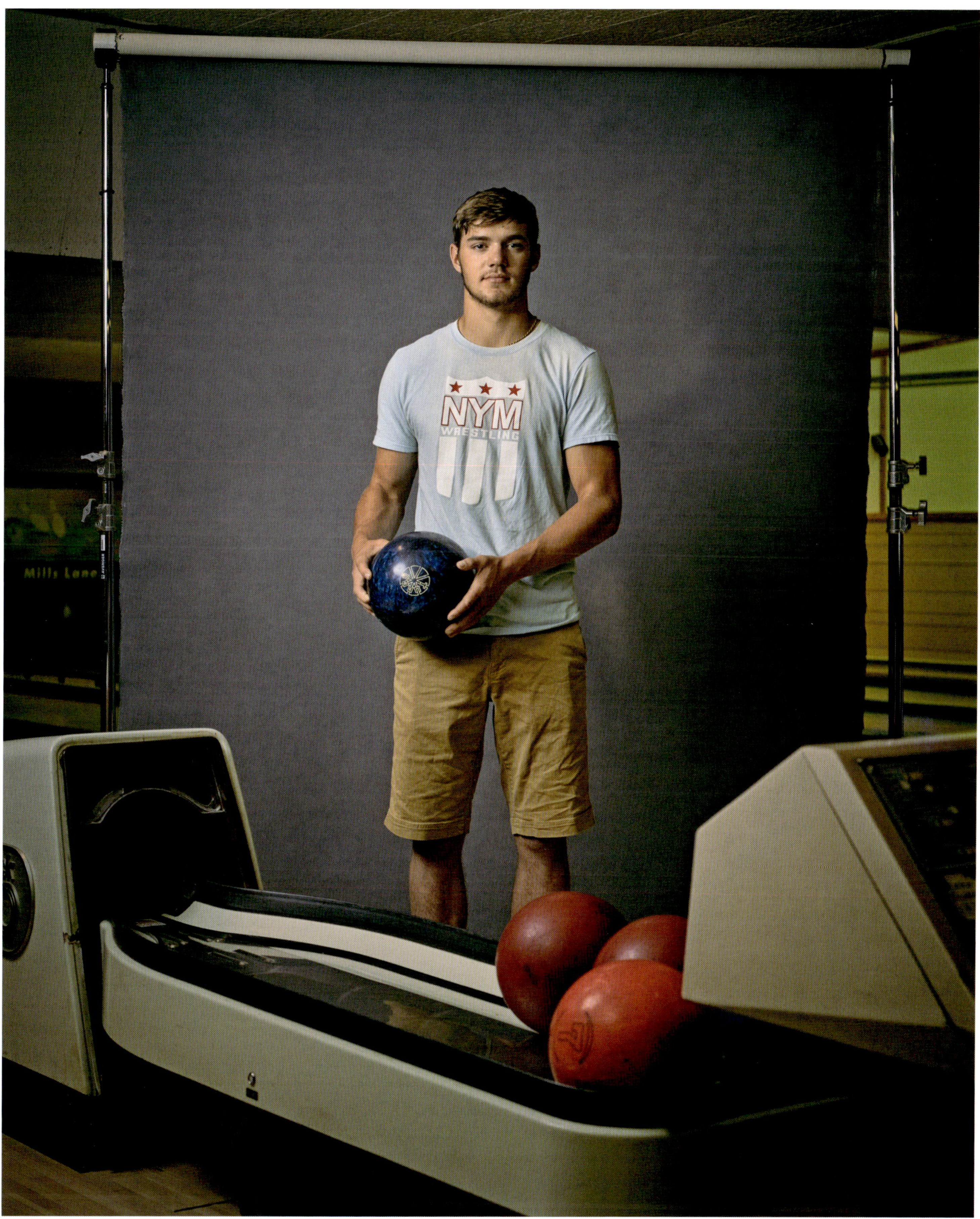

Gabe, 2020

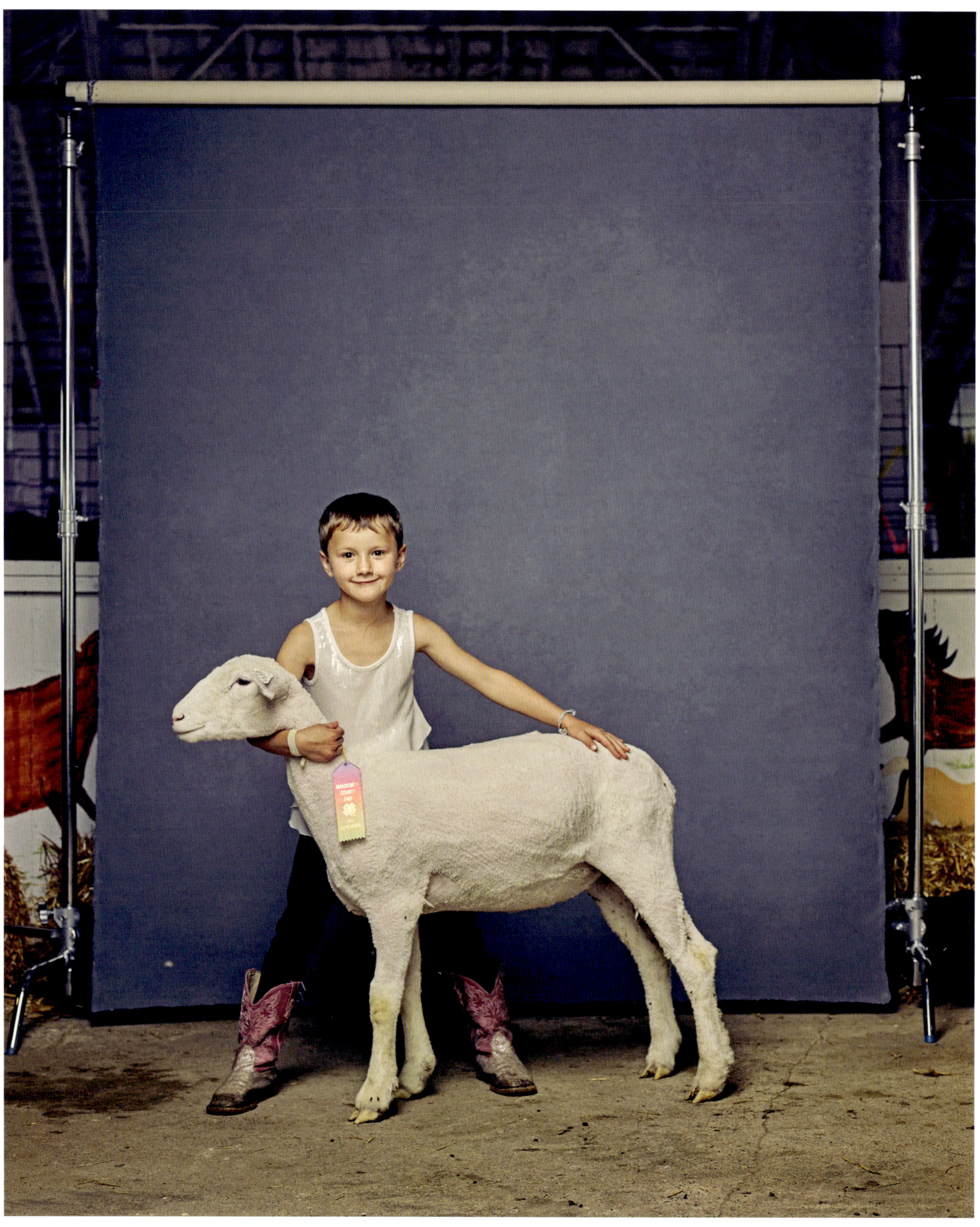

Natalie and Sheep, 2016

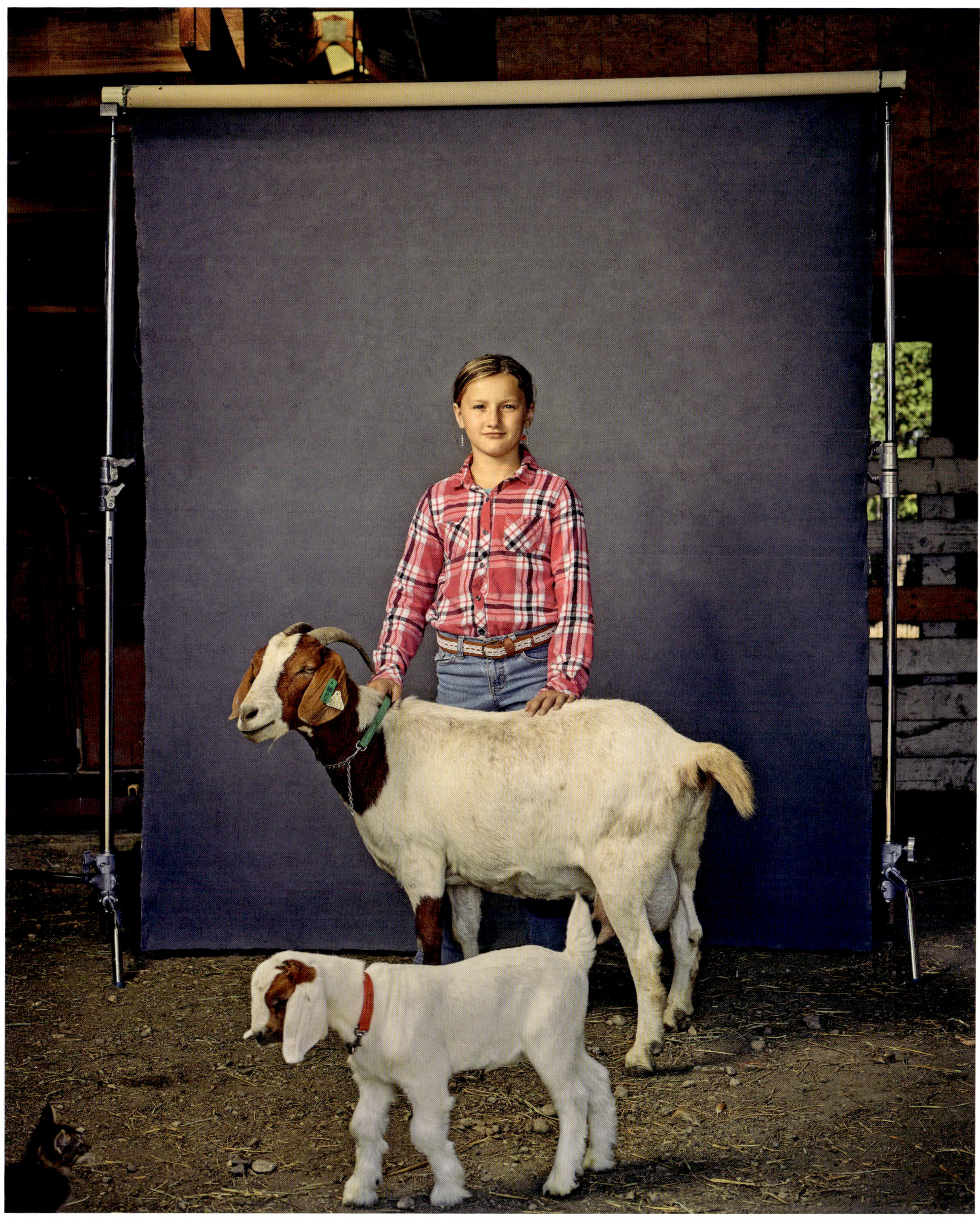

Natalie and Goats, 2020

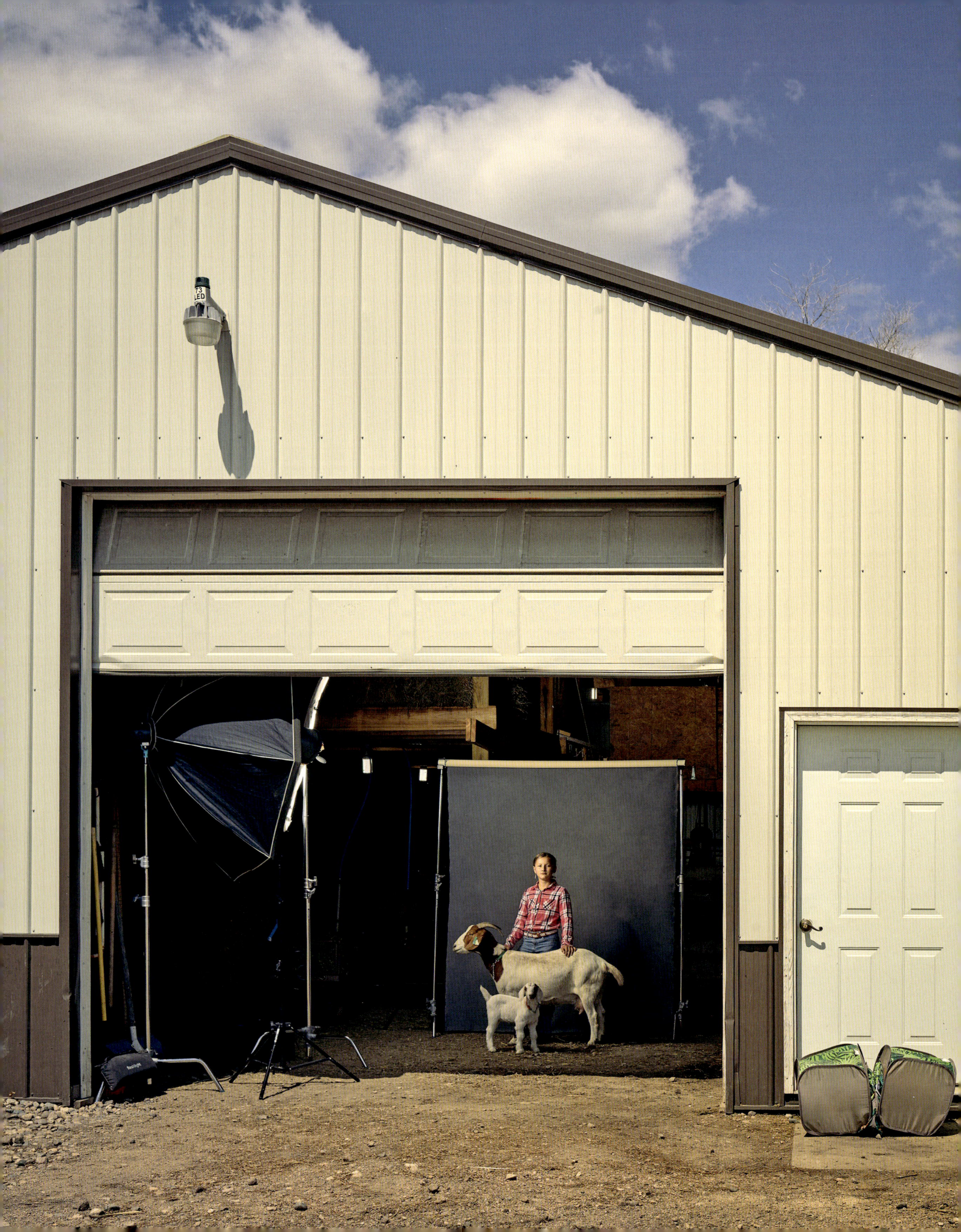

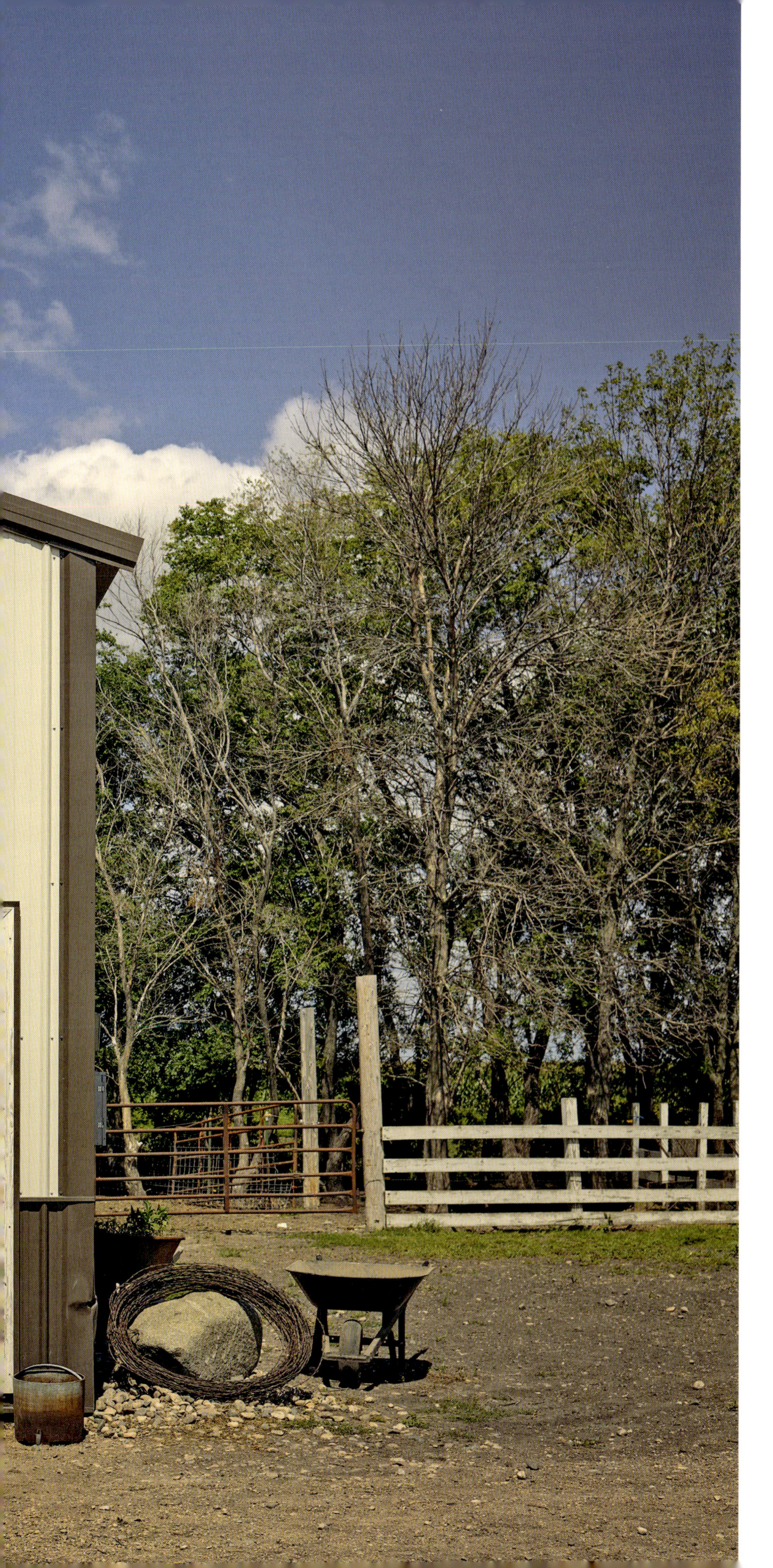

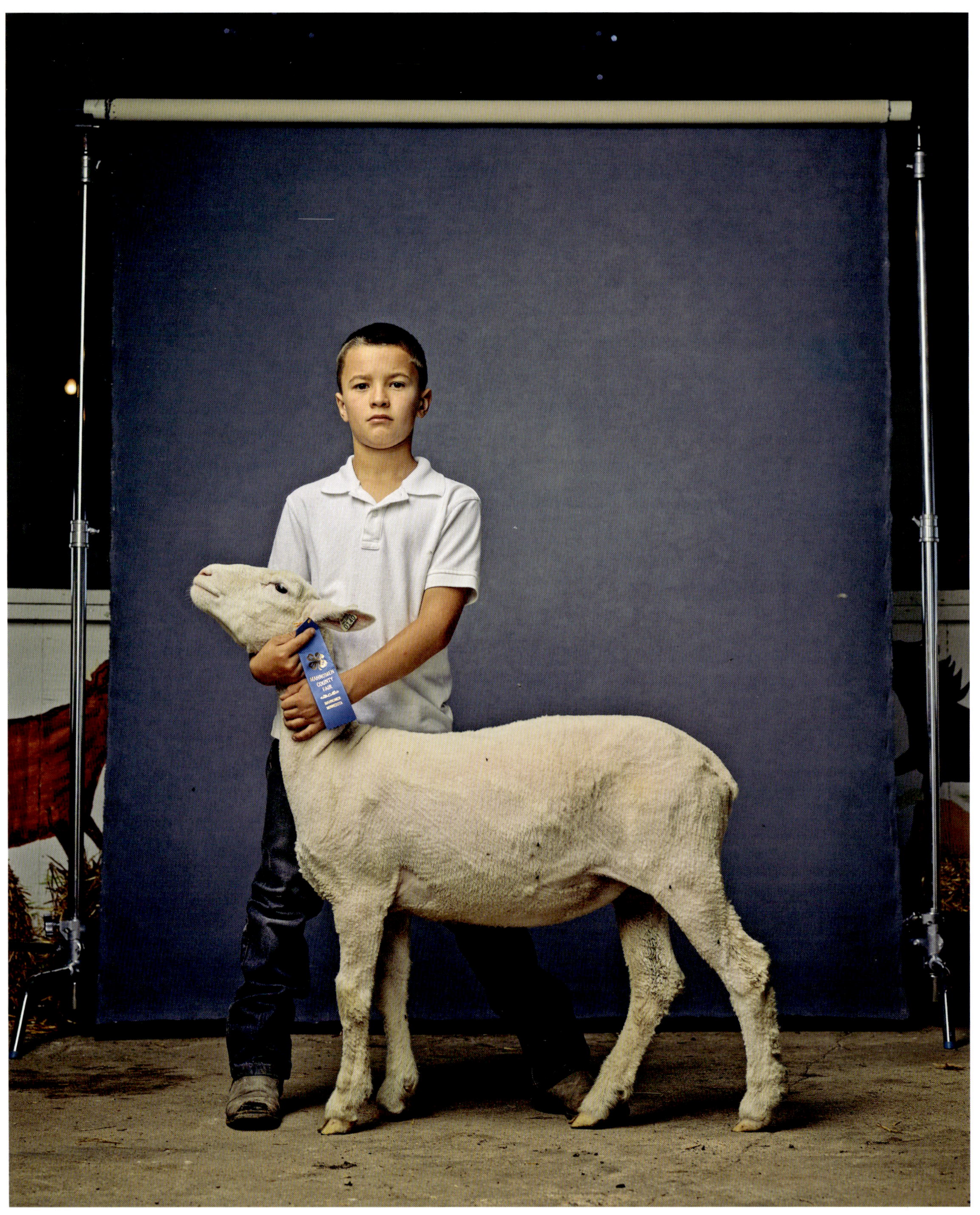

Kaden and Sheep, 2016

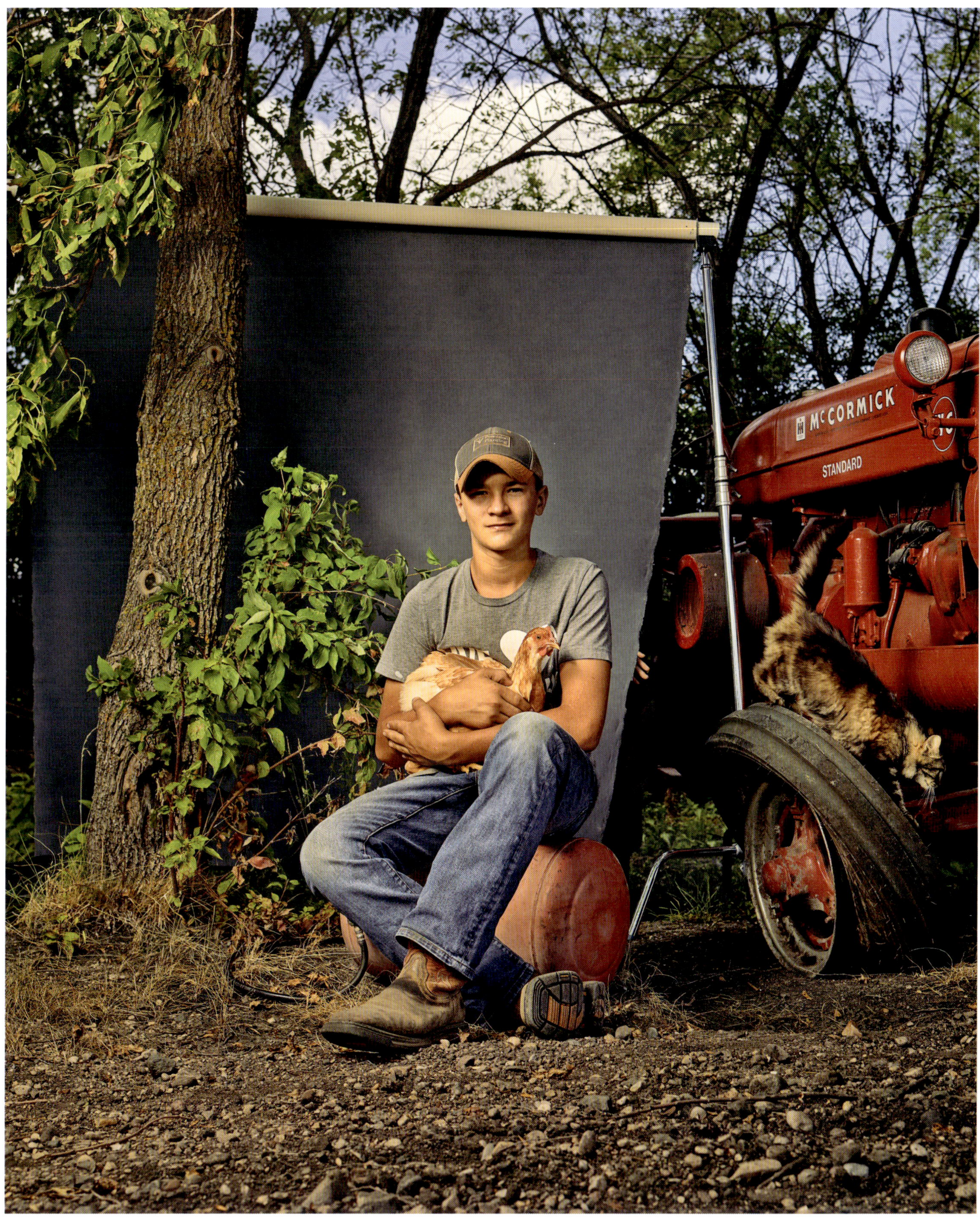

Kaden, 2020

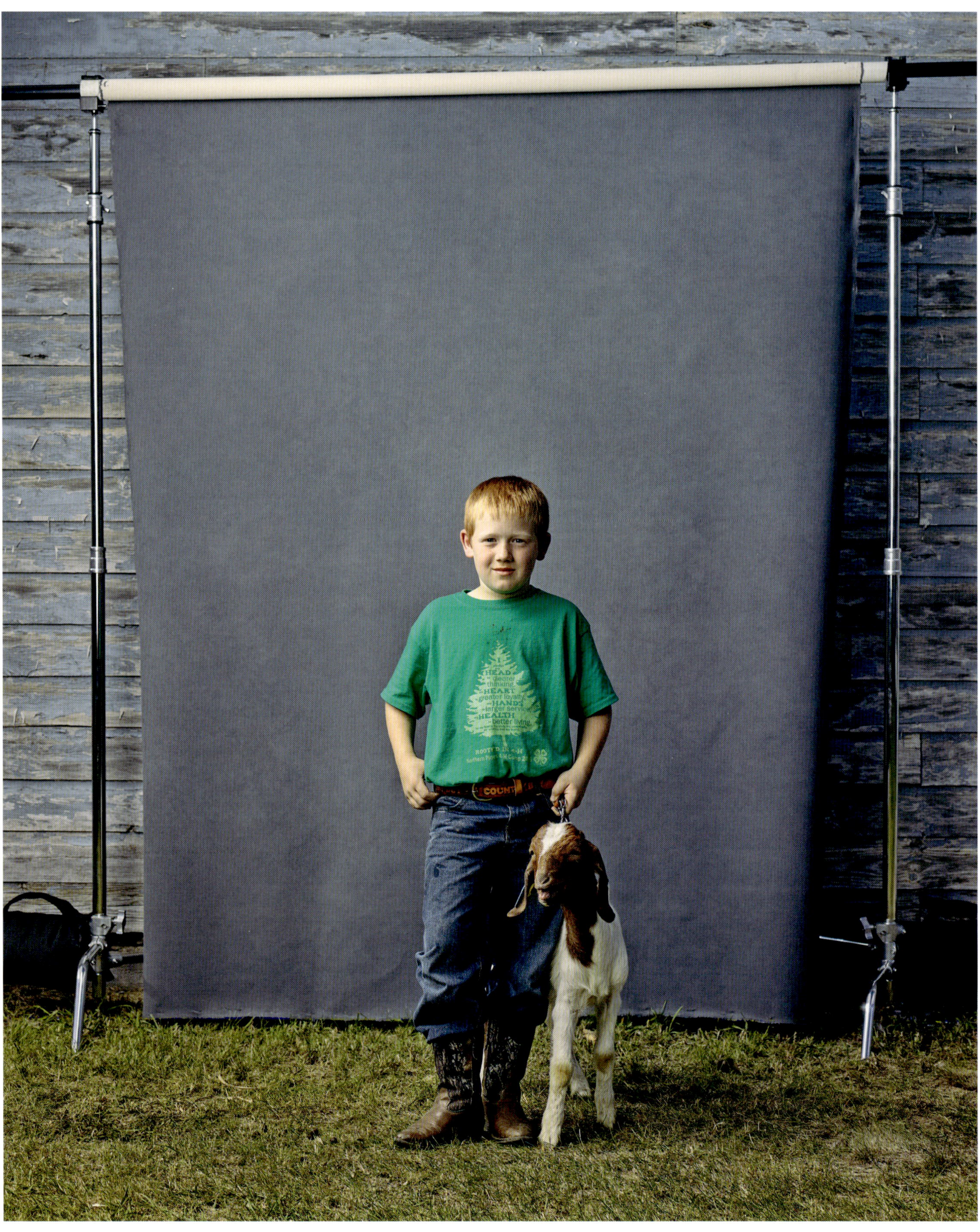

Blake and Bolt, 2016

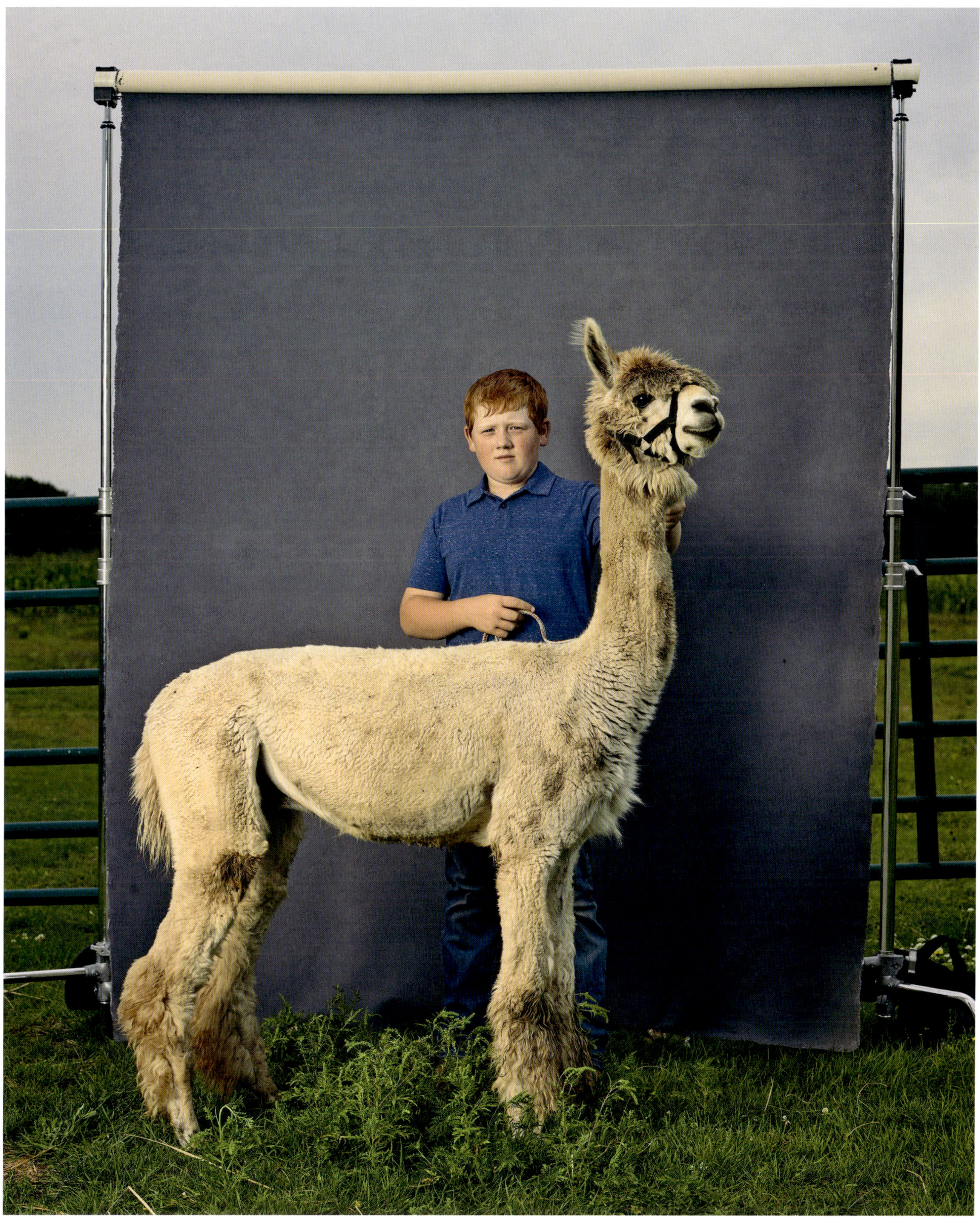

Blake and P. T., 2020

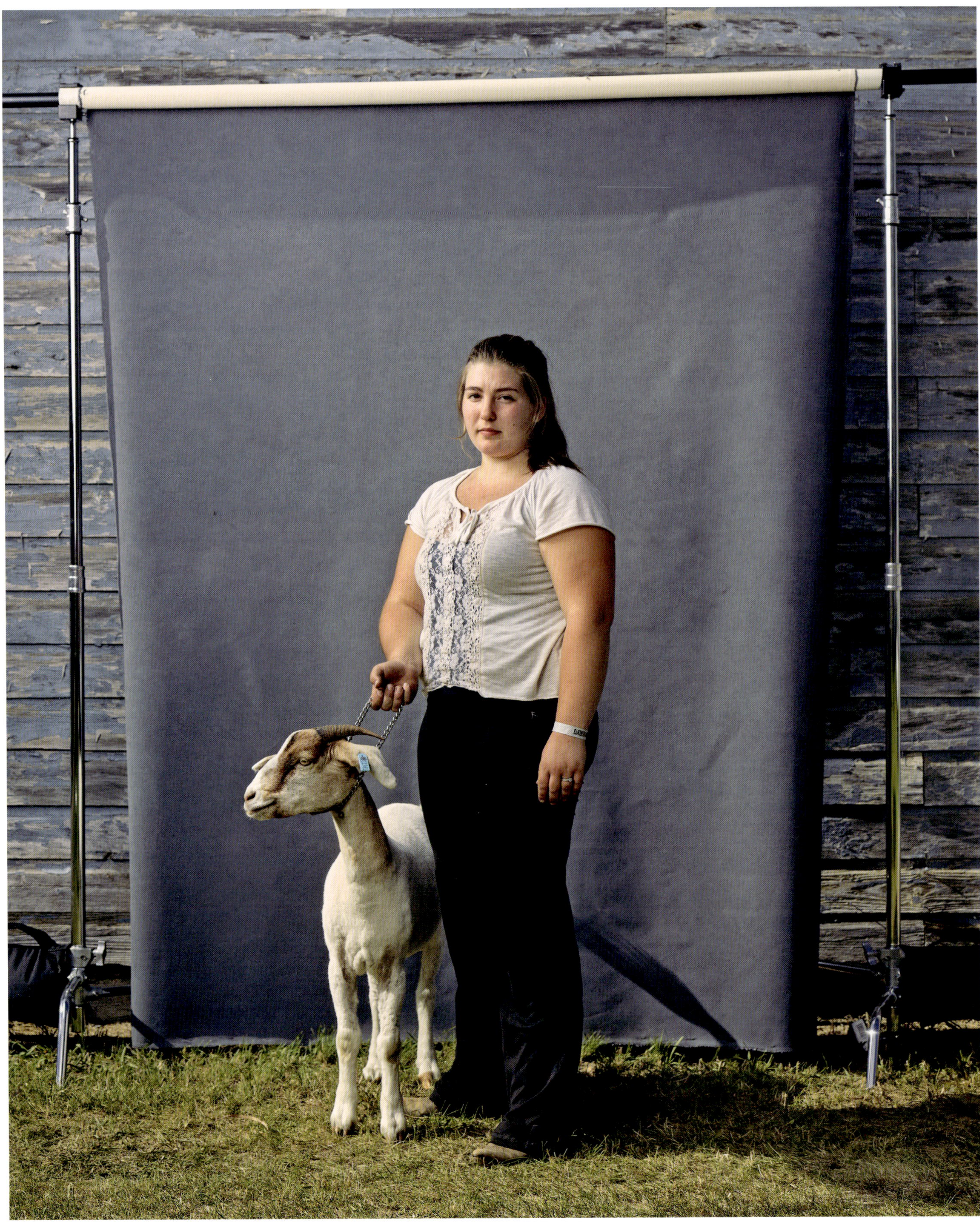

Sabrina and Molly, 2016

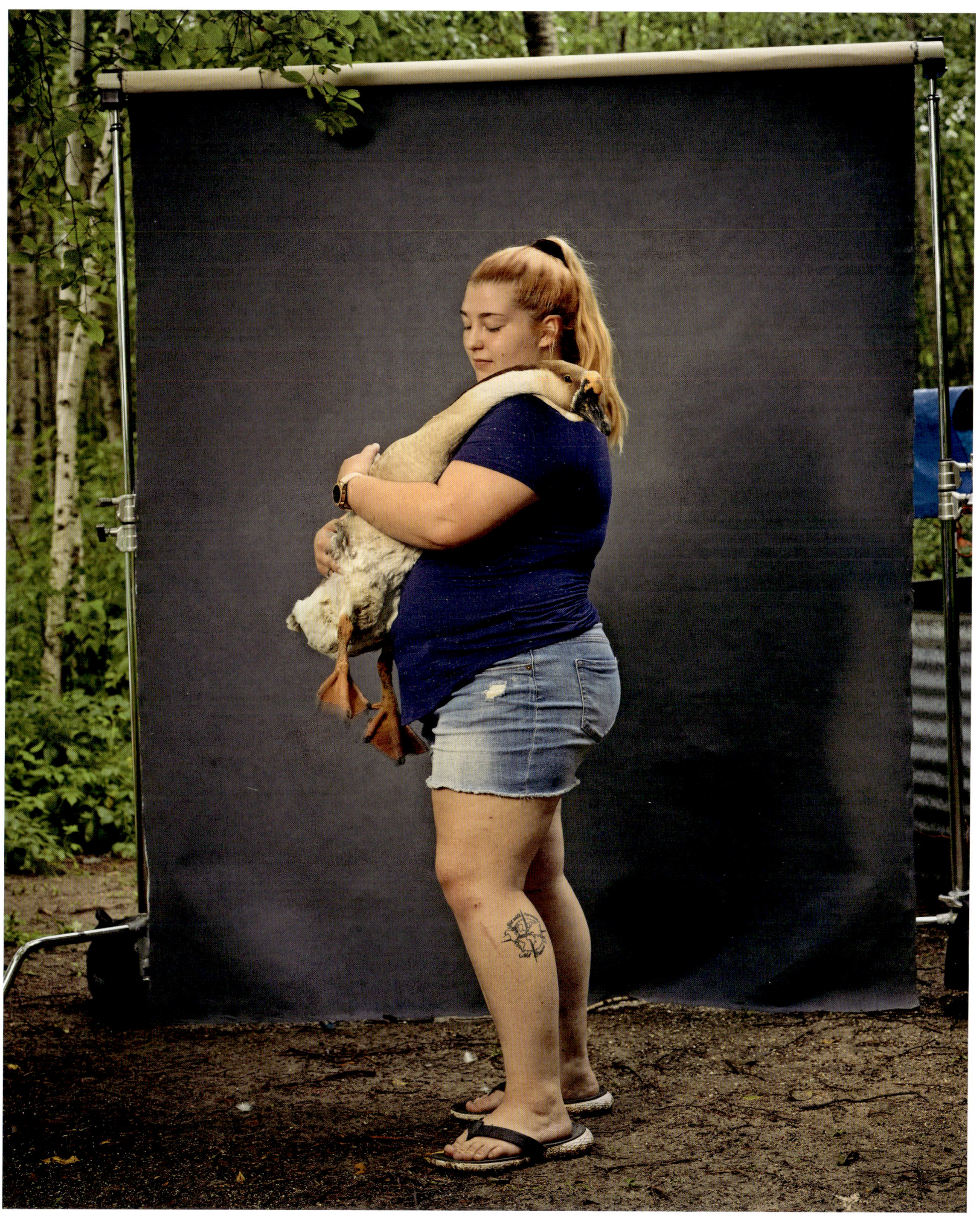

Sabrina and Freddy, 2020

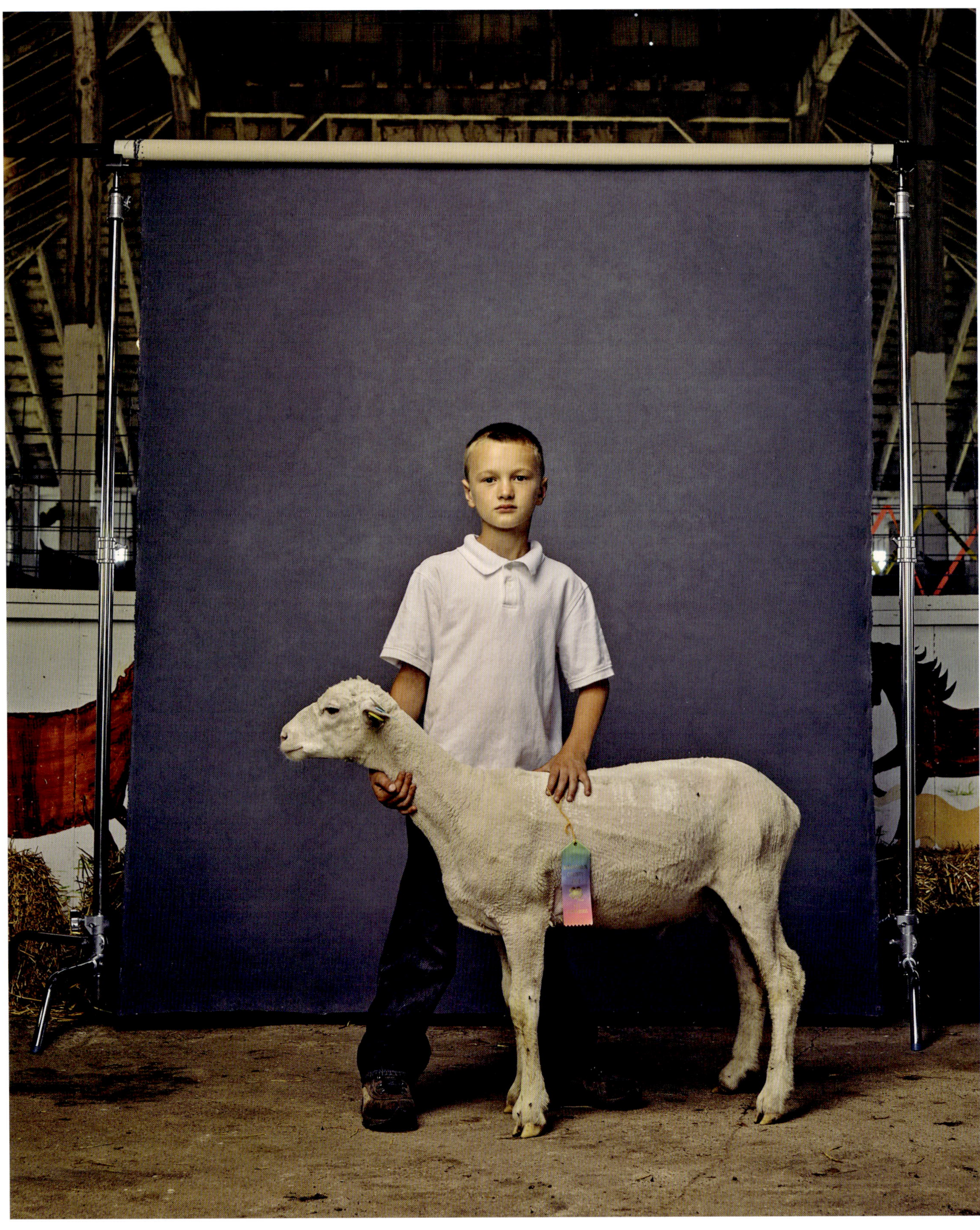

Marcus and Sheep, 2016

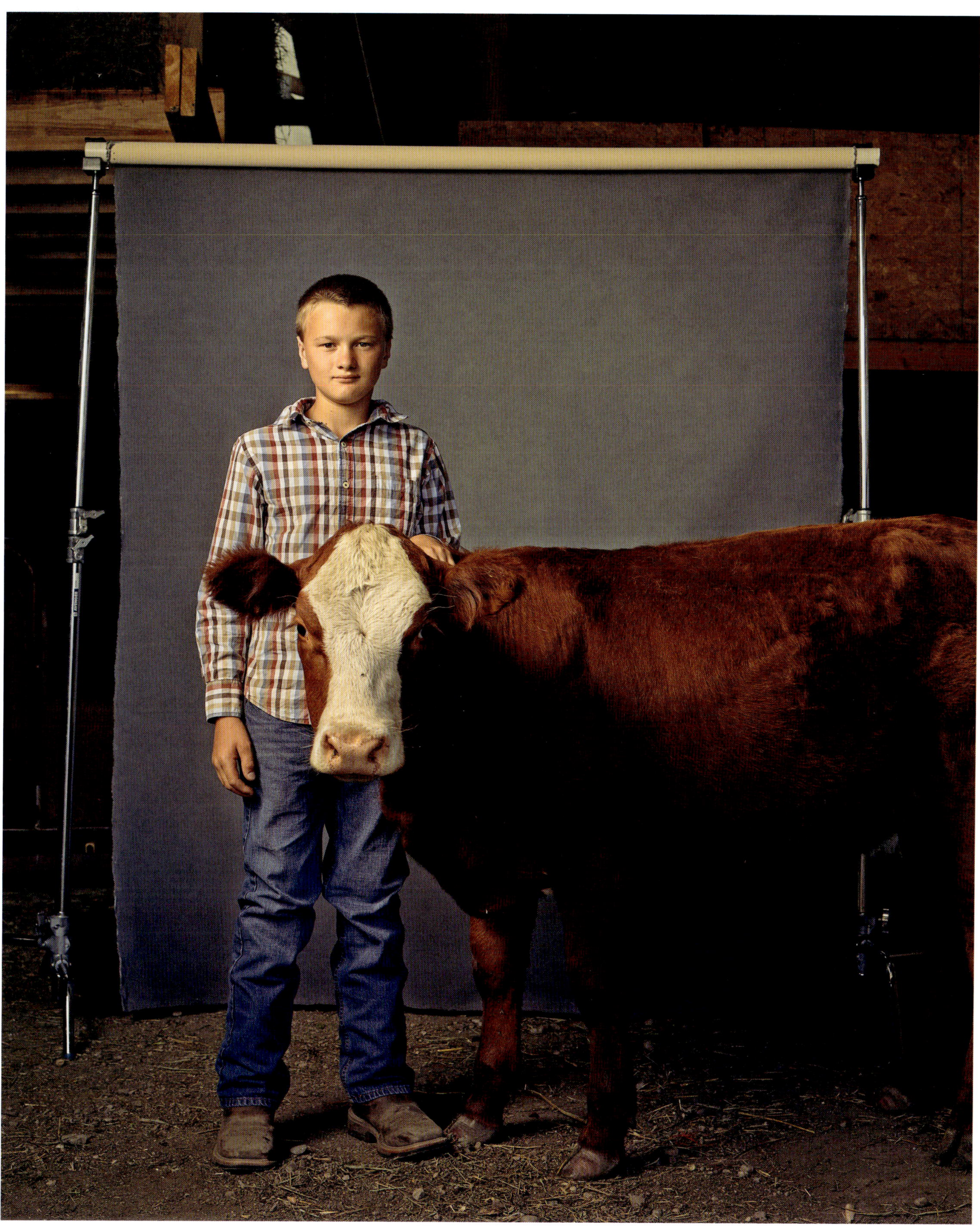

Marcus and Tiffany, 2020

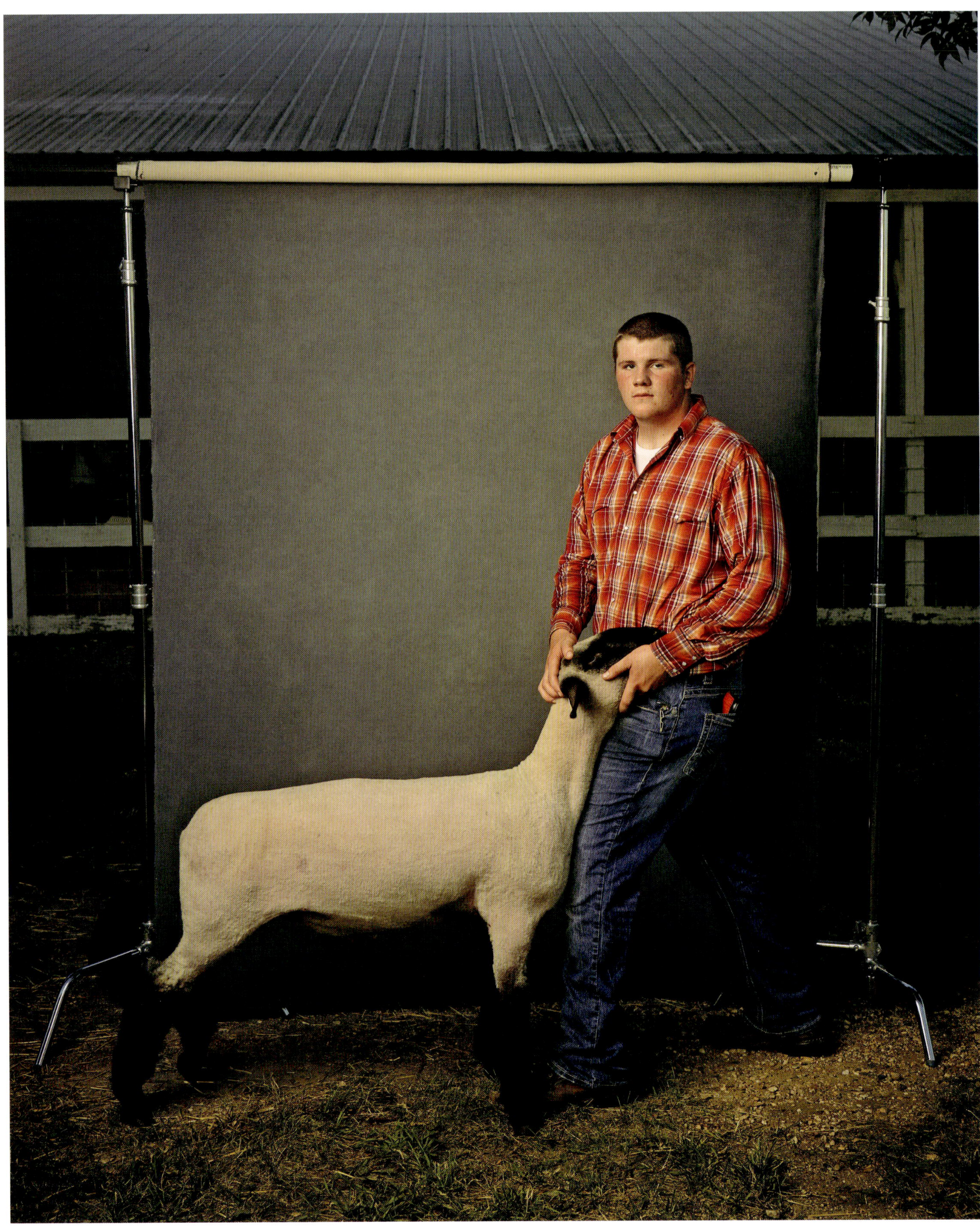

Eric and Sheep, 2016

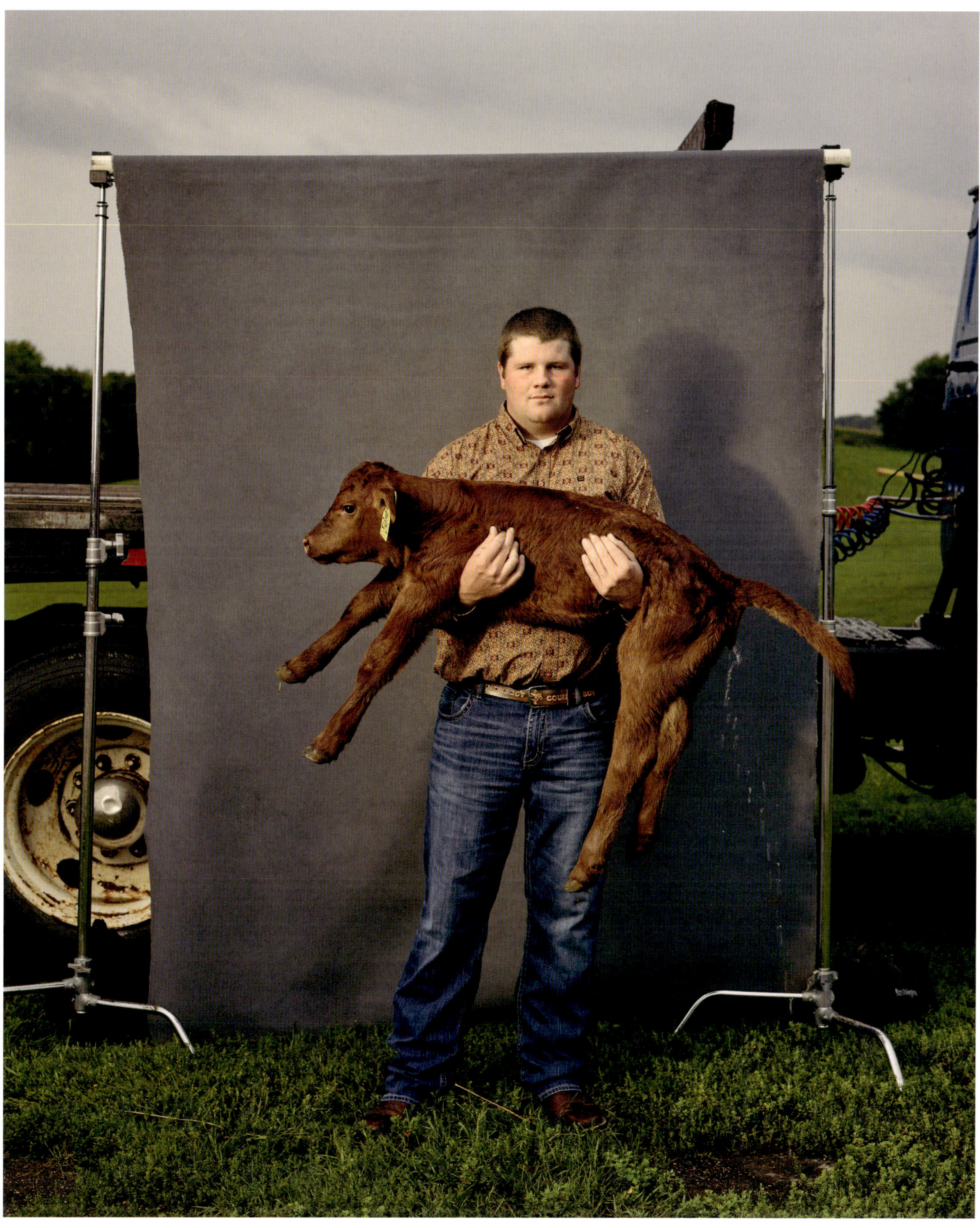

Eric and R. J., 2020

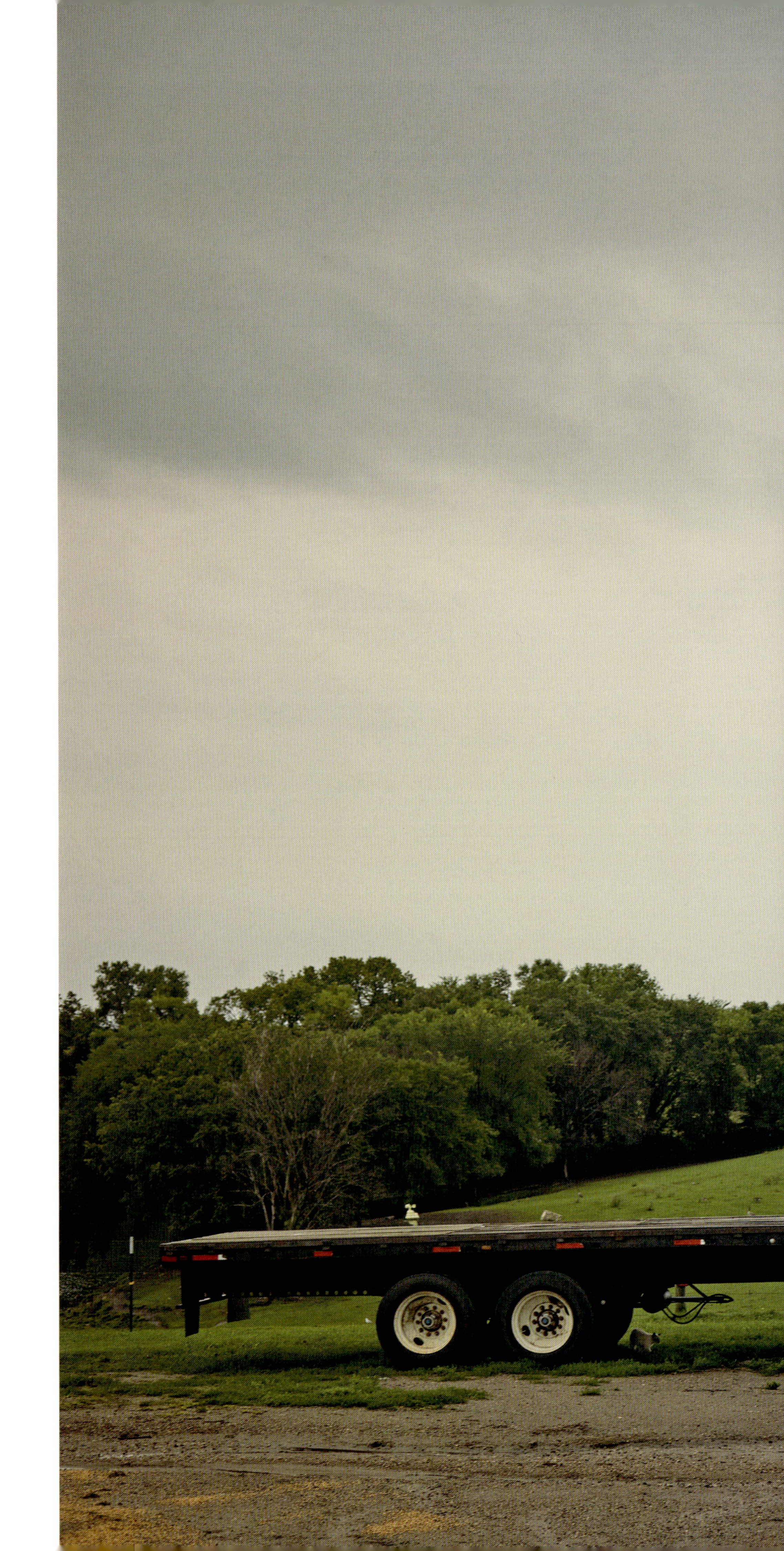

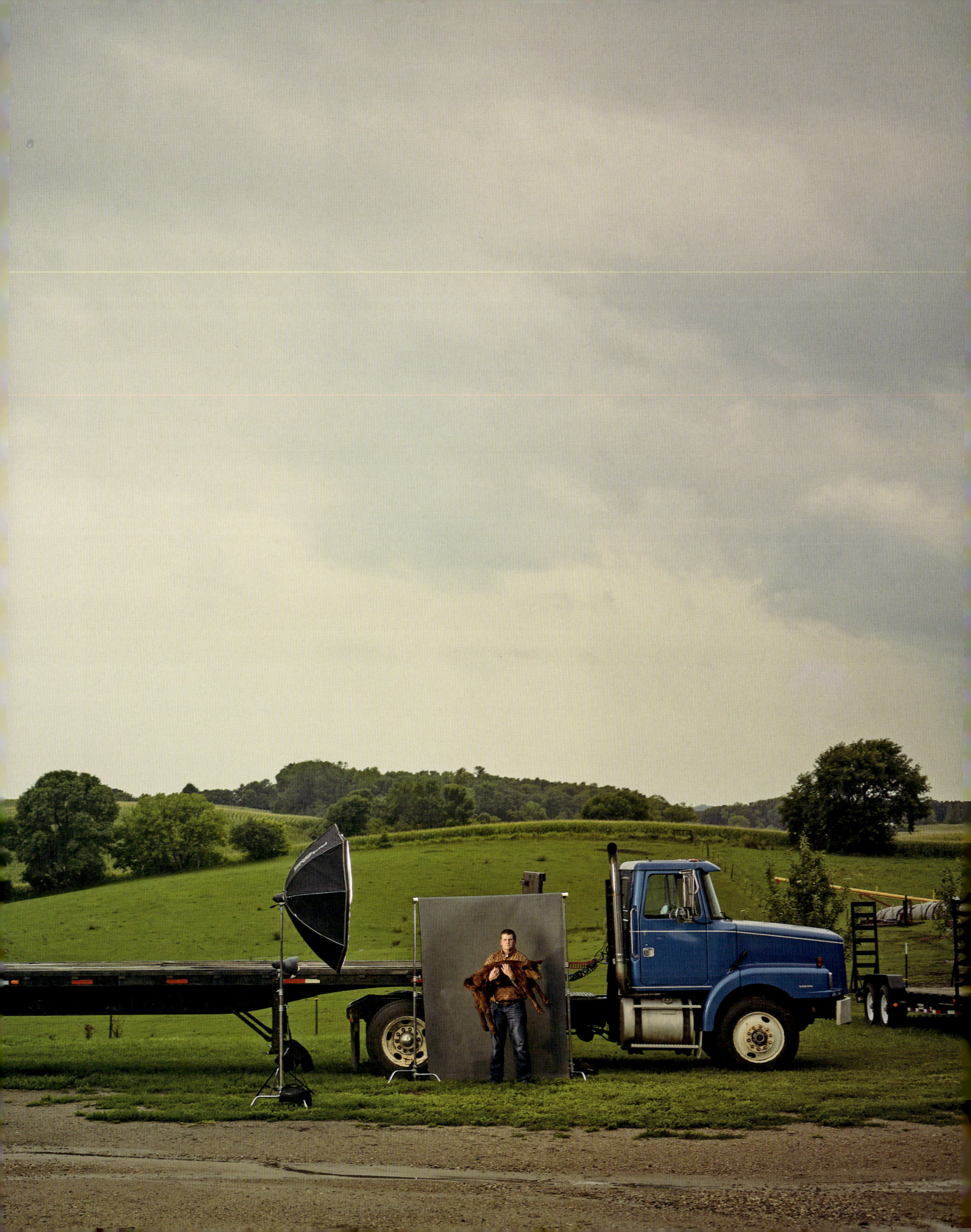

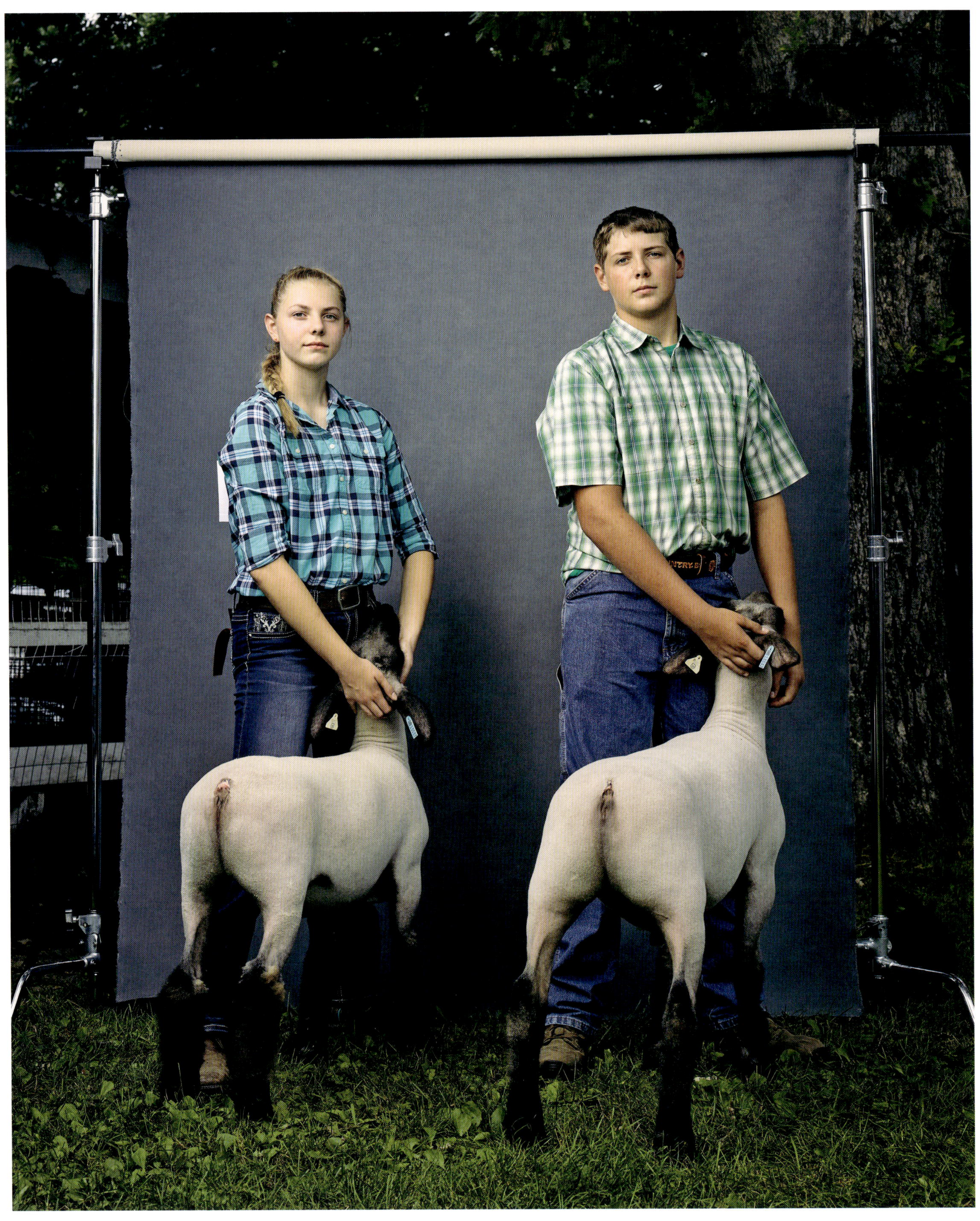

Emma and Ethan with Sheep, 2016

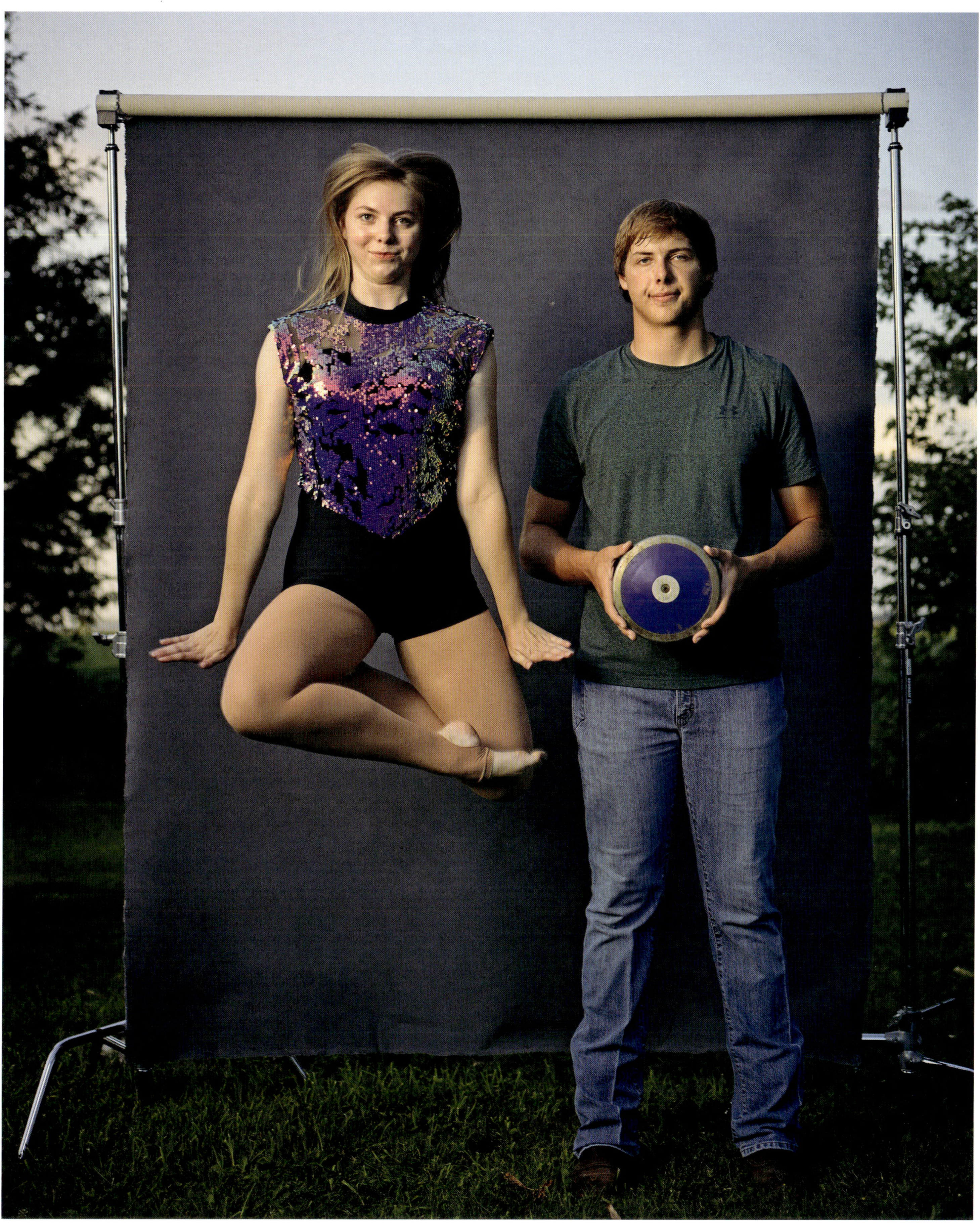

Emma and Ethan, 2020

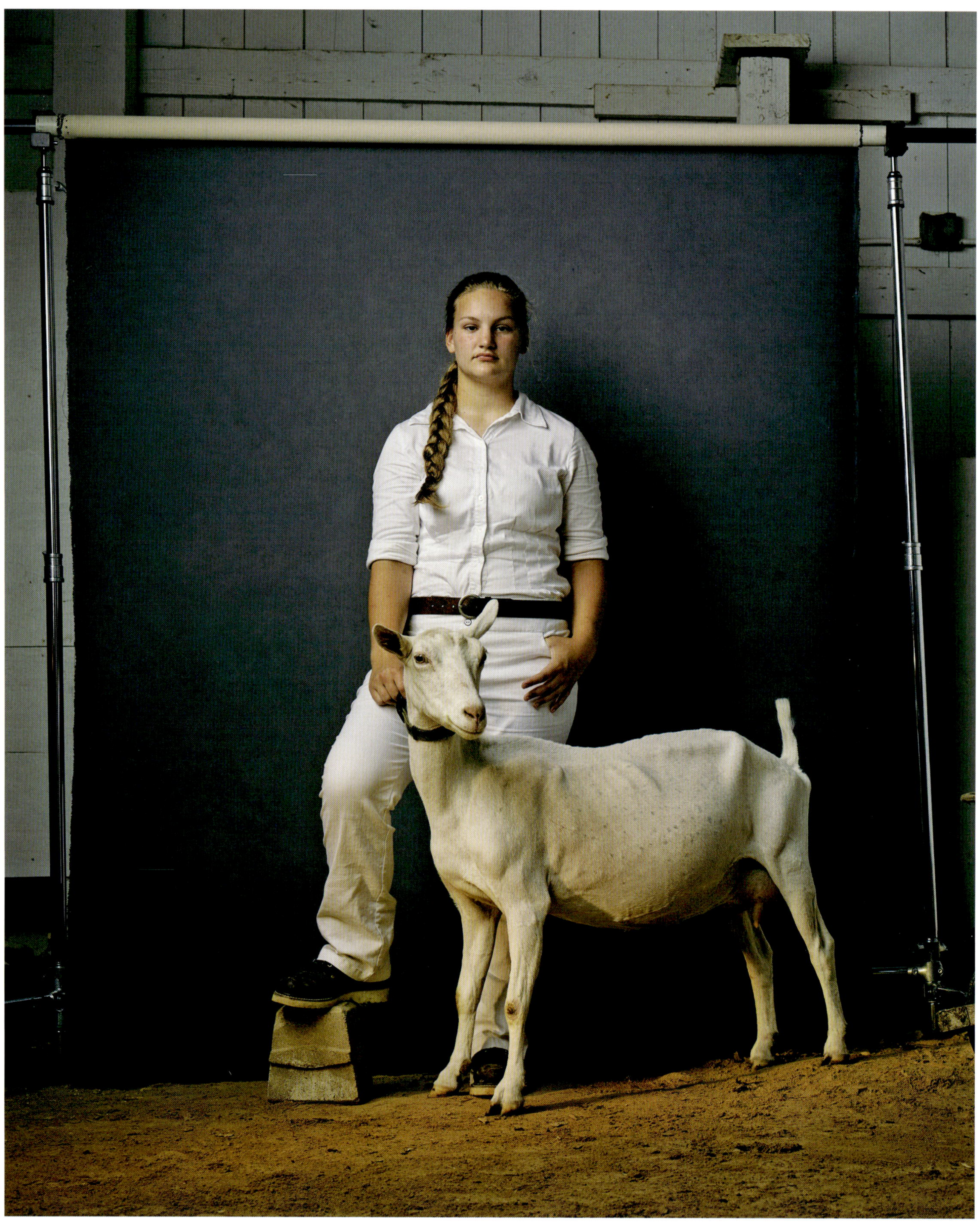

Gigi and Reba, 2016

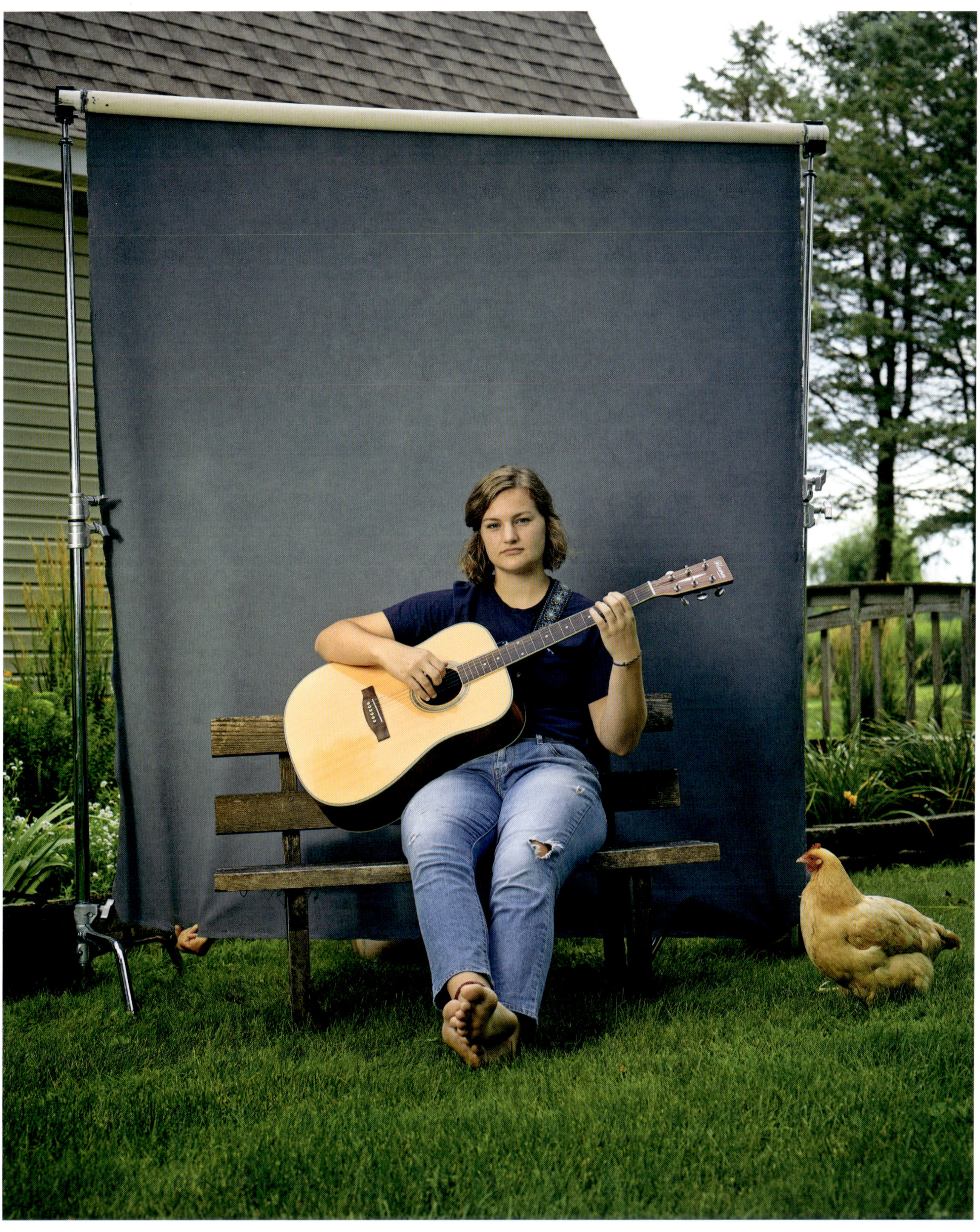

Gigi, 2020

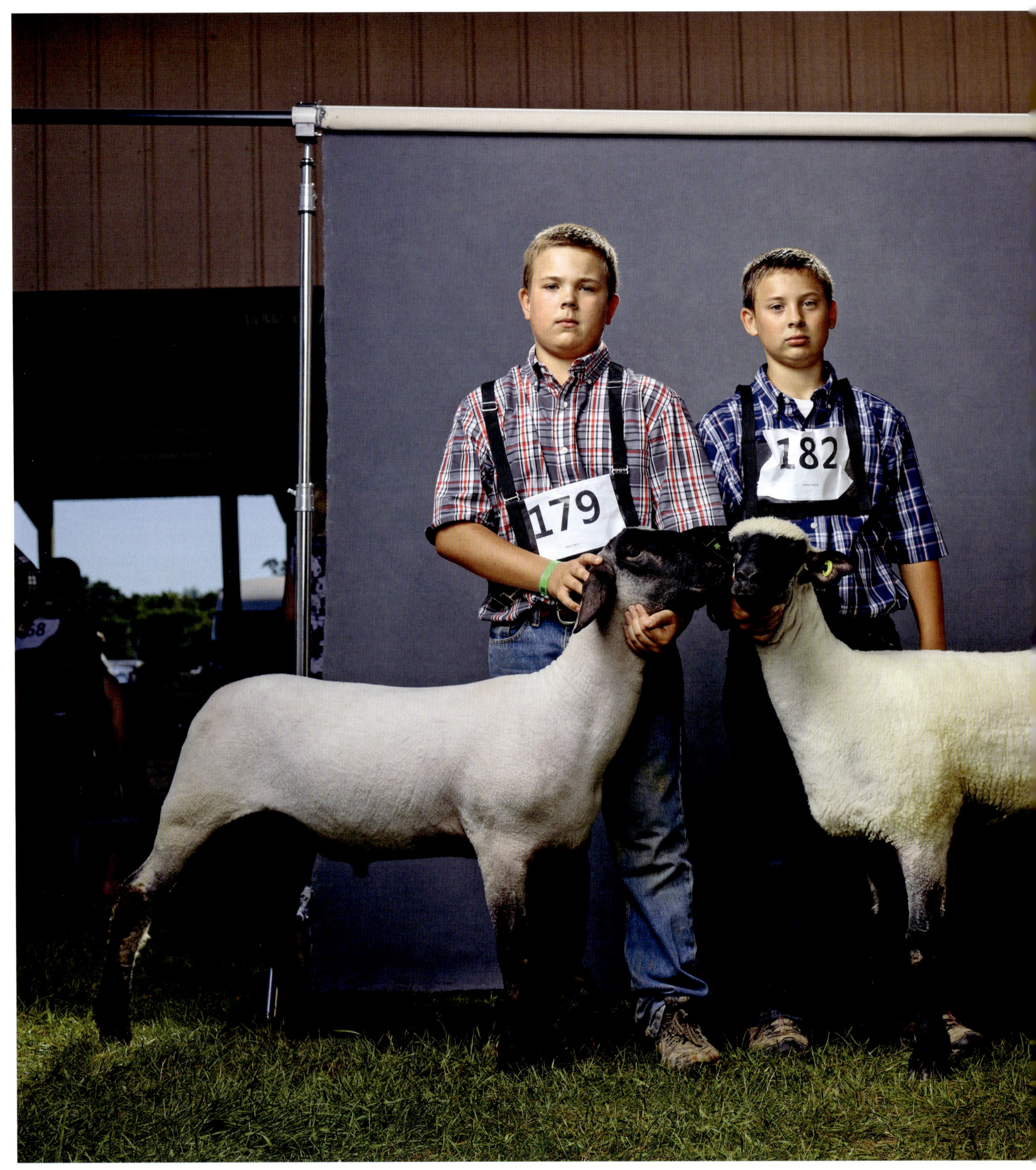

Bryce with Freaky Freddy and Nathan with Skittles, 2016

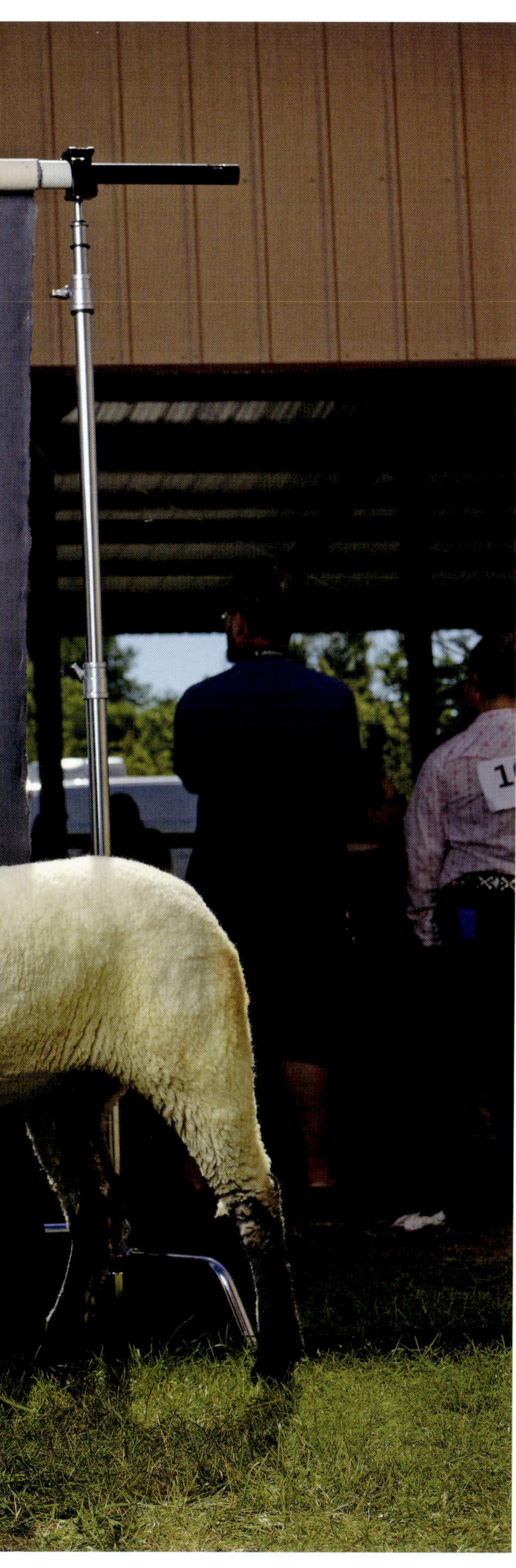

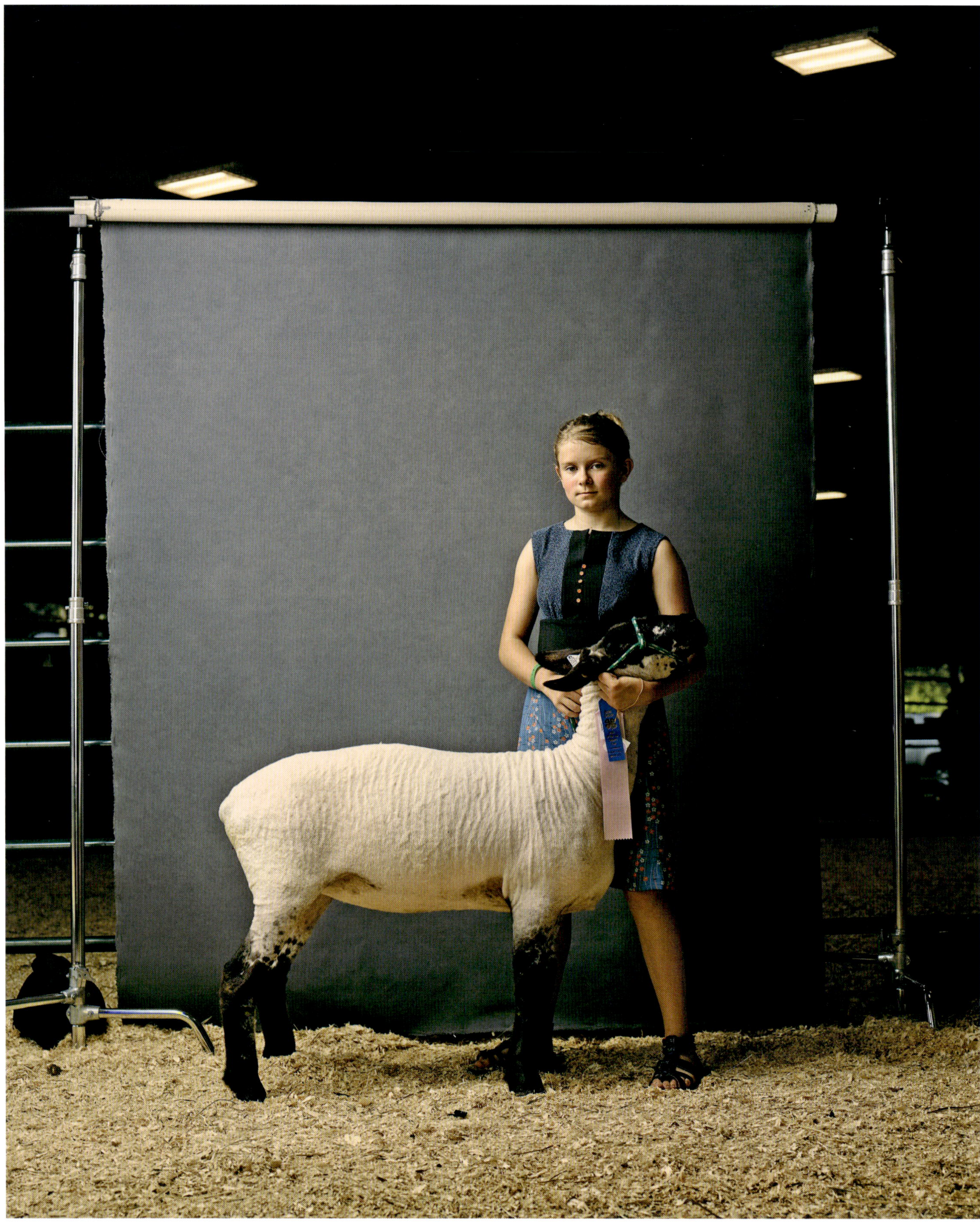

Erika and Paint, 2016

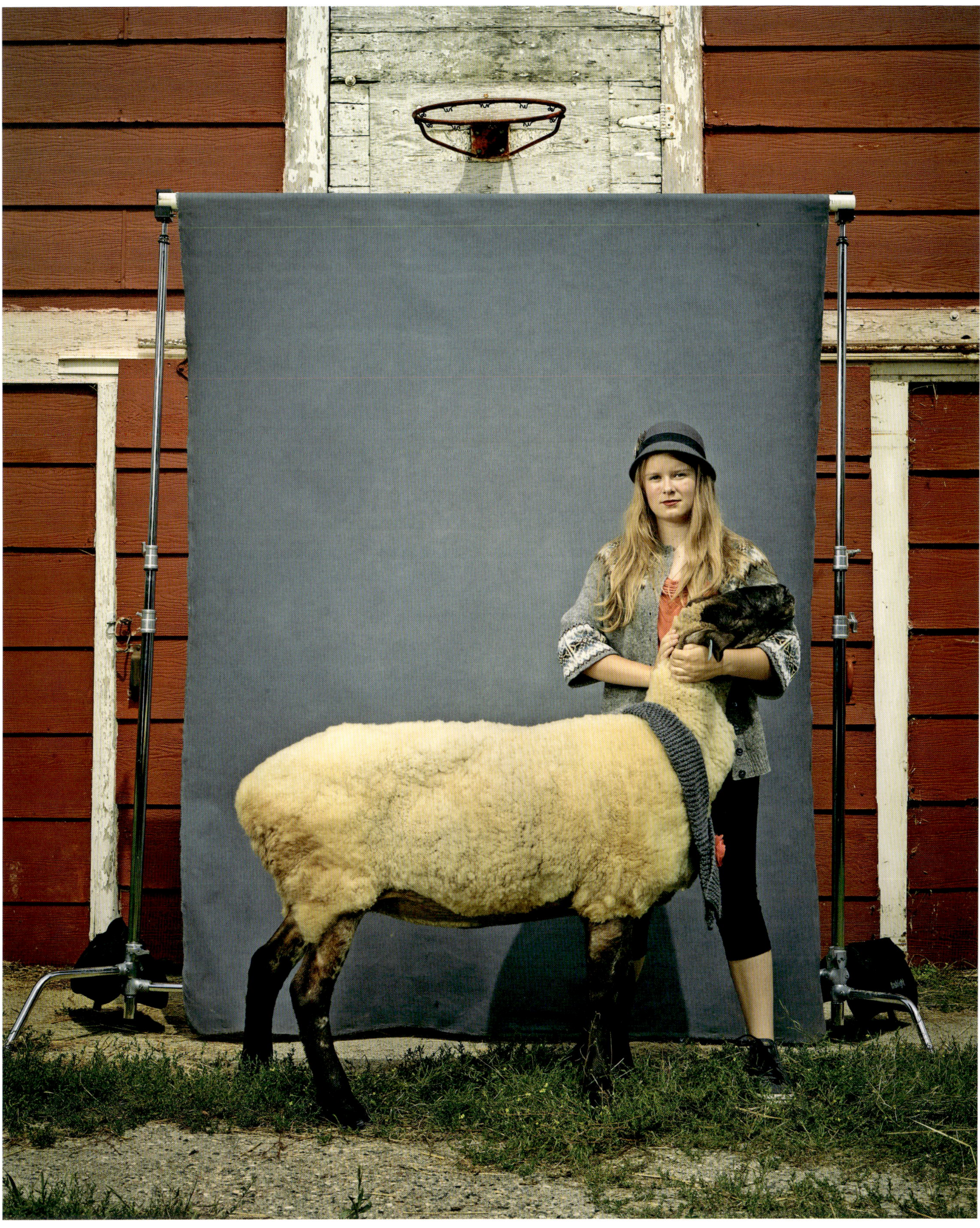

Erika and Paint, 2020

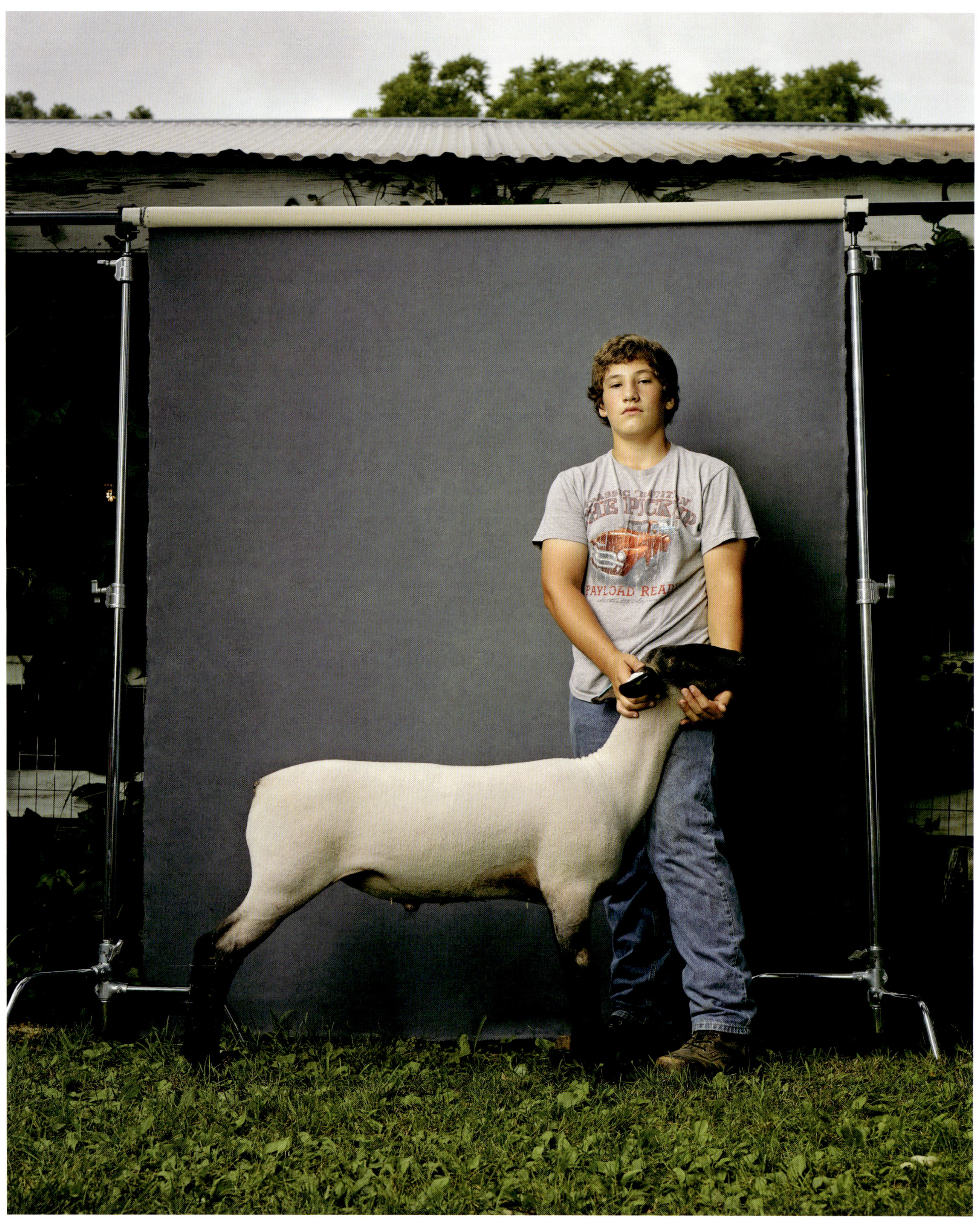

David and Sheep, 2016

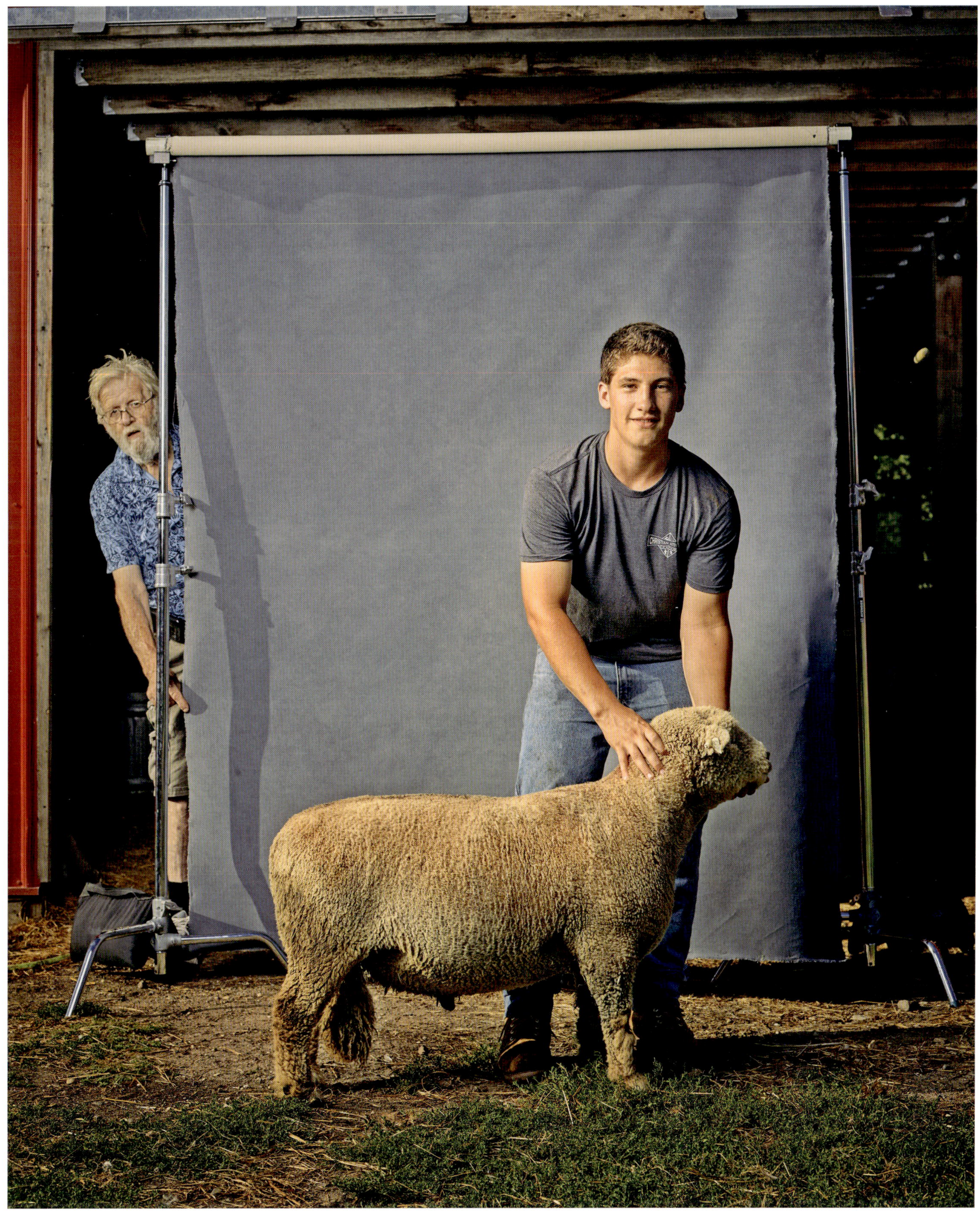

David and Sheep, 2020

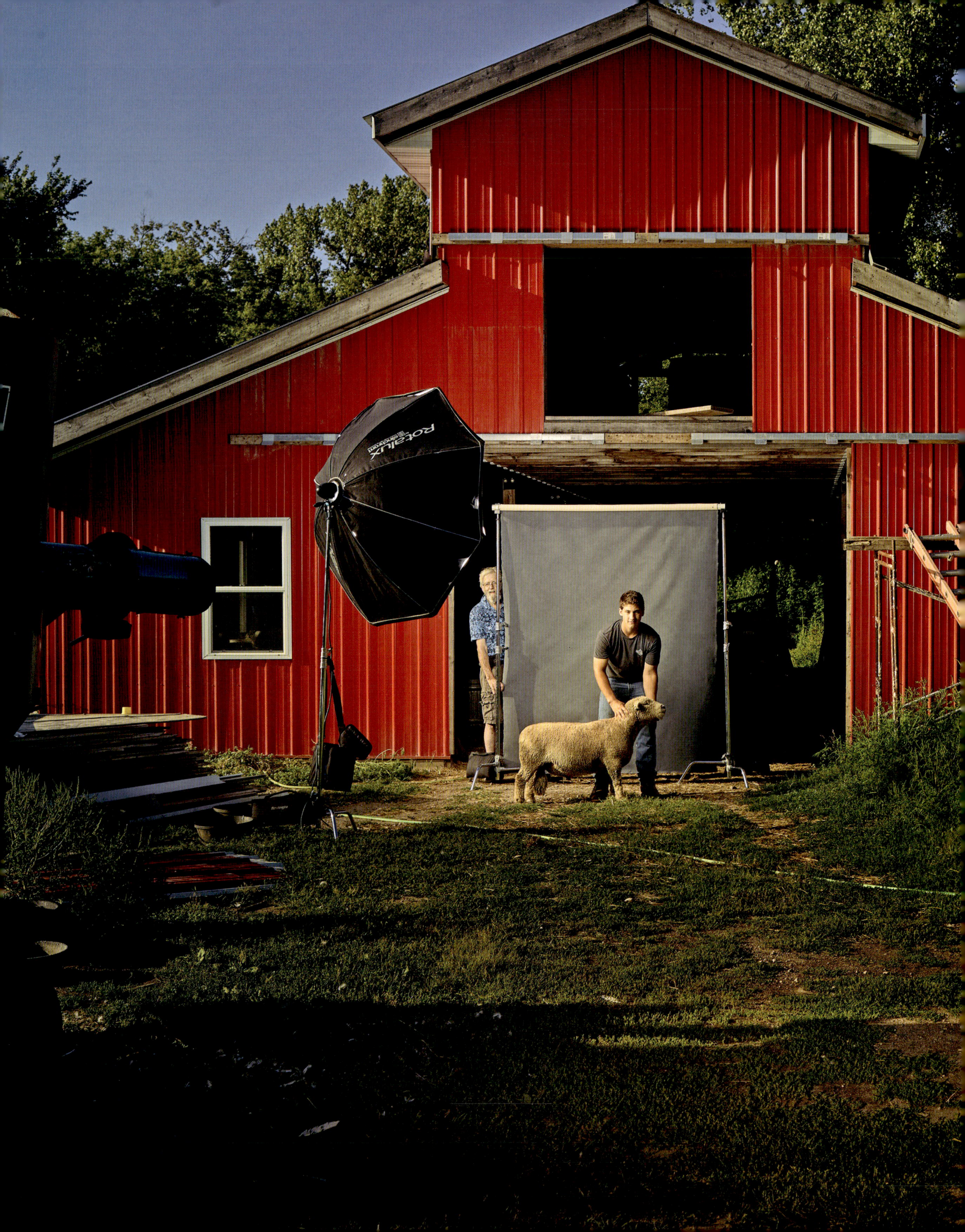

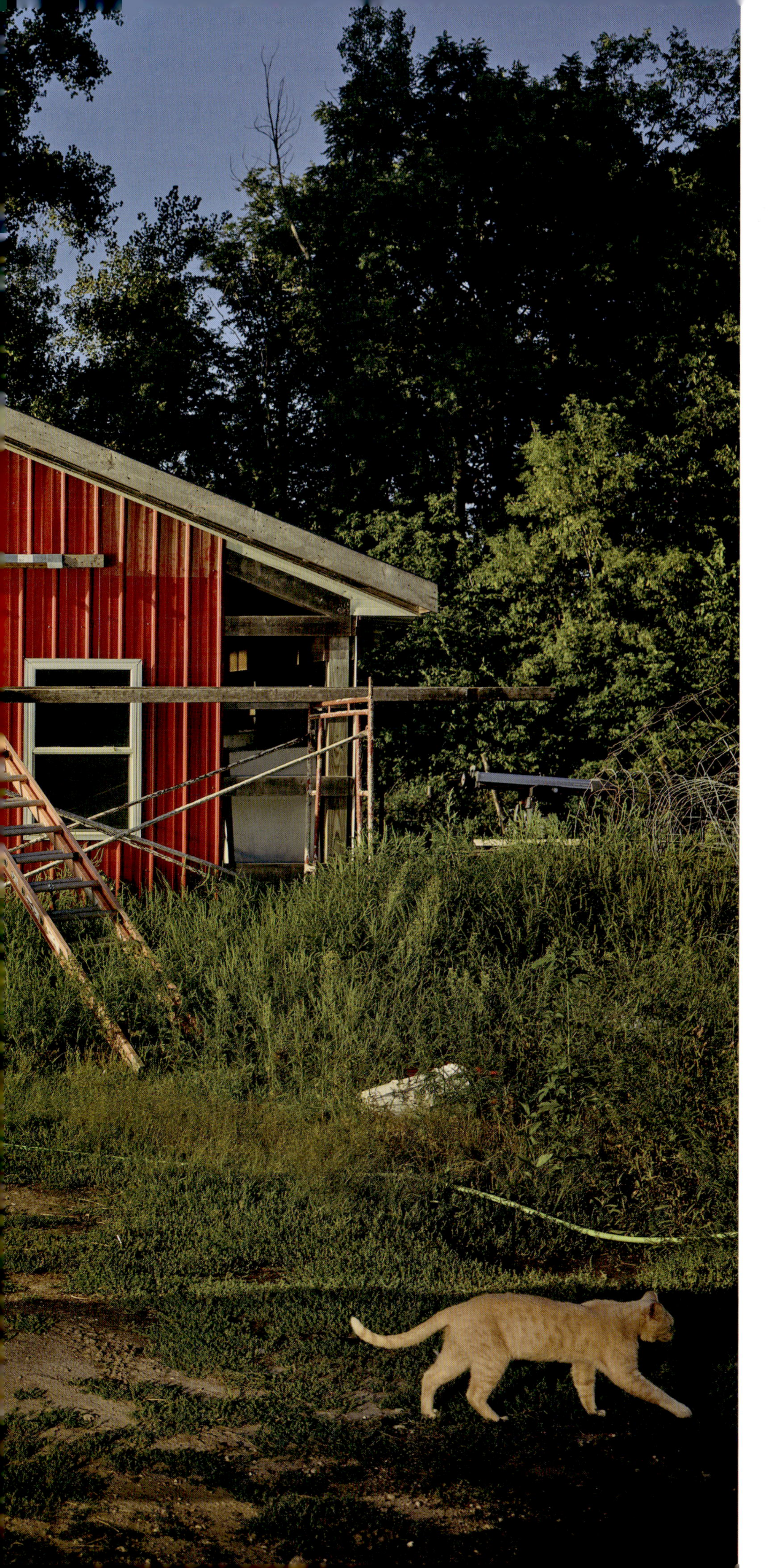

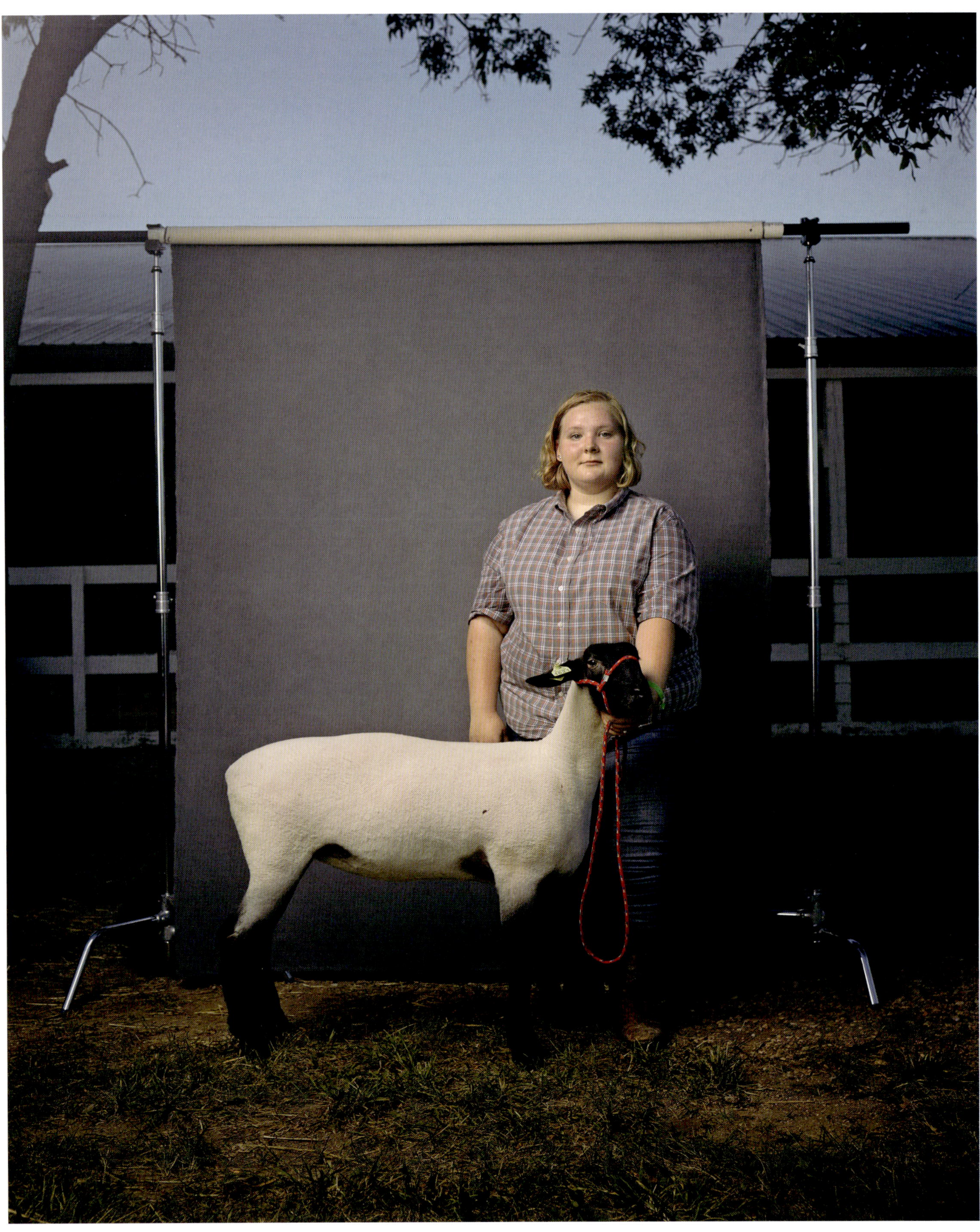

Katherine and Cagney, 2016

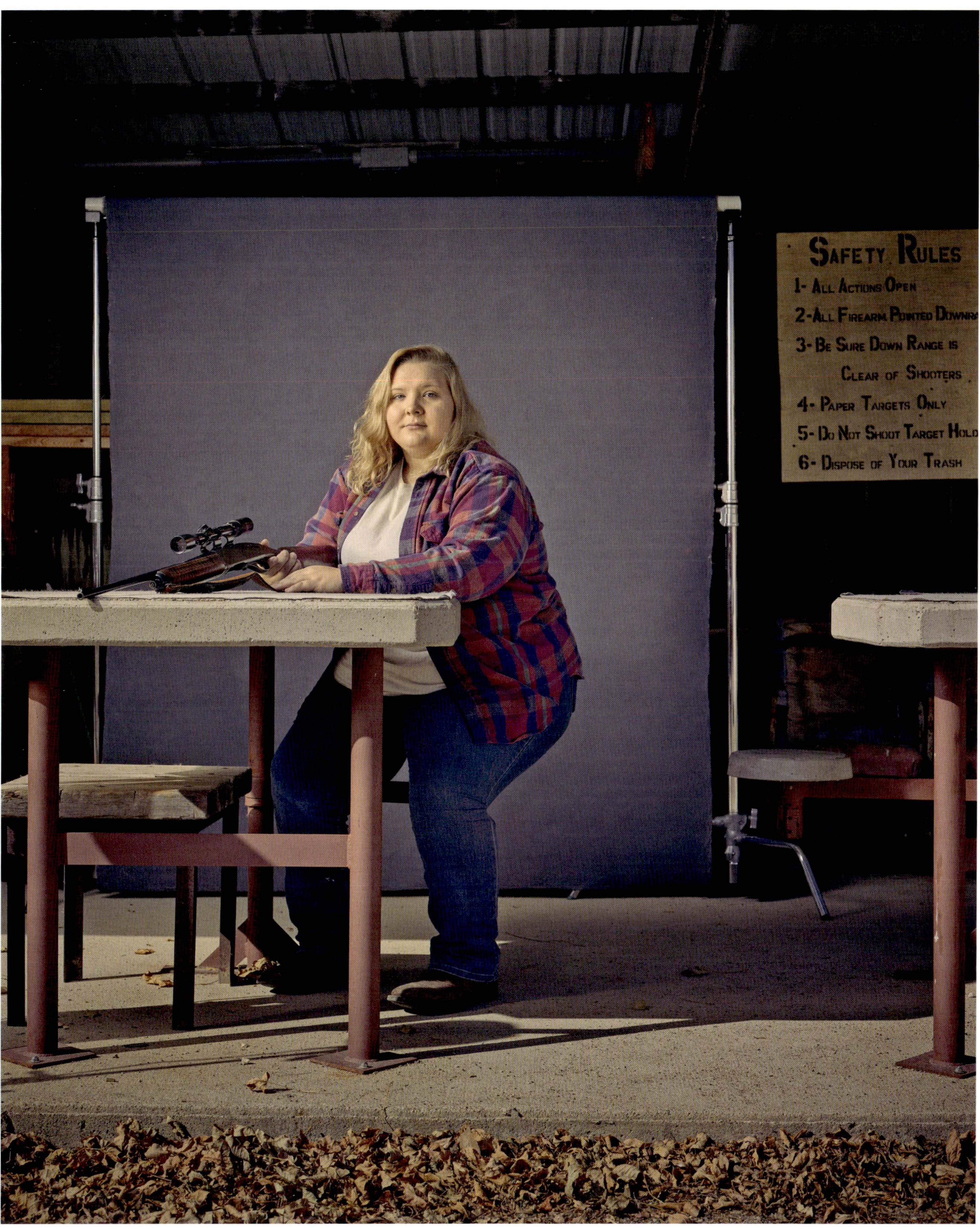

Katherine, 2020

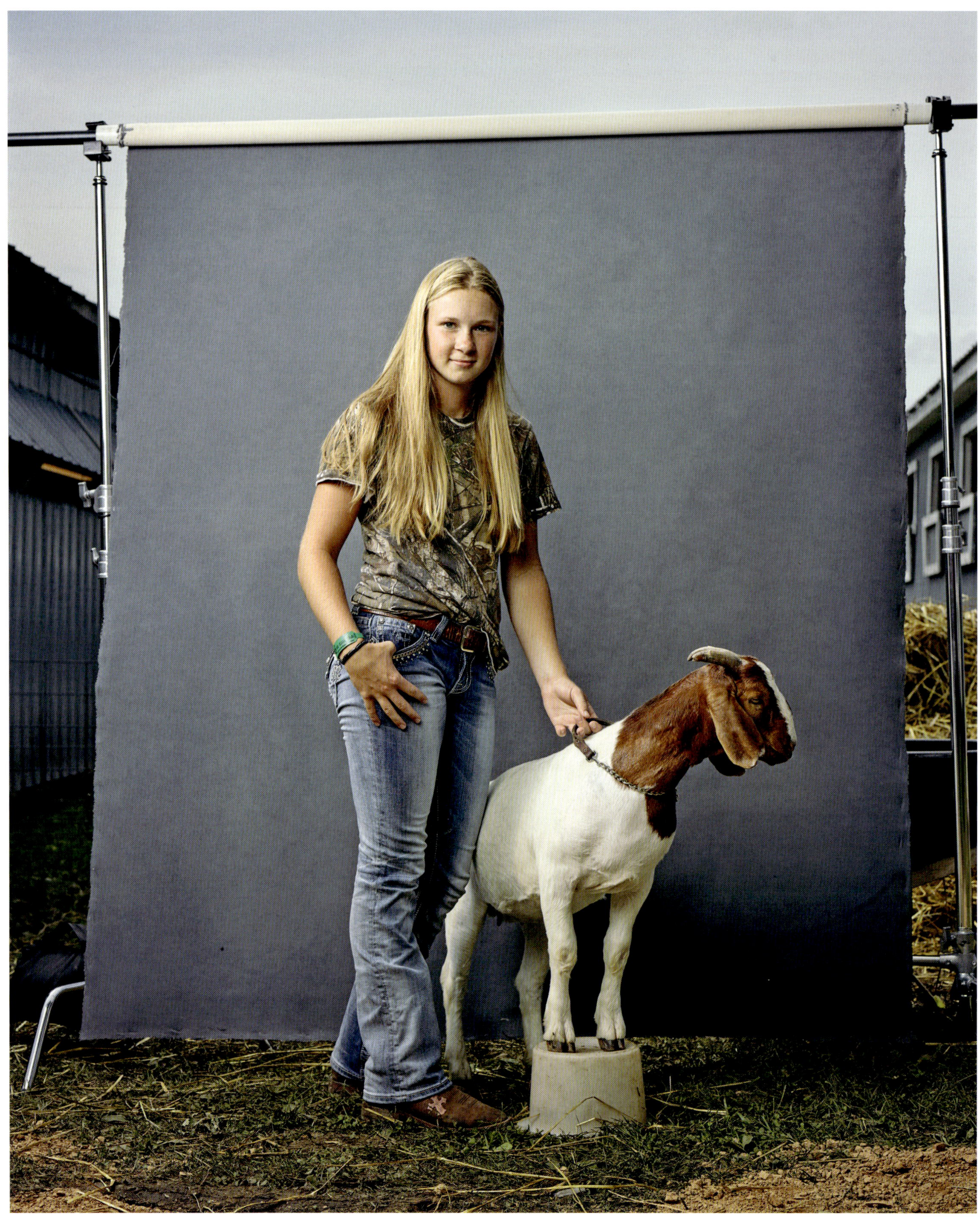

Audrey and Stella, 2016

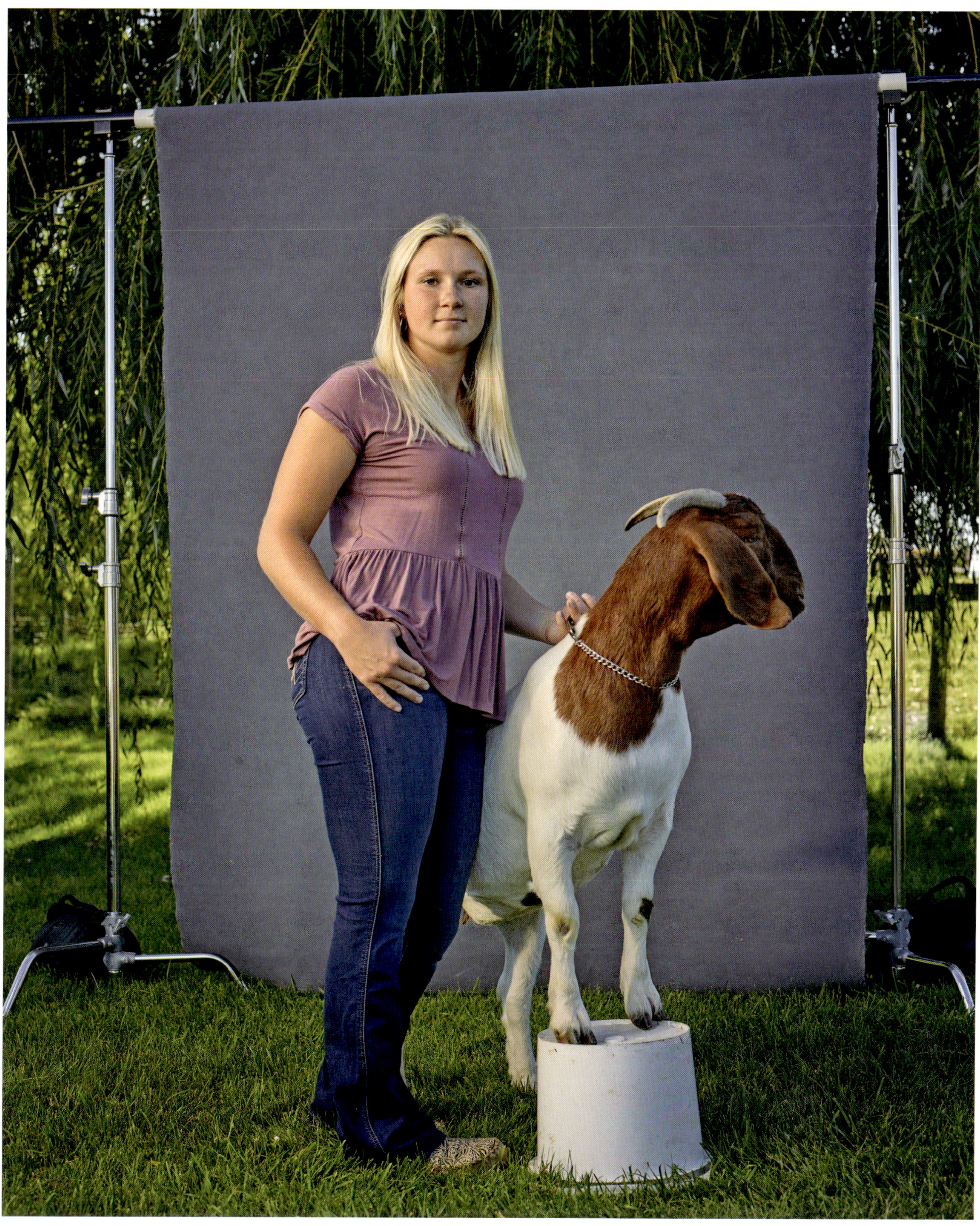

Audrey and Stella, 2020

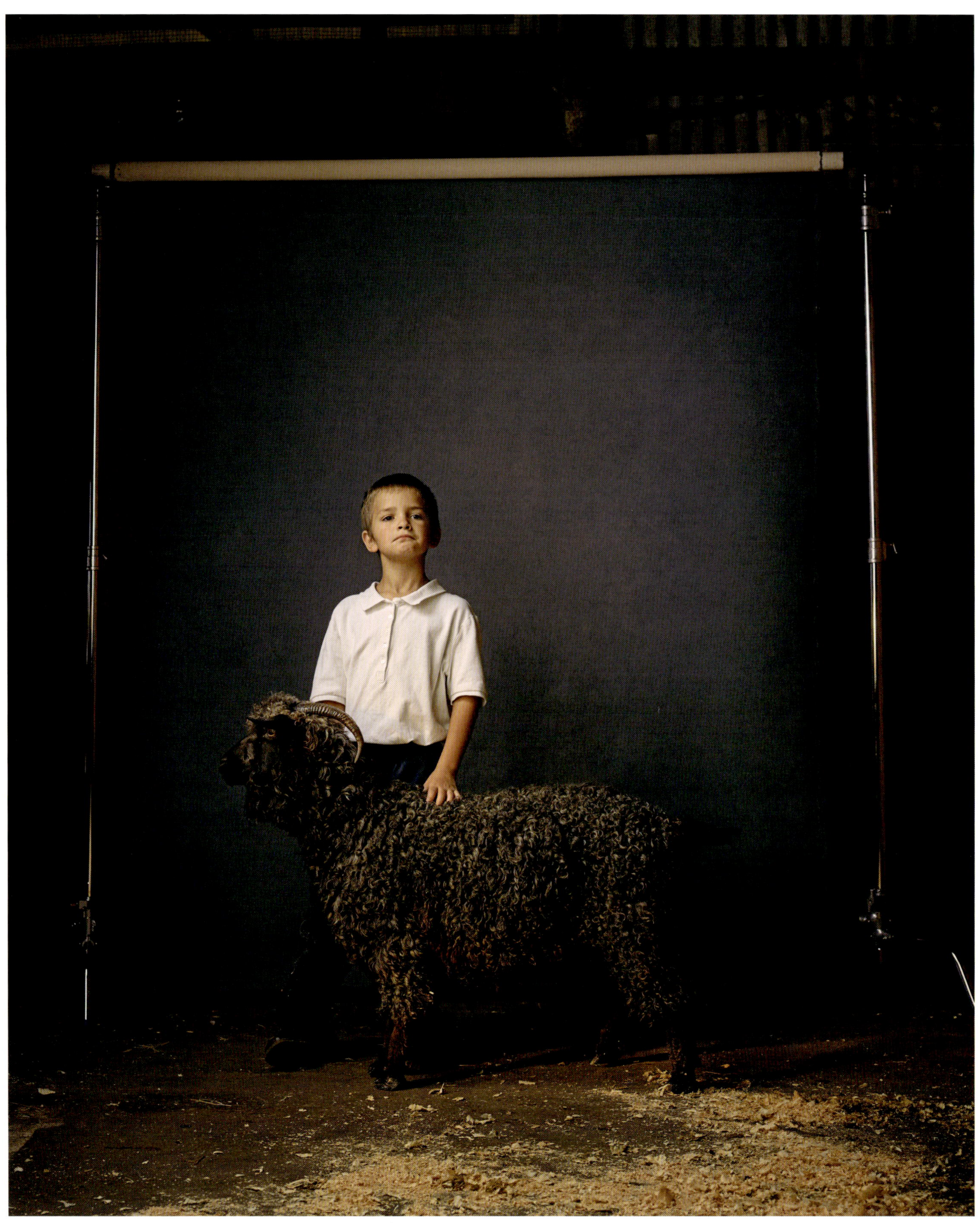

Kol and Annabelle, 2016

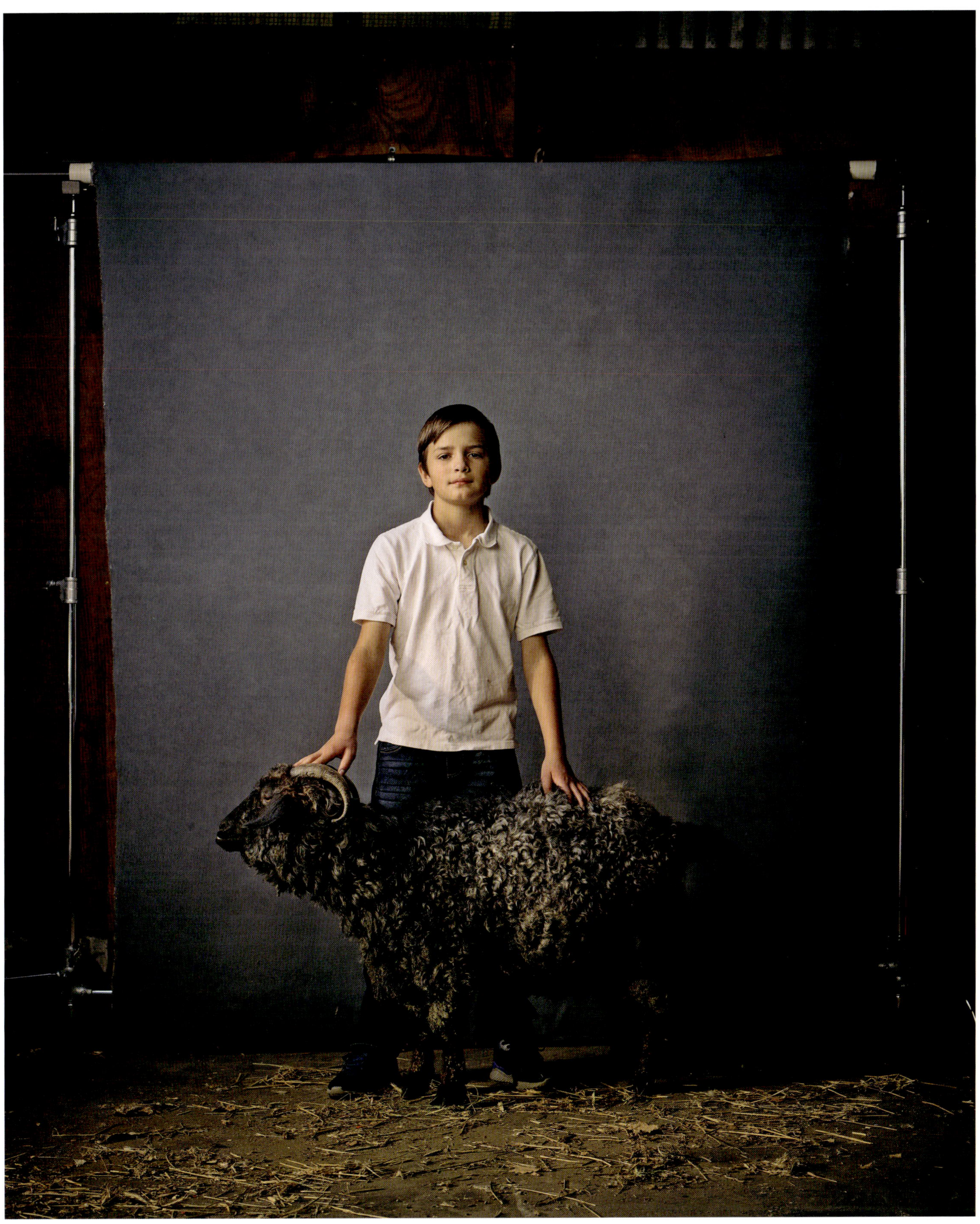

Kol and Annabelle, 2020

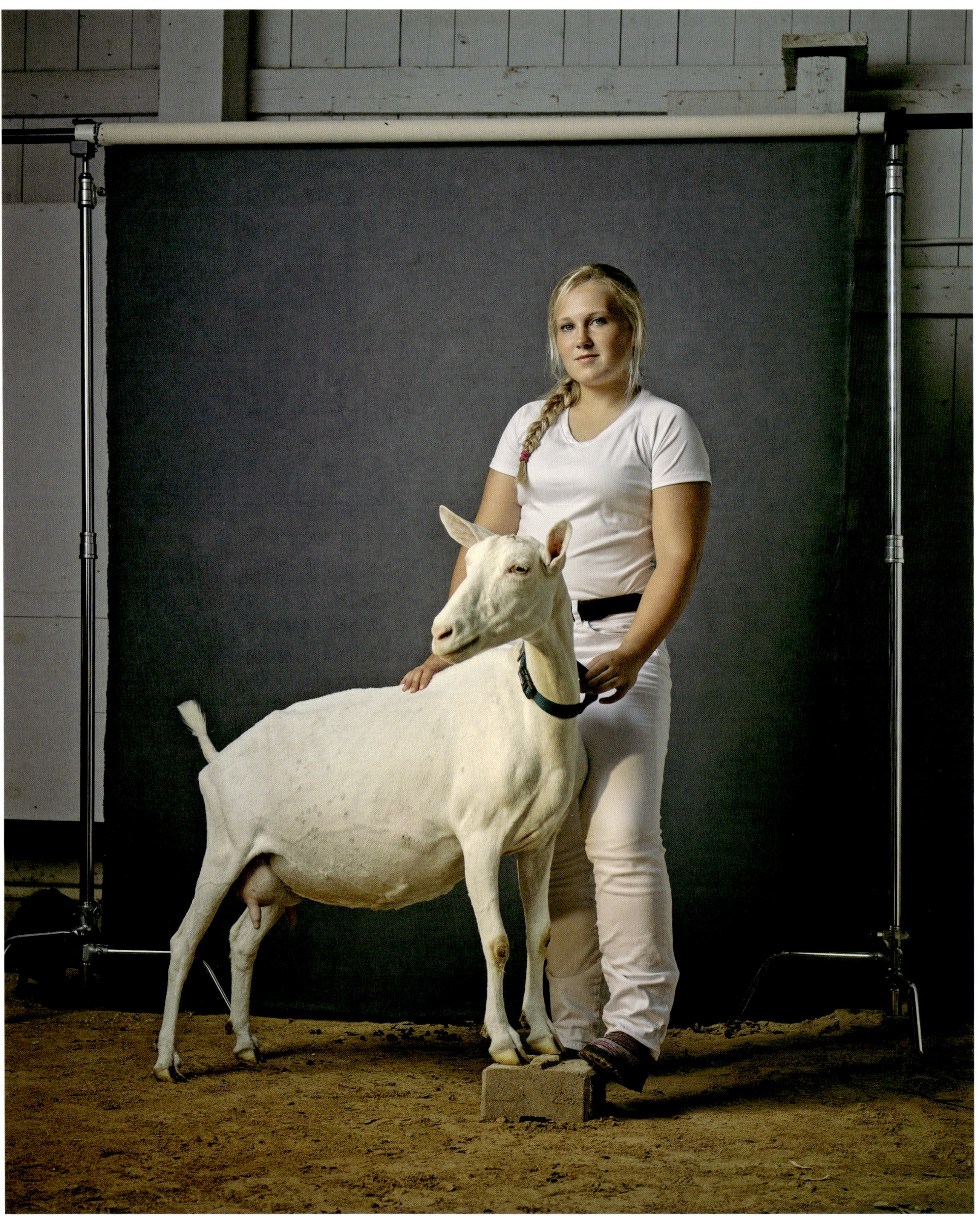

Bethany and Roxy, 2016

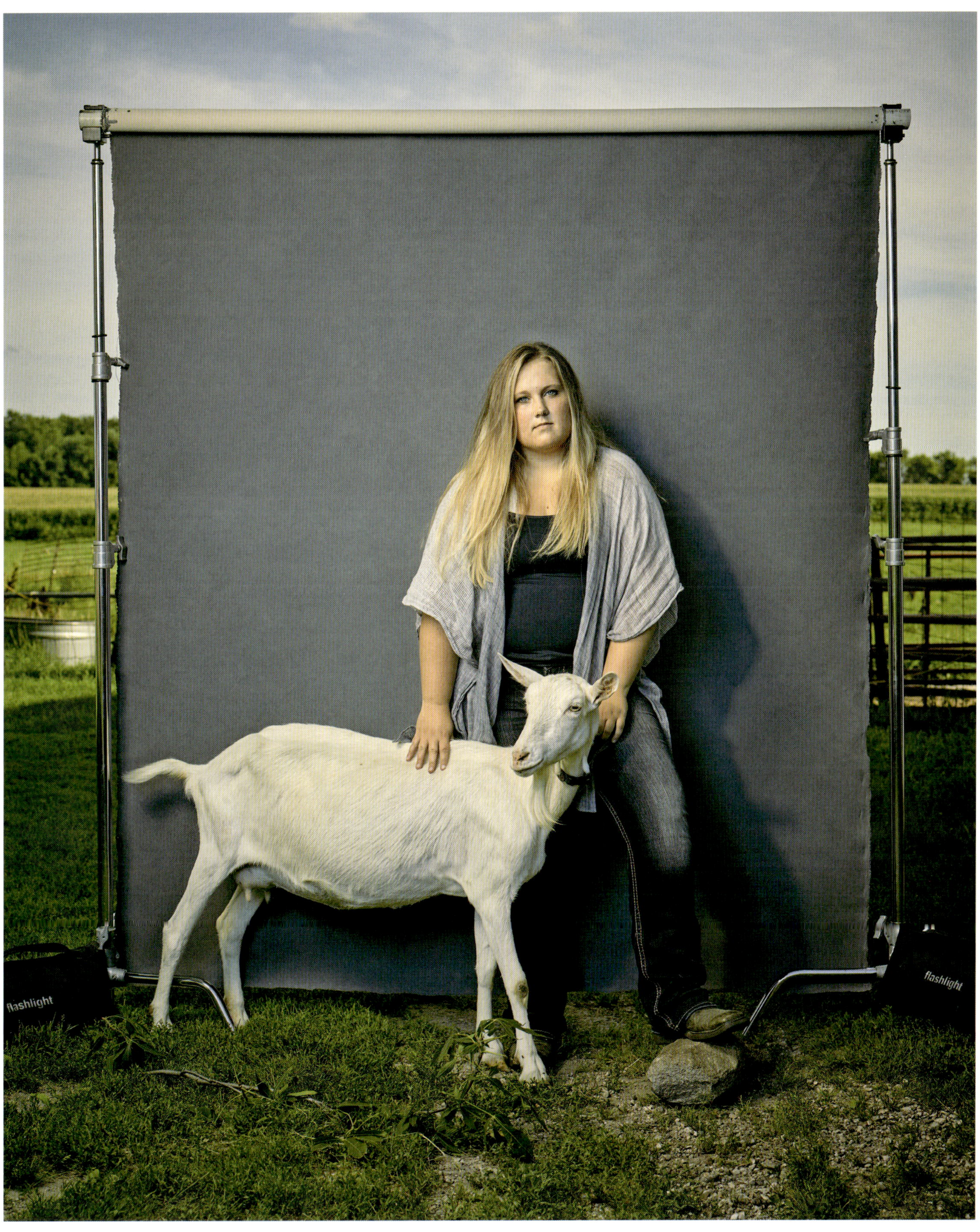

Bethany and Roxy, 2020

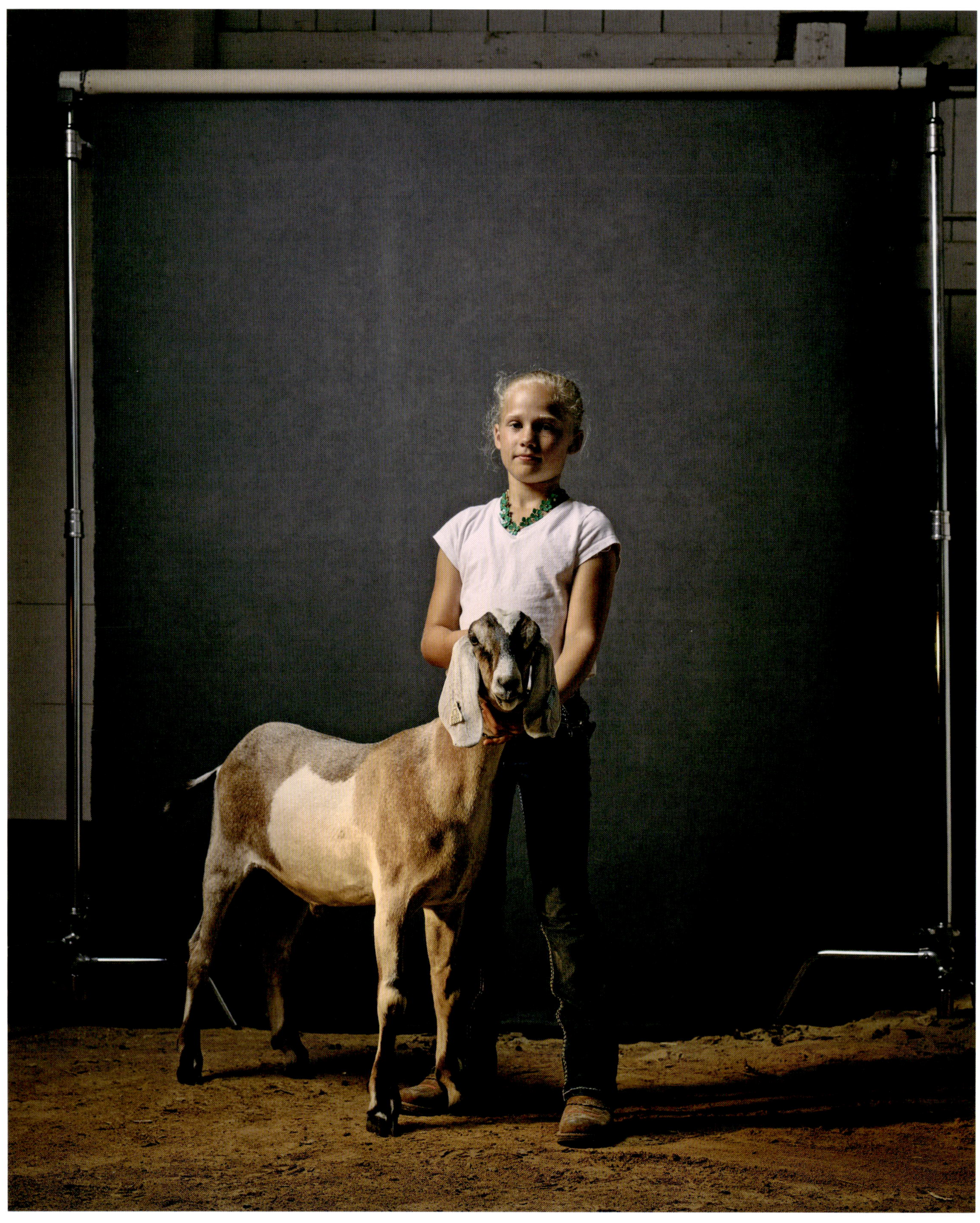

Hannah and Matthew, 2016

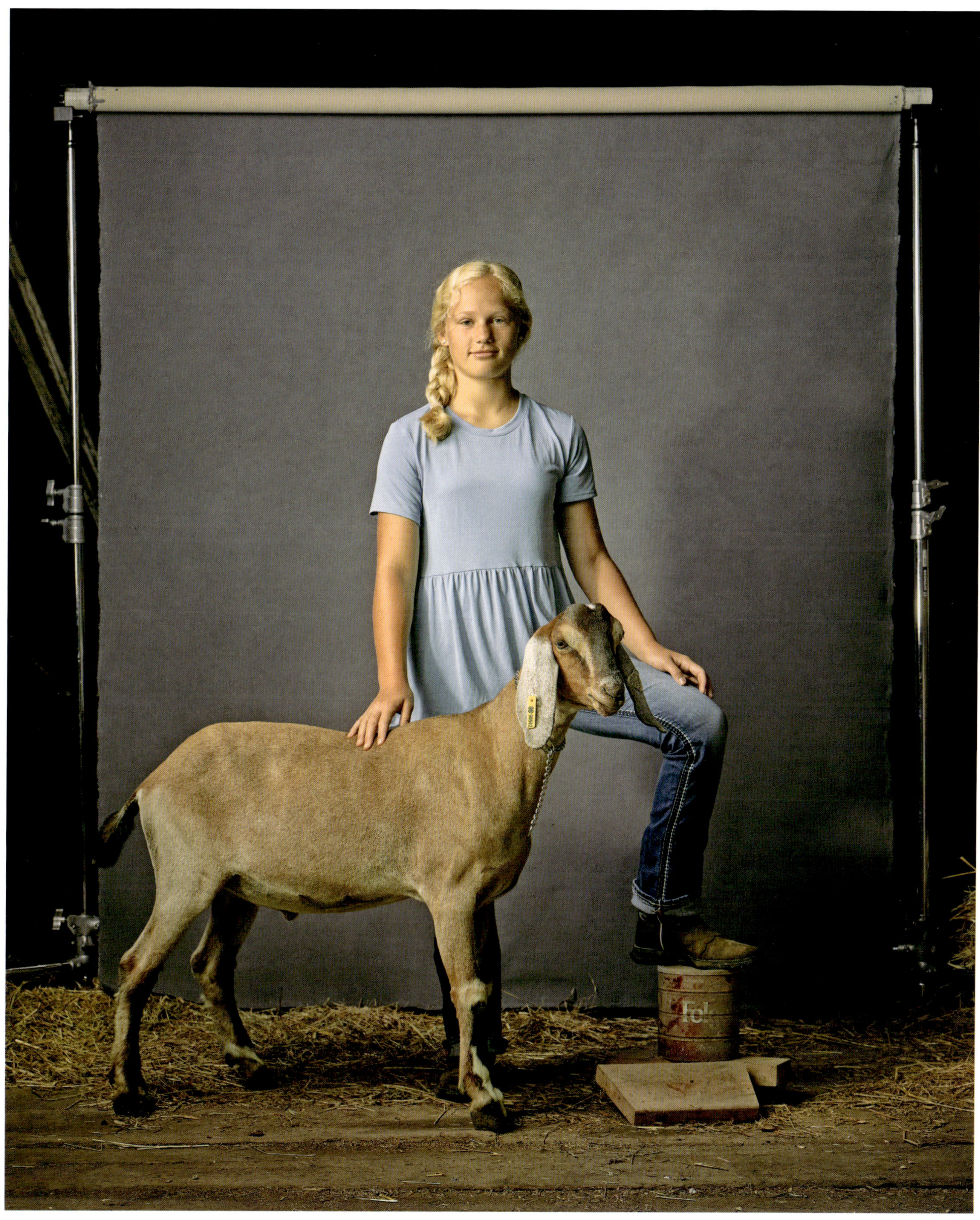

Hannah and Howard, 2020

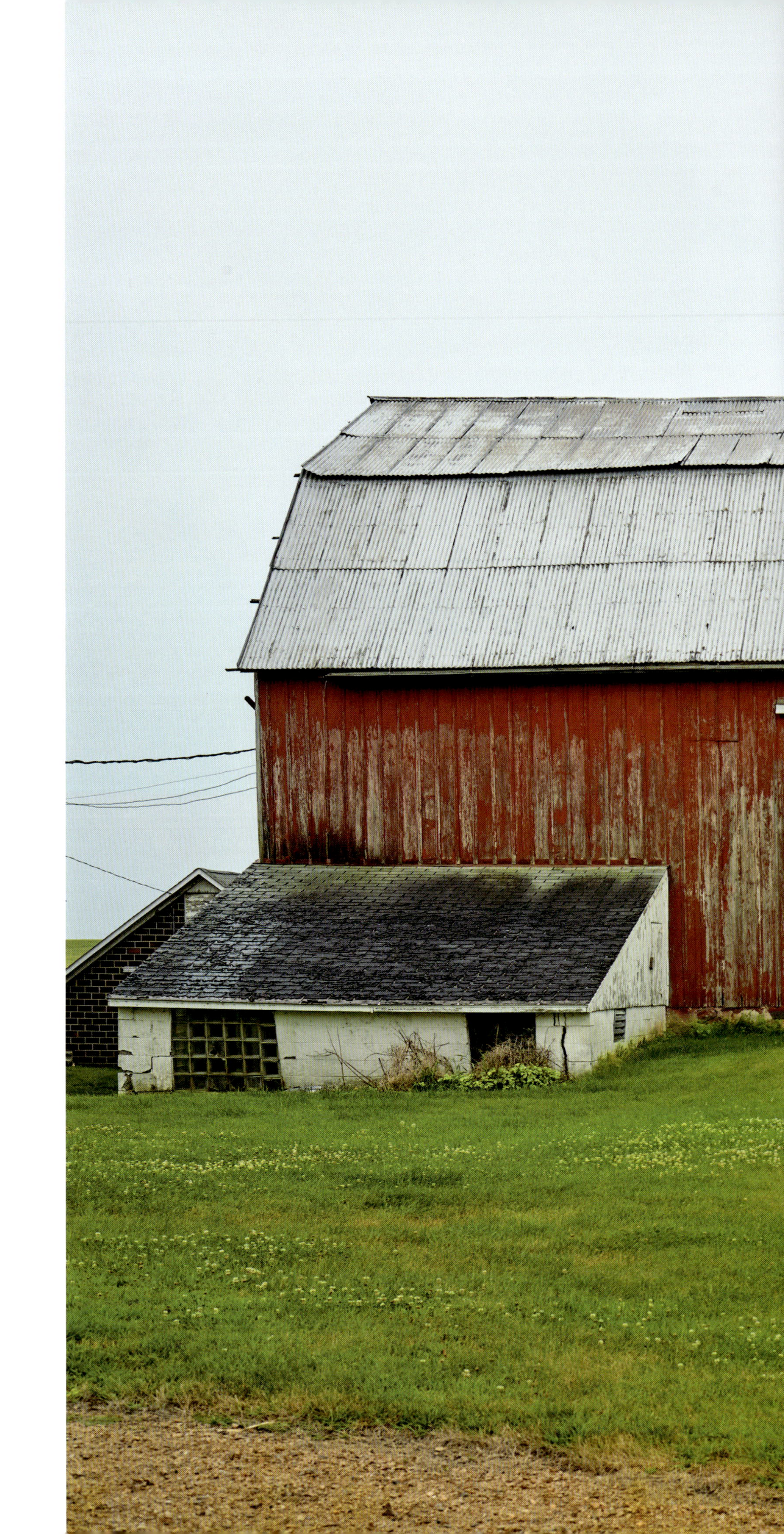

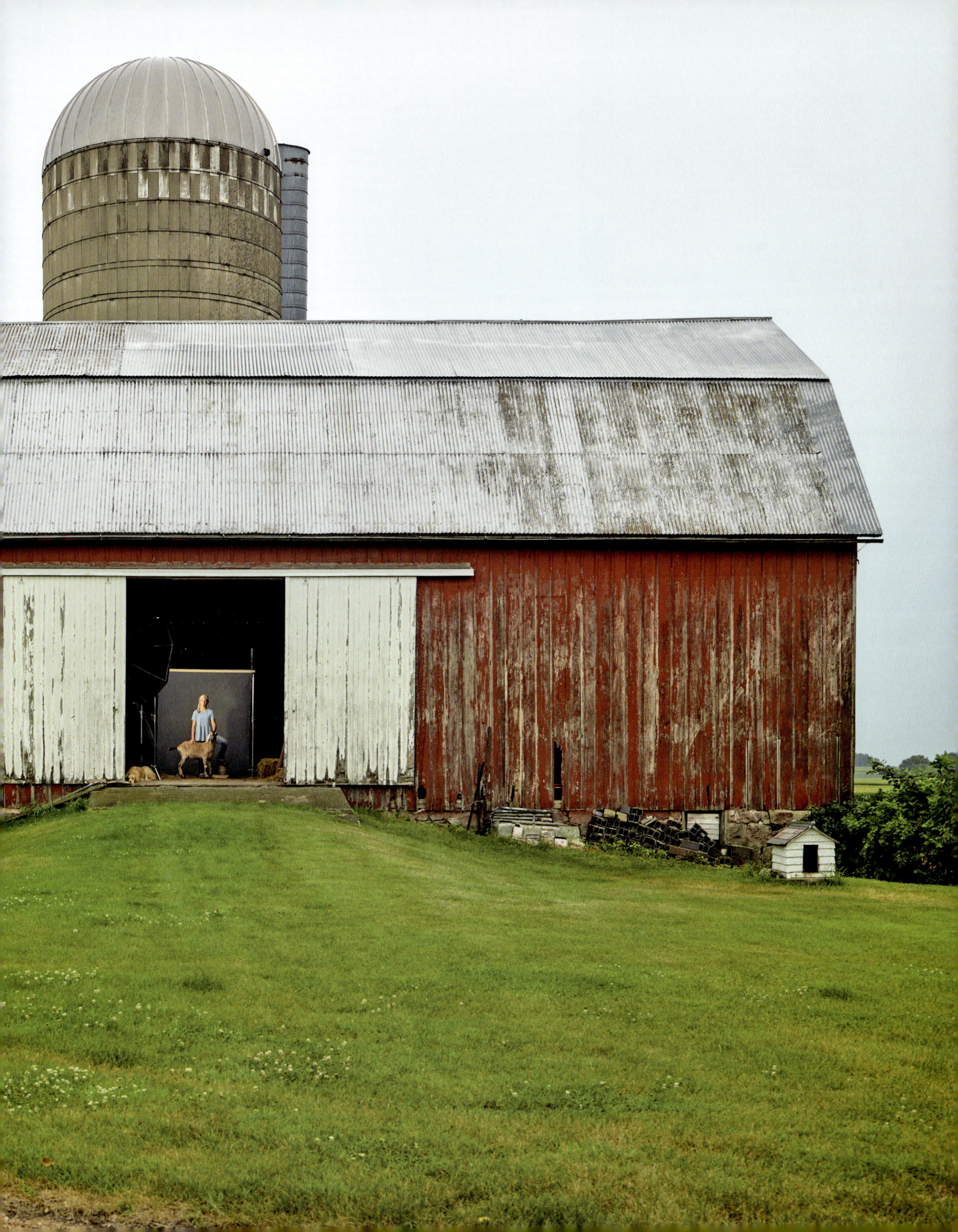

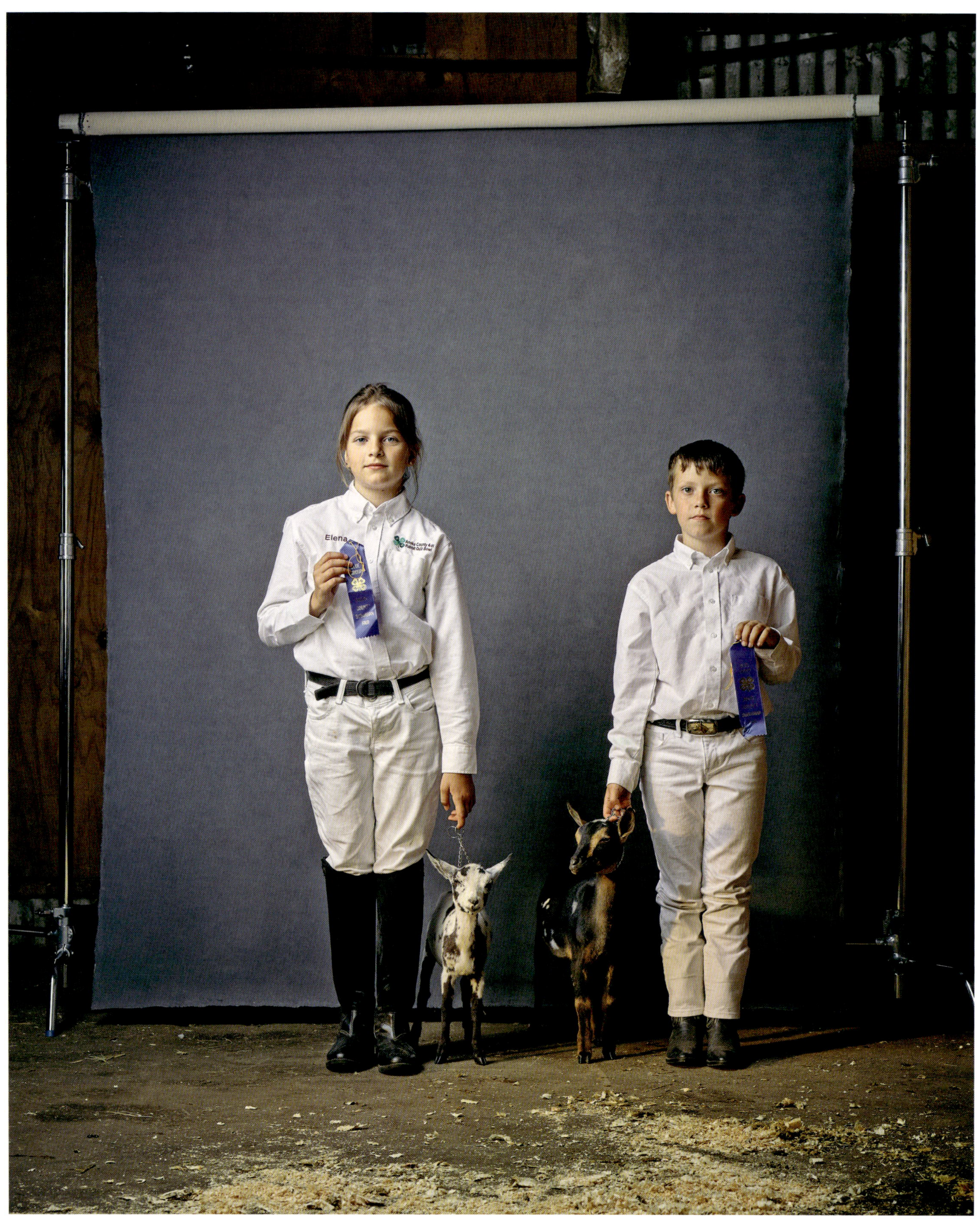

Elena with Tigerlily and Will with Tulip, 2016

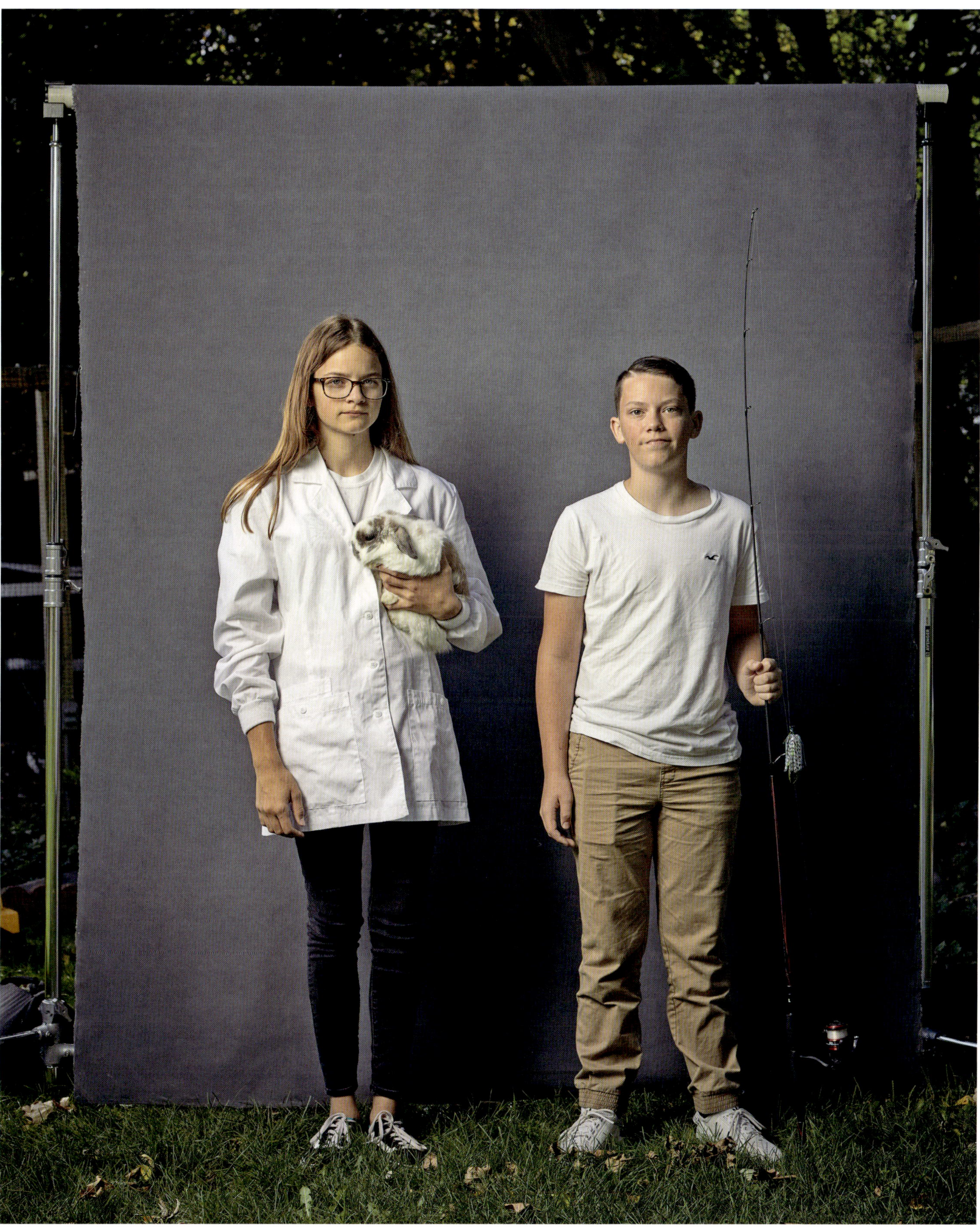

Elena and Will, 2020

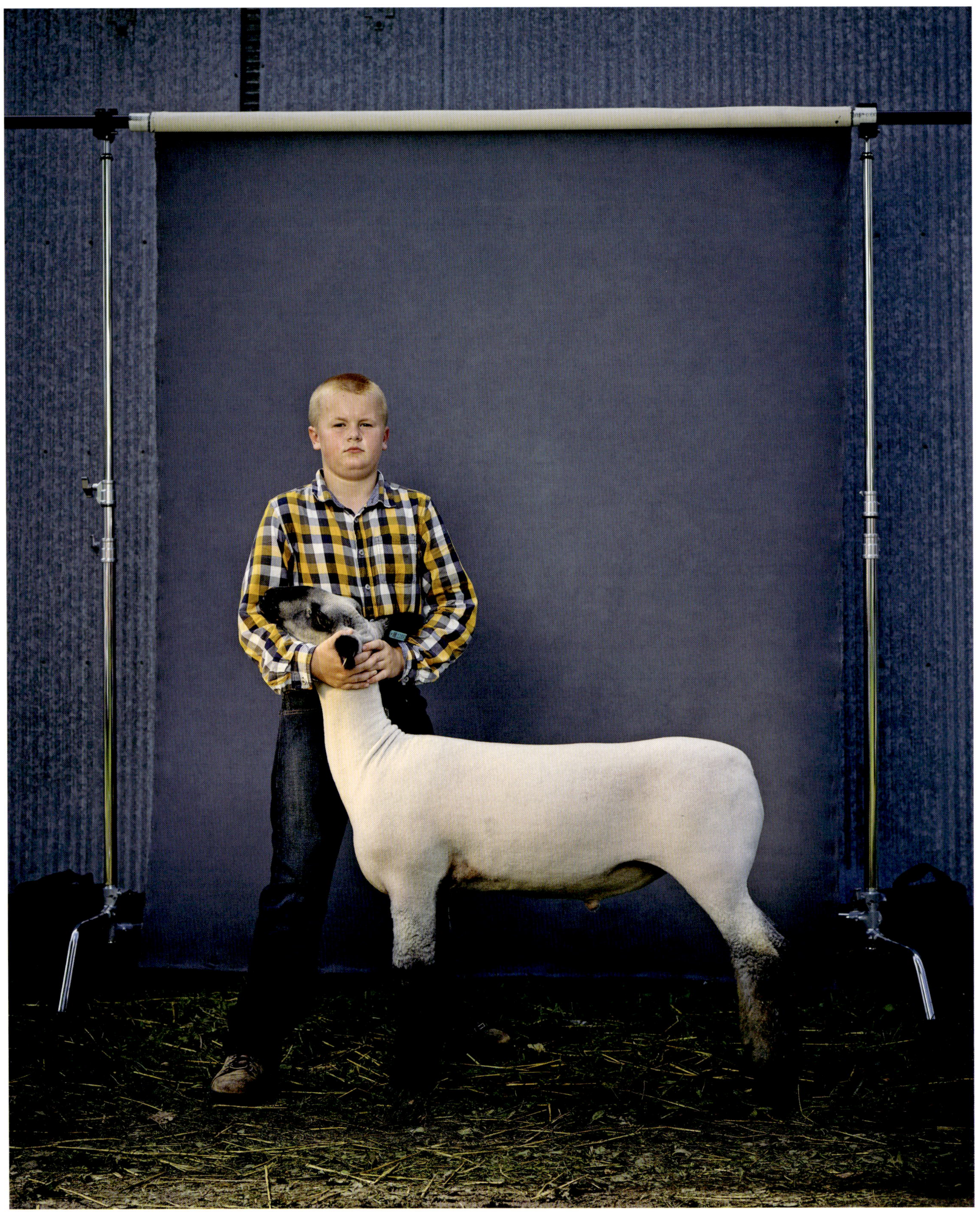

Dustin and Mack, 2016

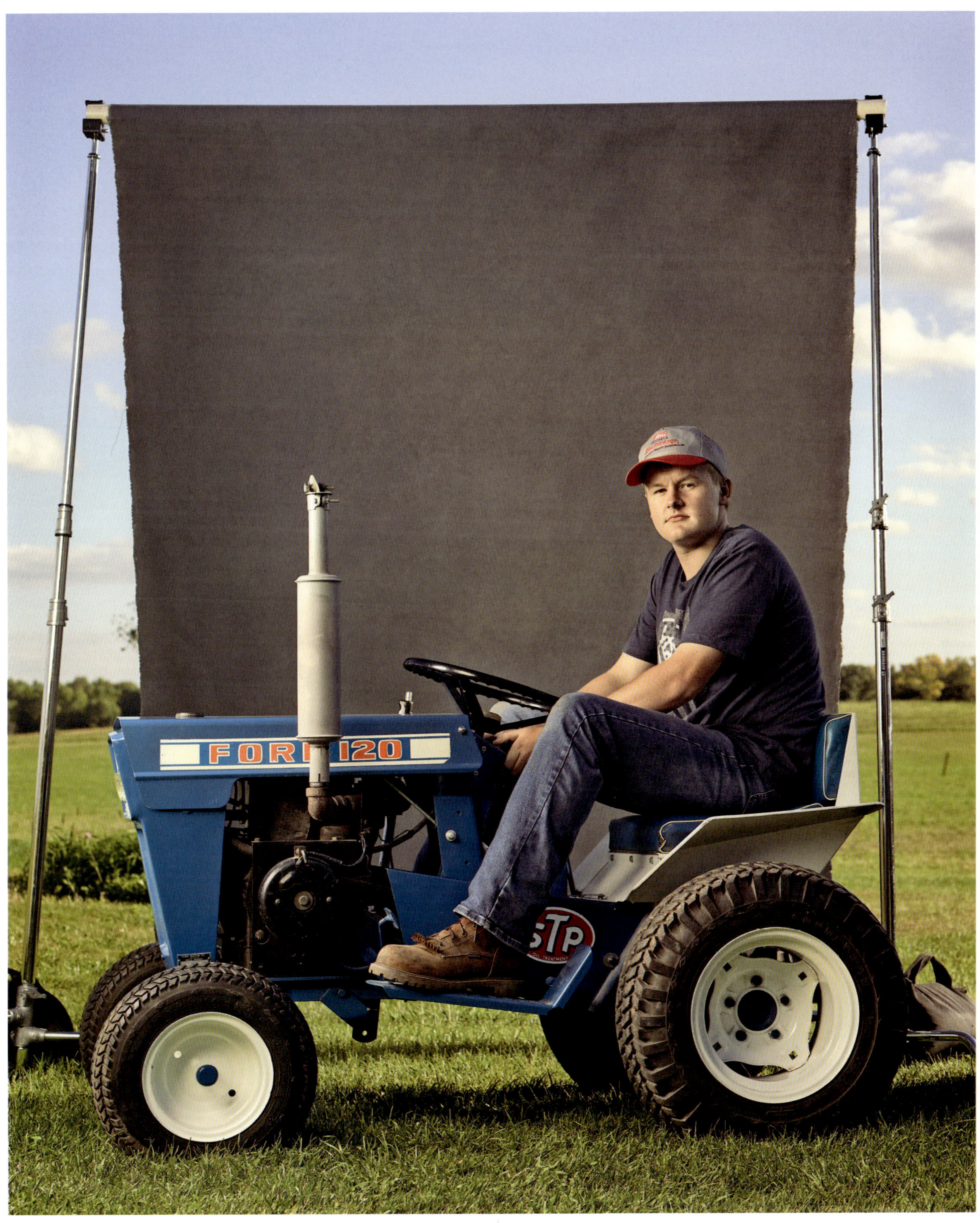

Dustin, 2020

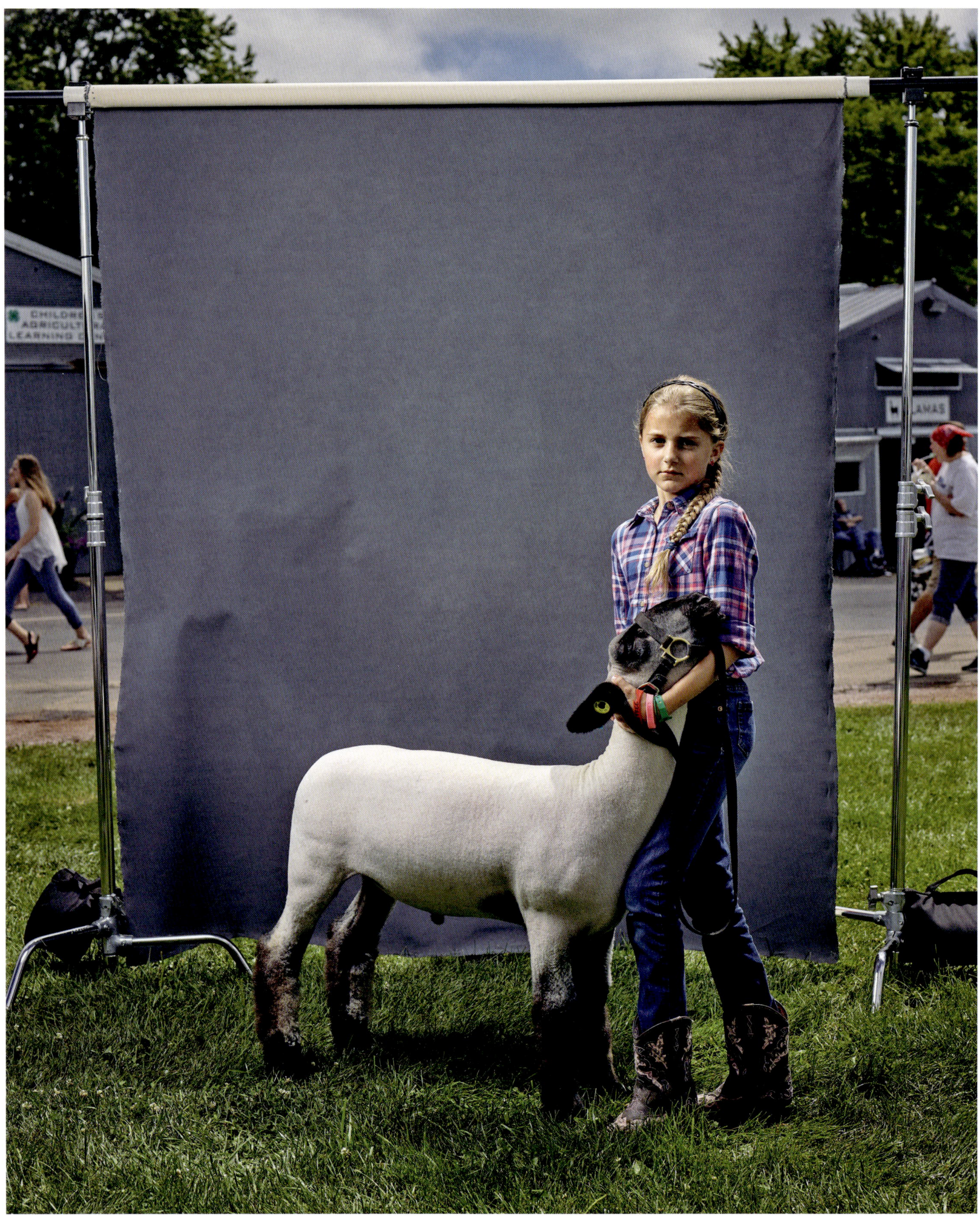

Cheyenne and Giraffe, 2016

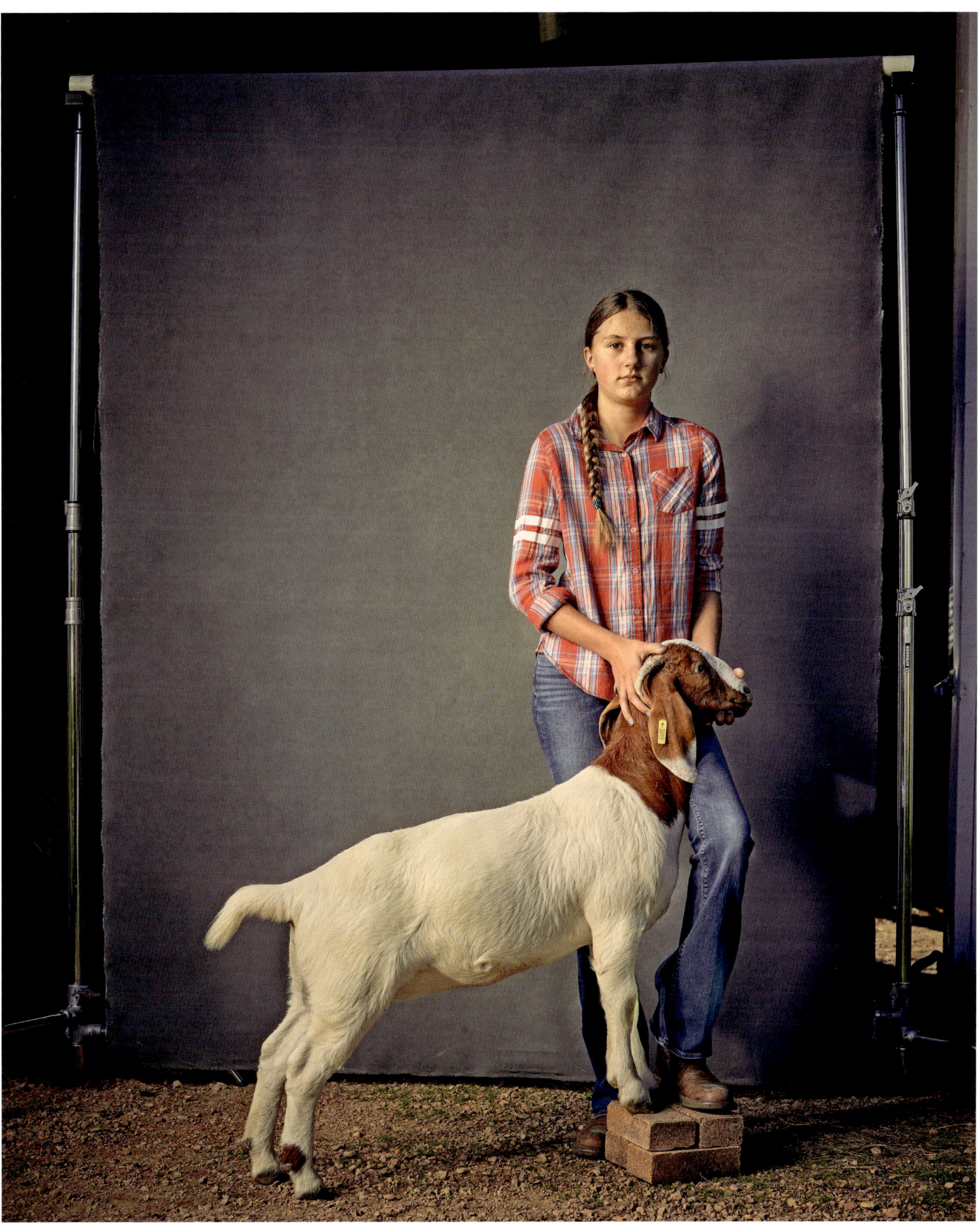

Cheyenne and Goat, 2020

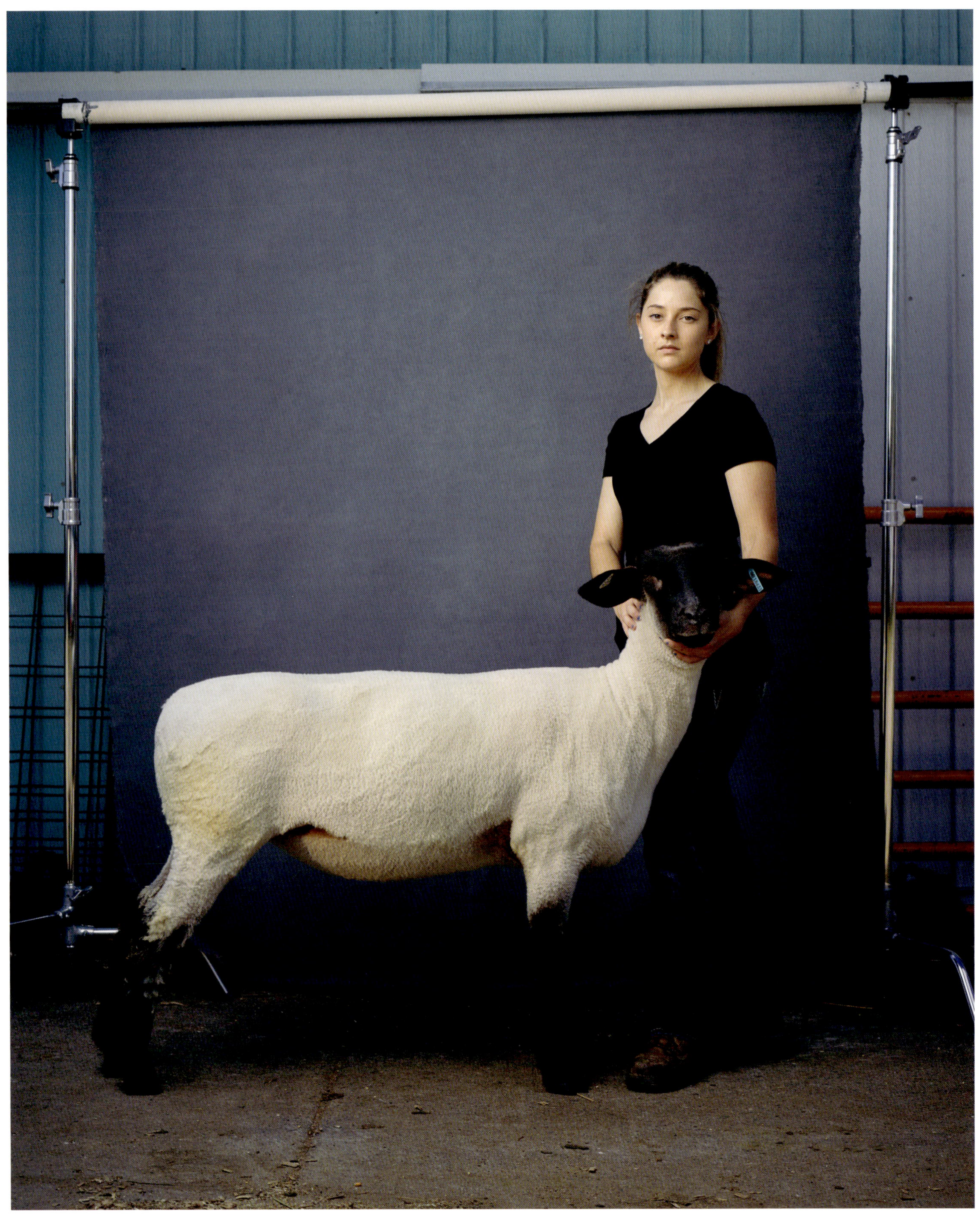

Chelsea and Chelsea's Crowdpleaser, 2016

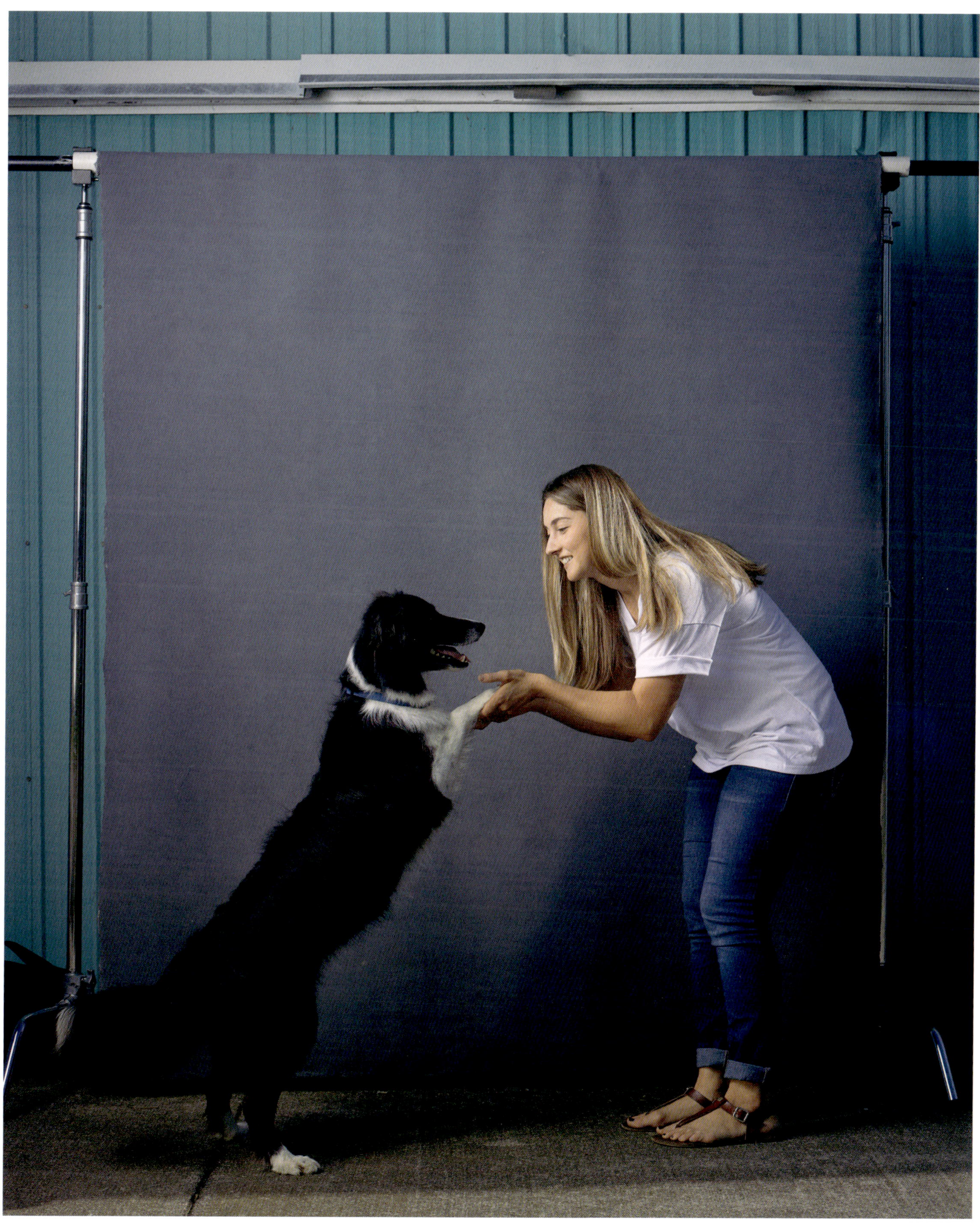

Chelsea and Willow, 2020

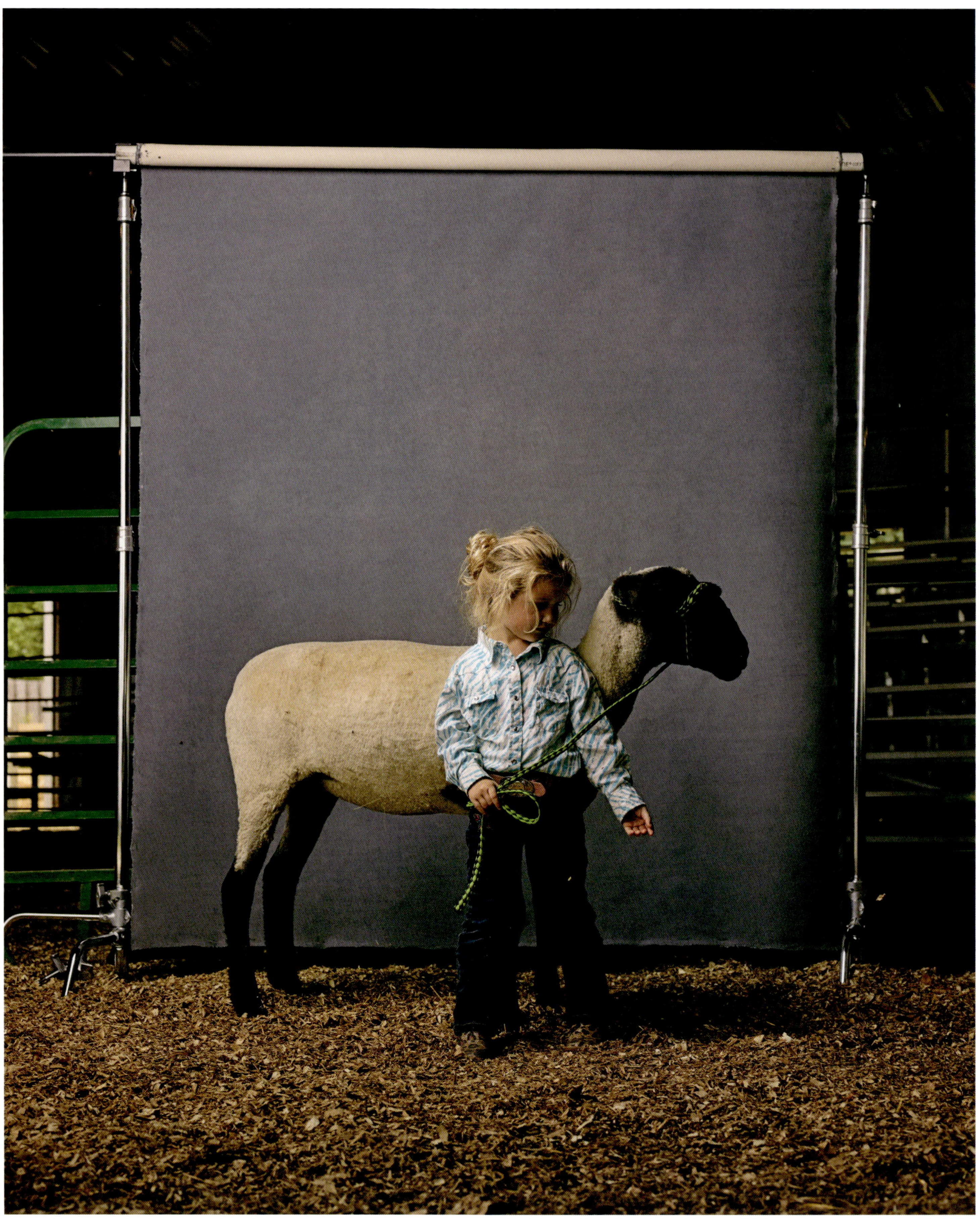

Rylee and Nelly, 2016

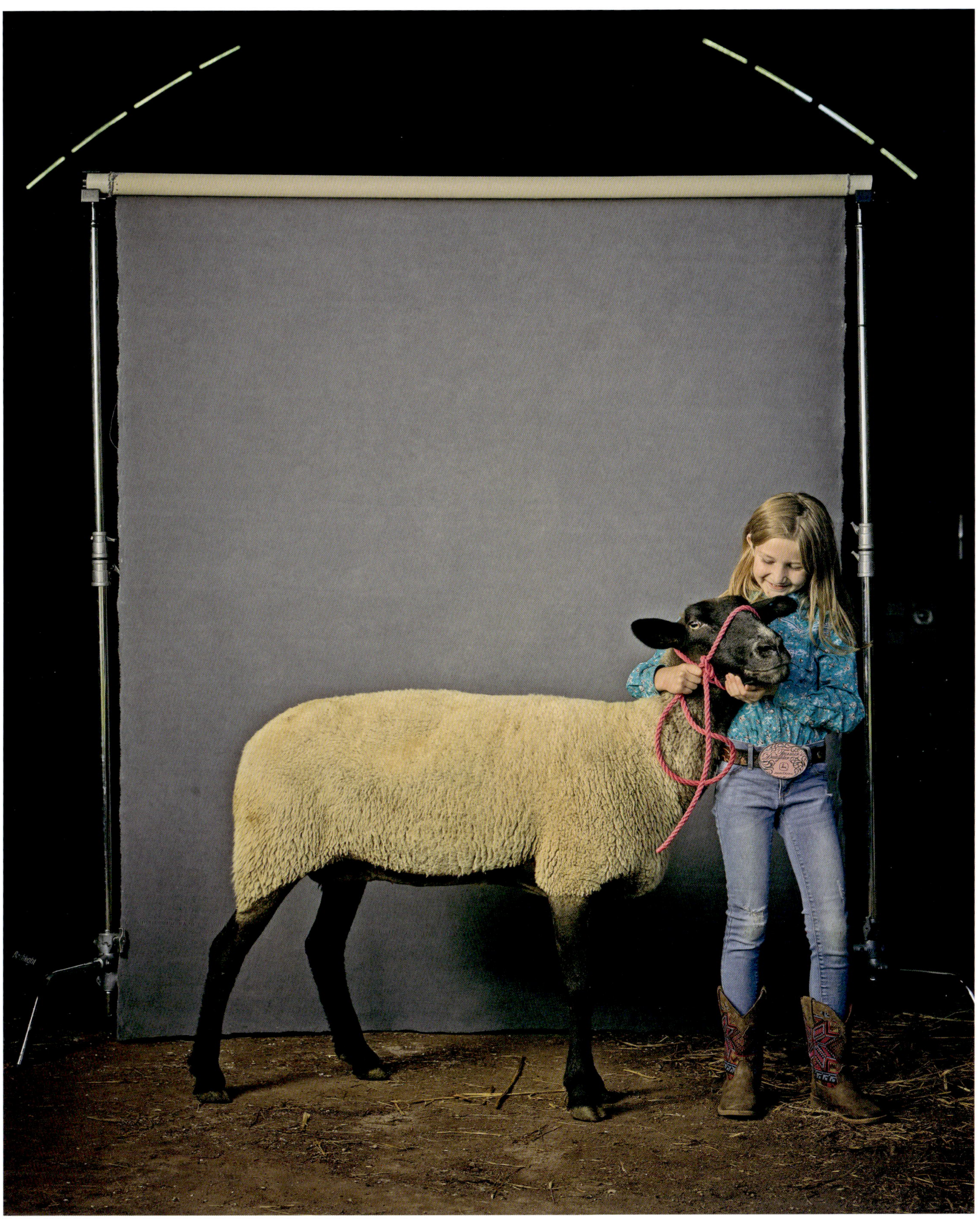

Rylee and Nelly, 2020

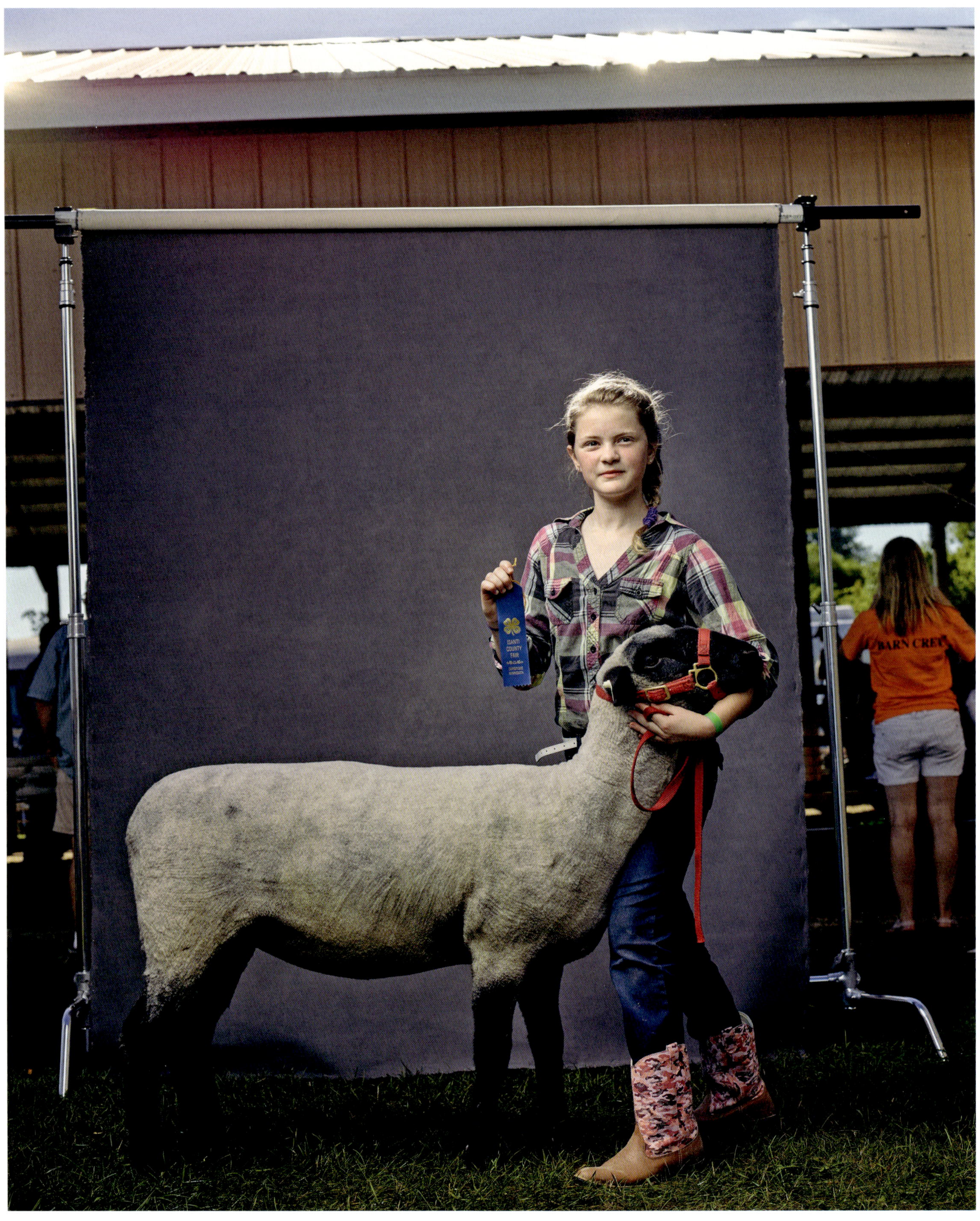

Mable and Stella, 2016

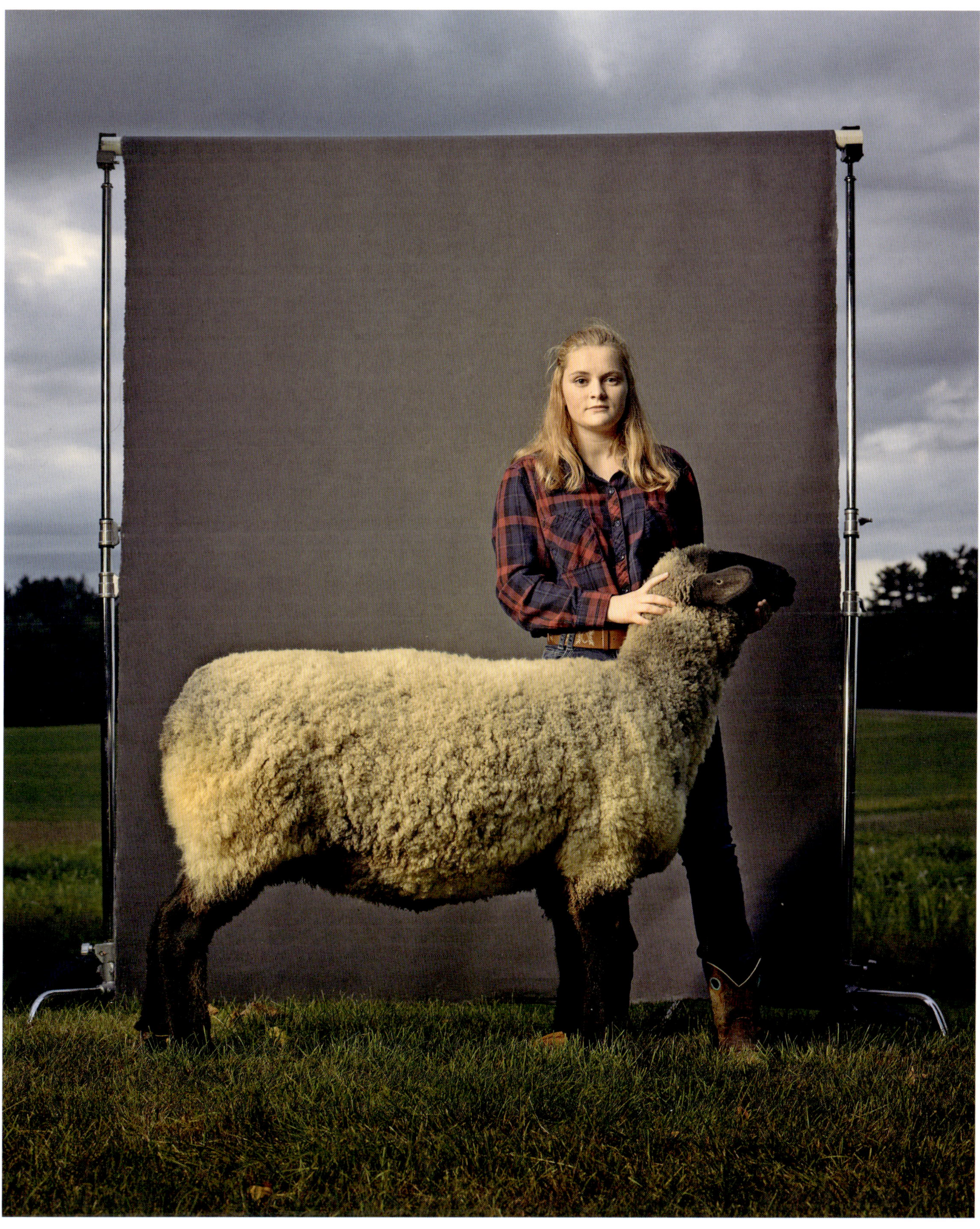

Mable and Stella, 2020

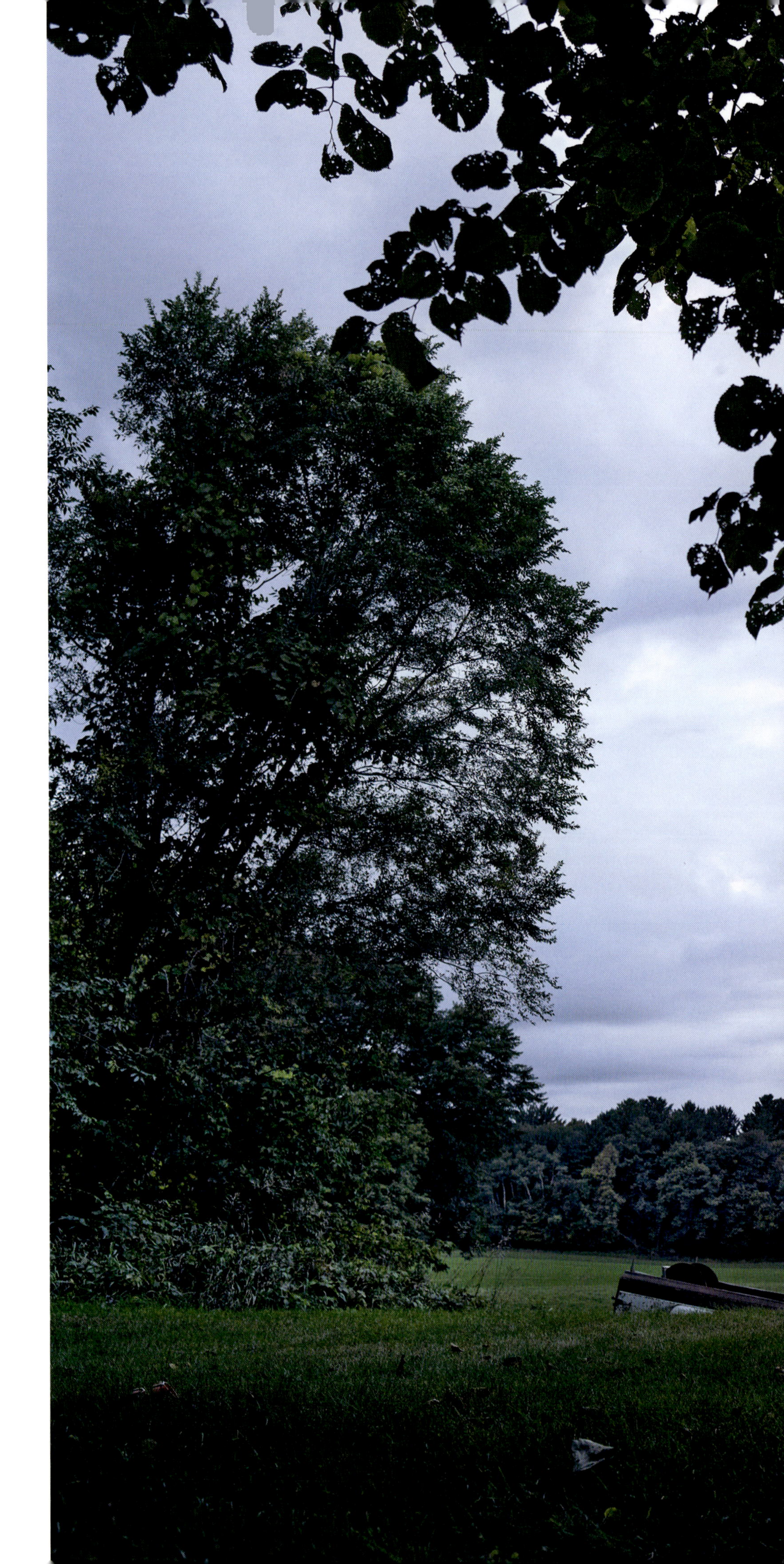

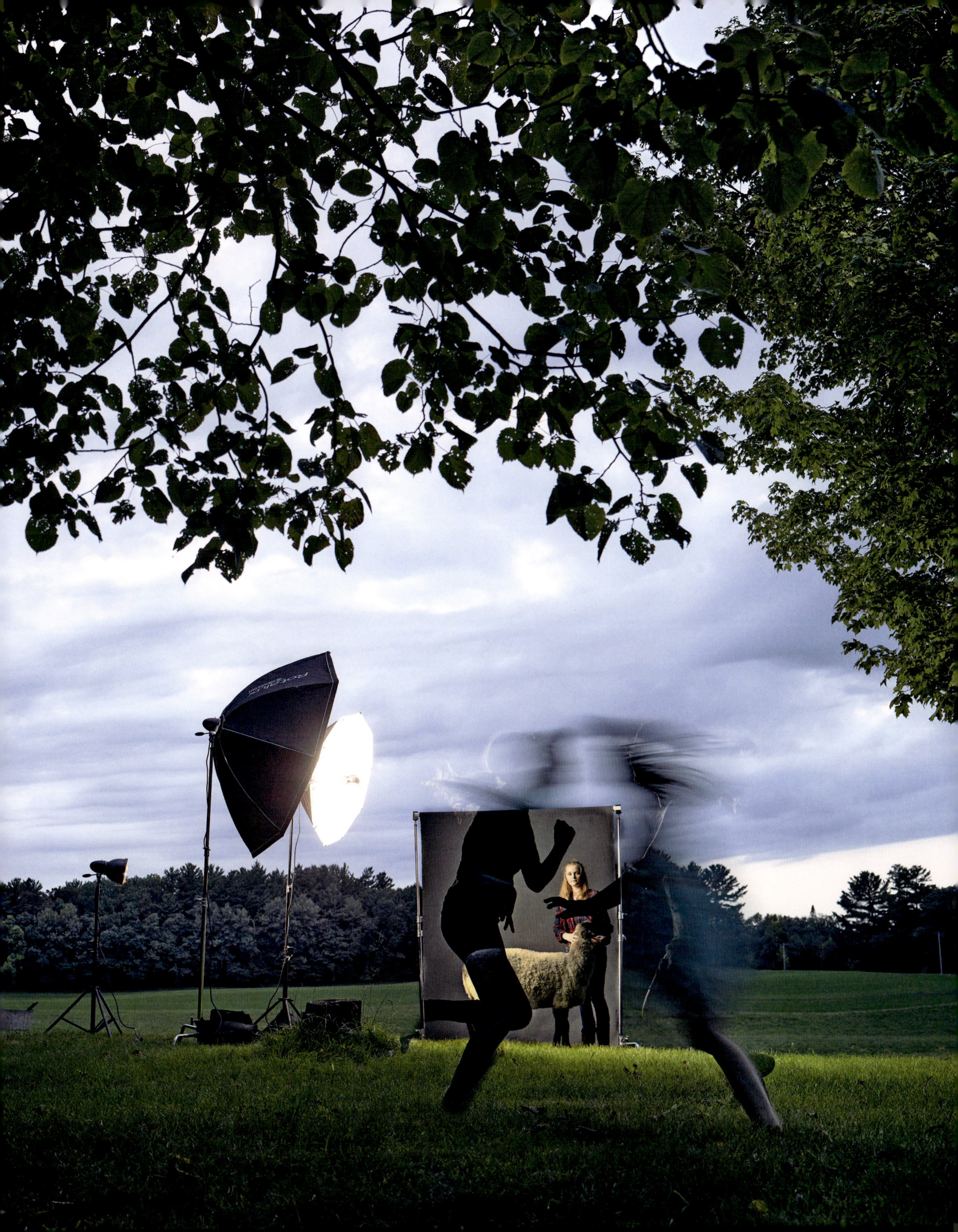

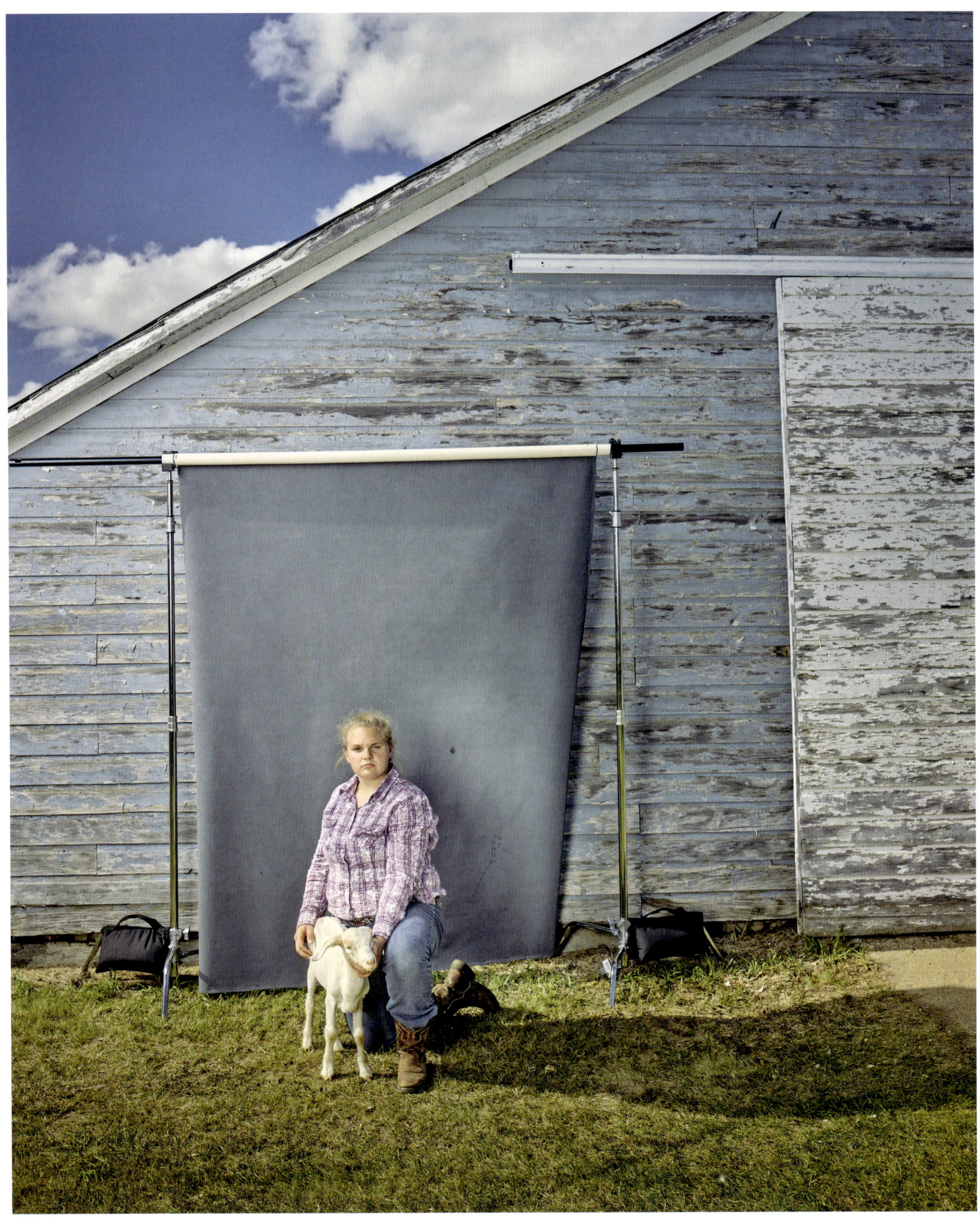

Emma and Margo, 2016

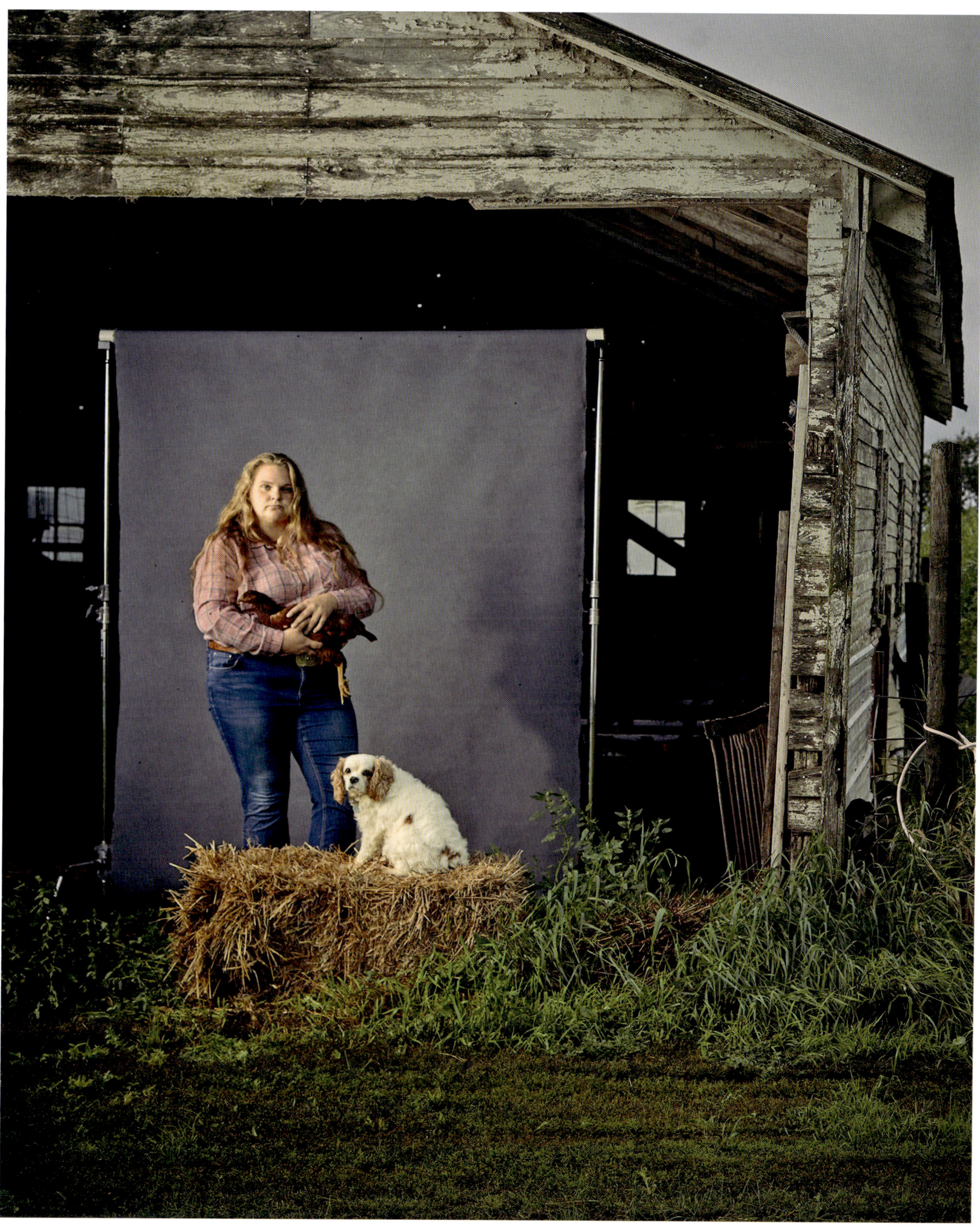

Emma, Bob and Chicken, 2020

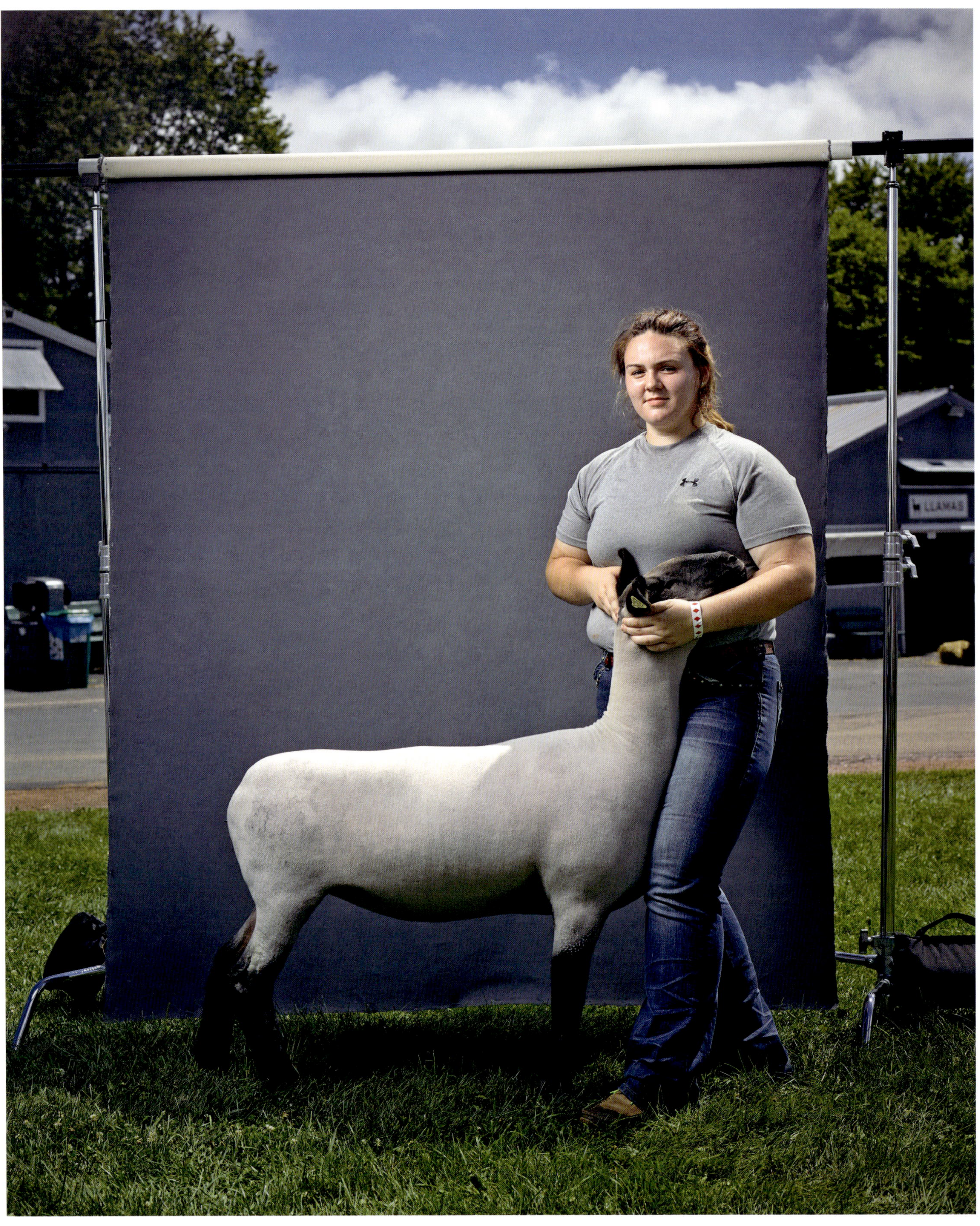

Grace and Wild Child, 2016

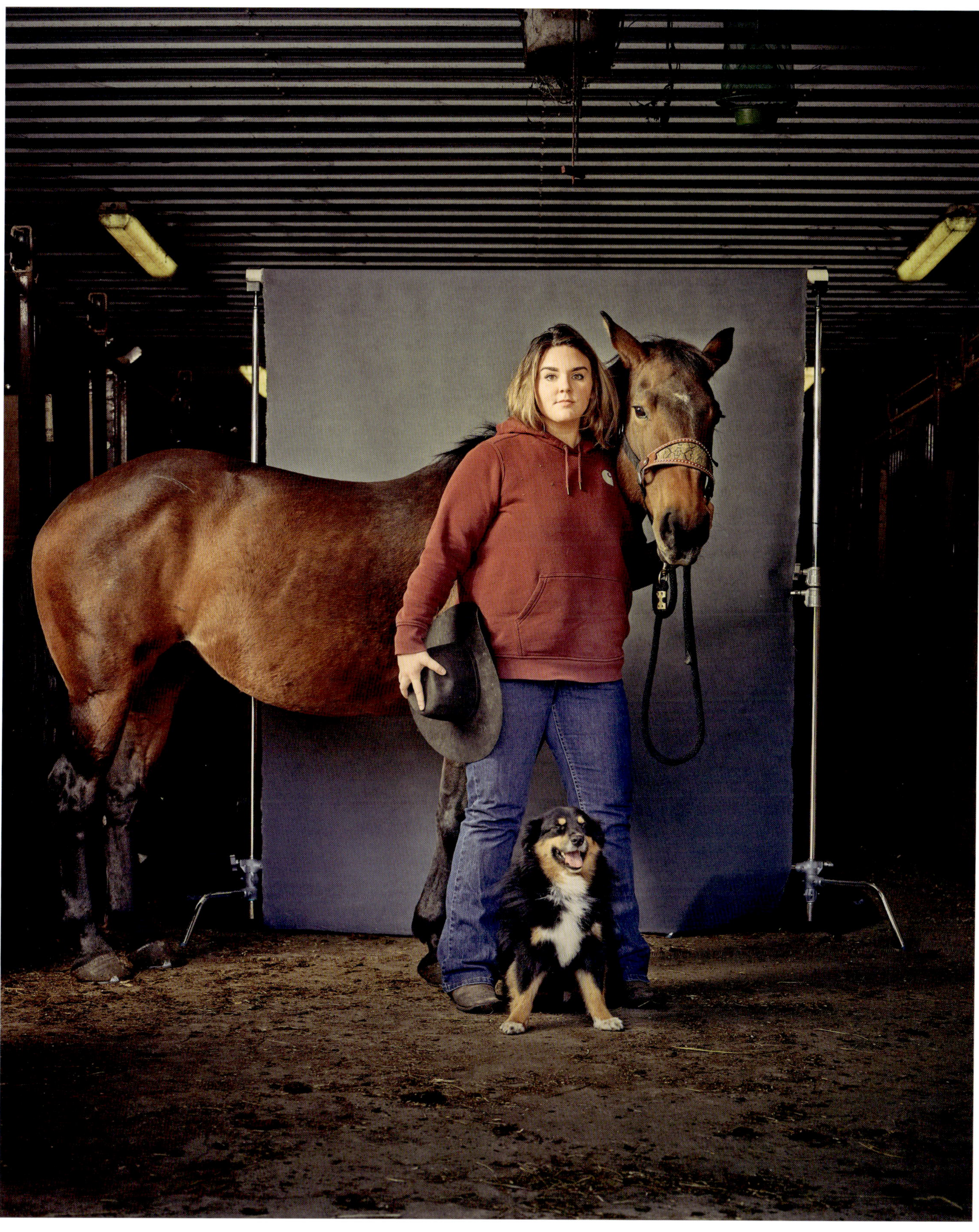

Grace with Coral and Walter, 2020

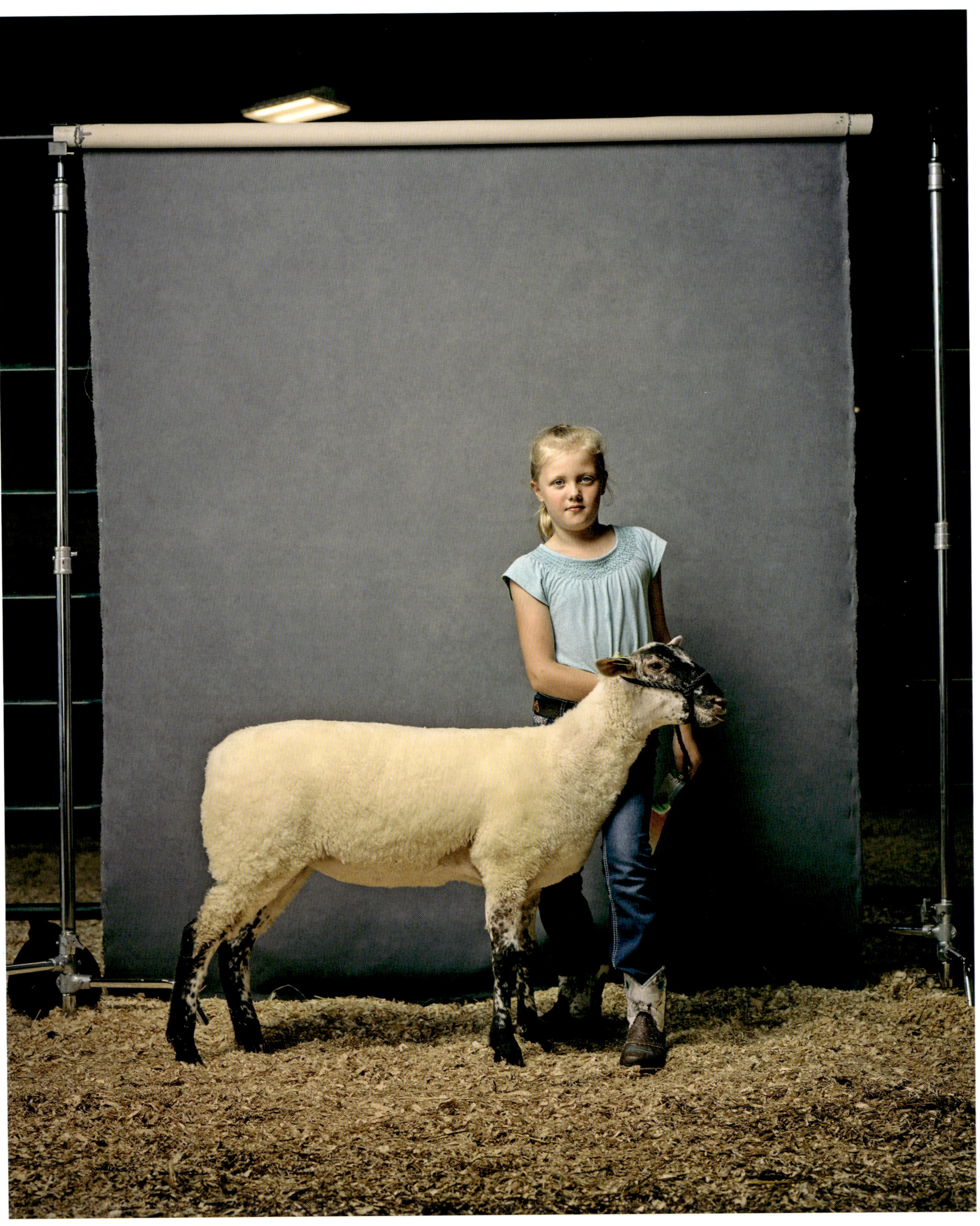

Ava and Sassy, 2016

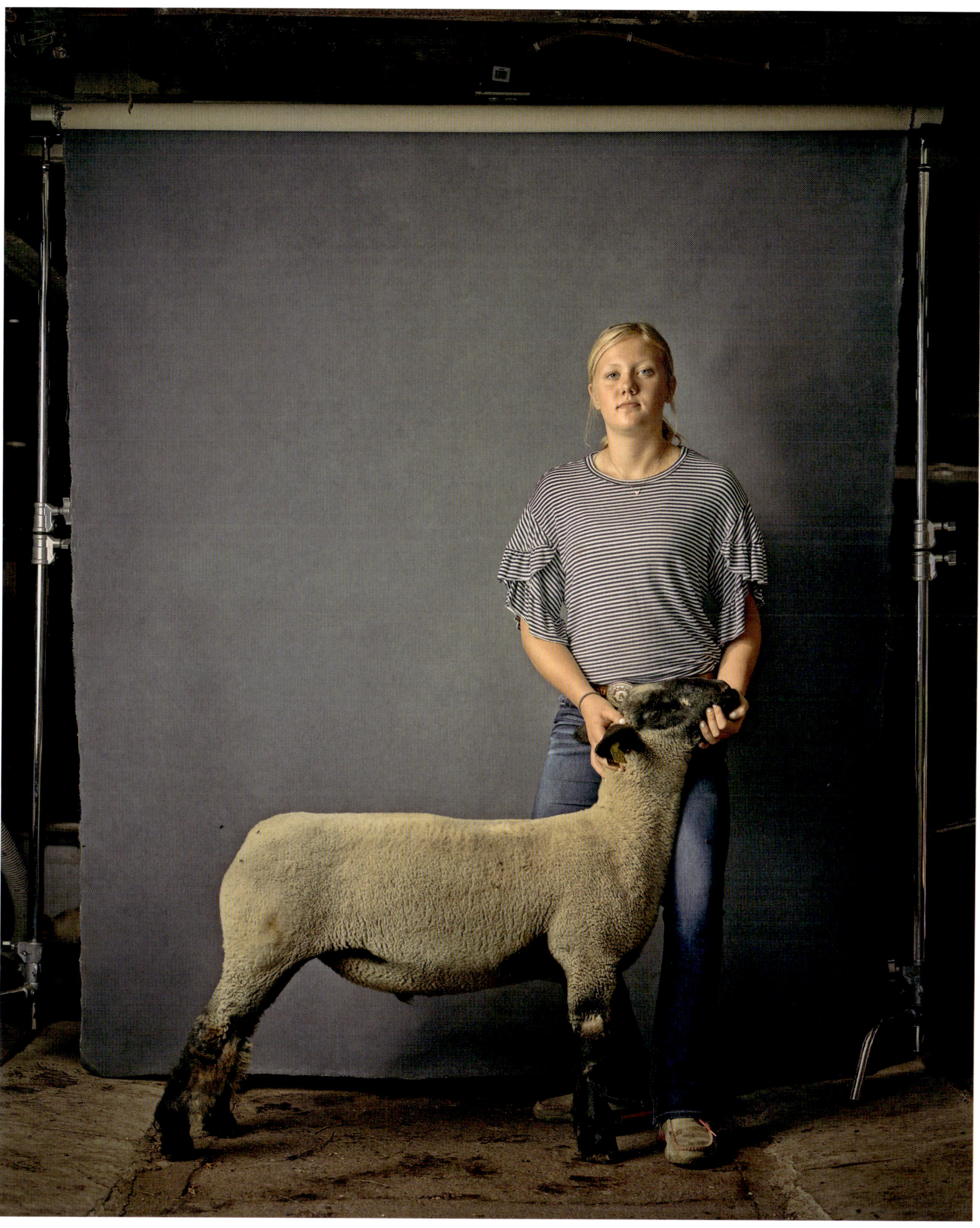

Ava and Smooth, 2020

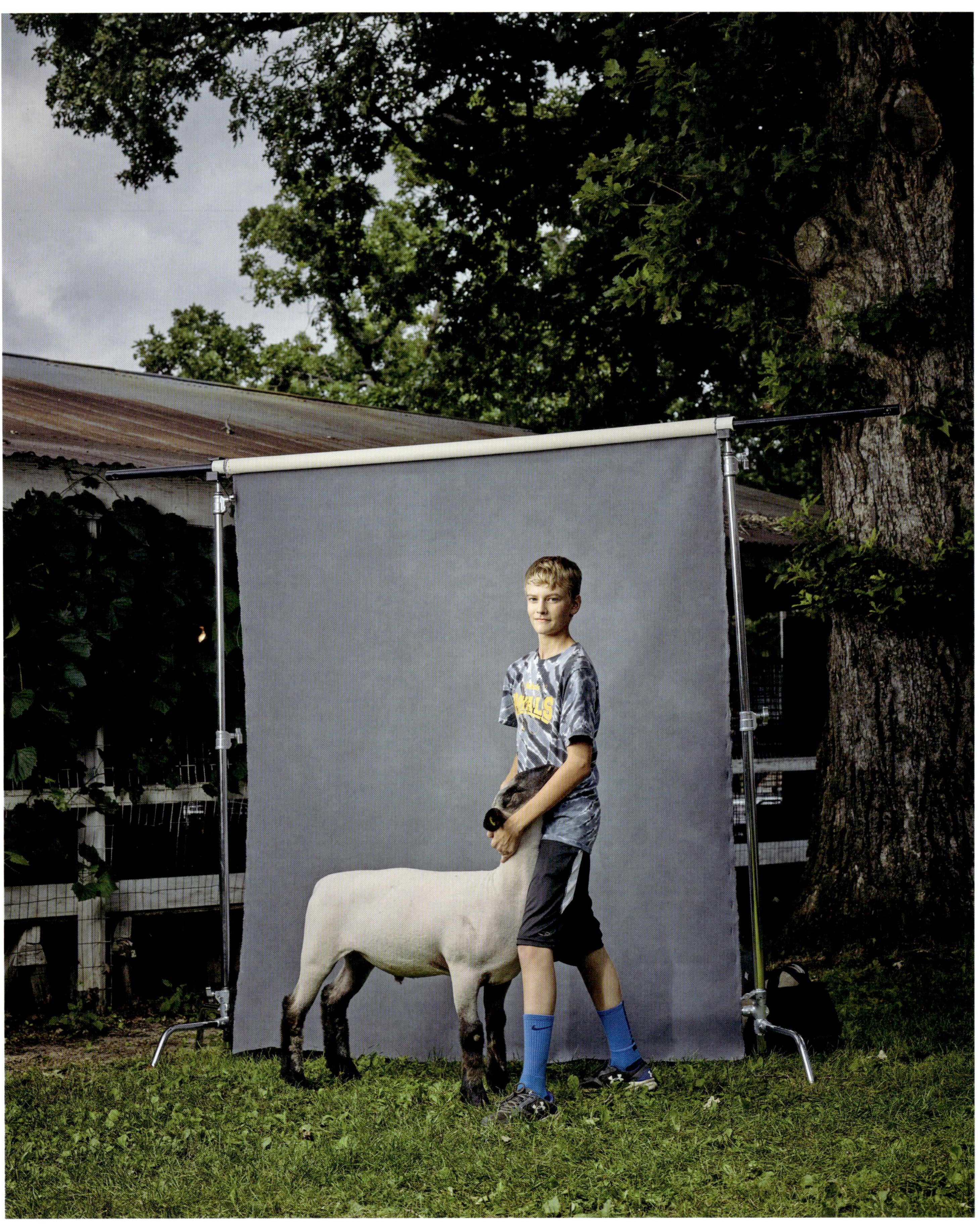

Matthew and Sheep, 2016

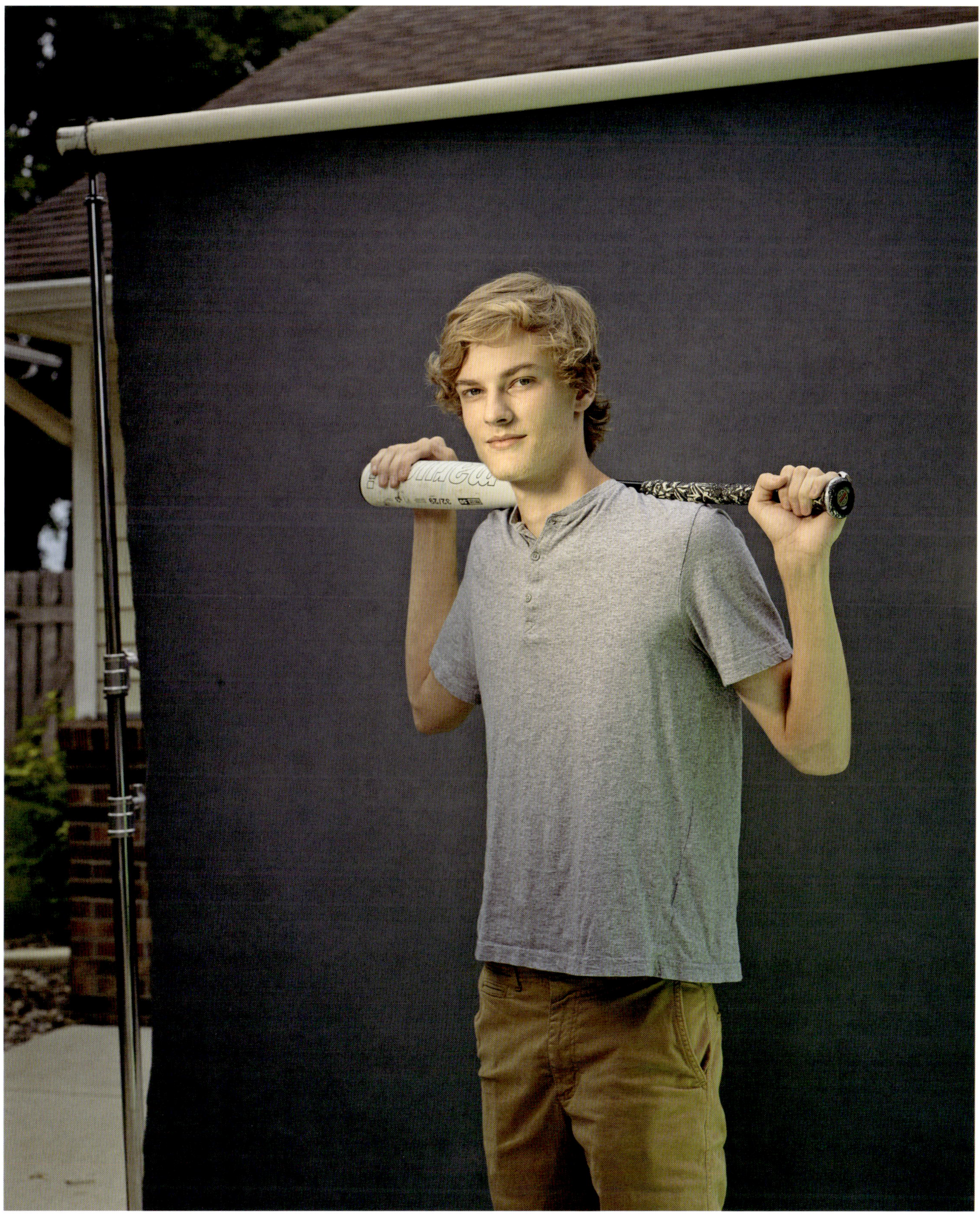

Matthew, 2020

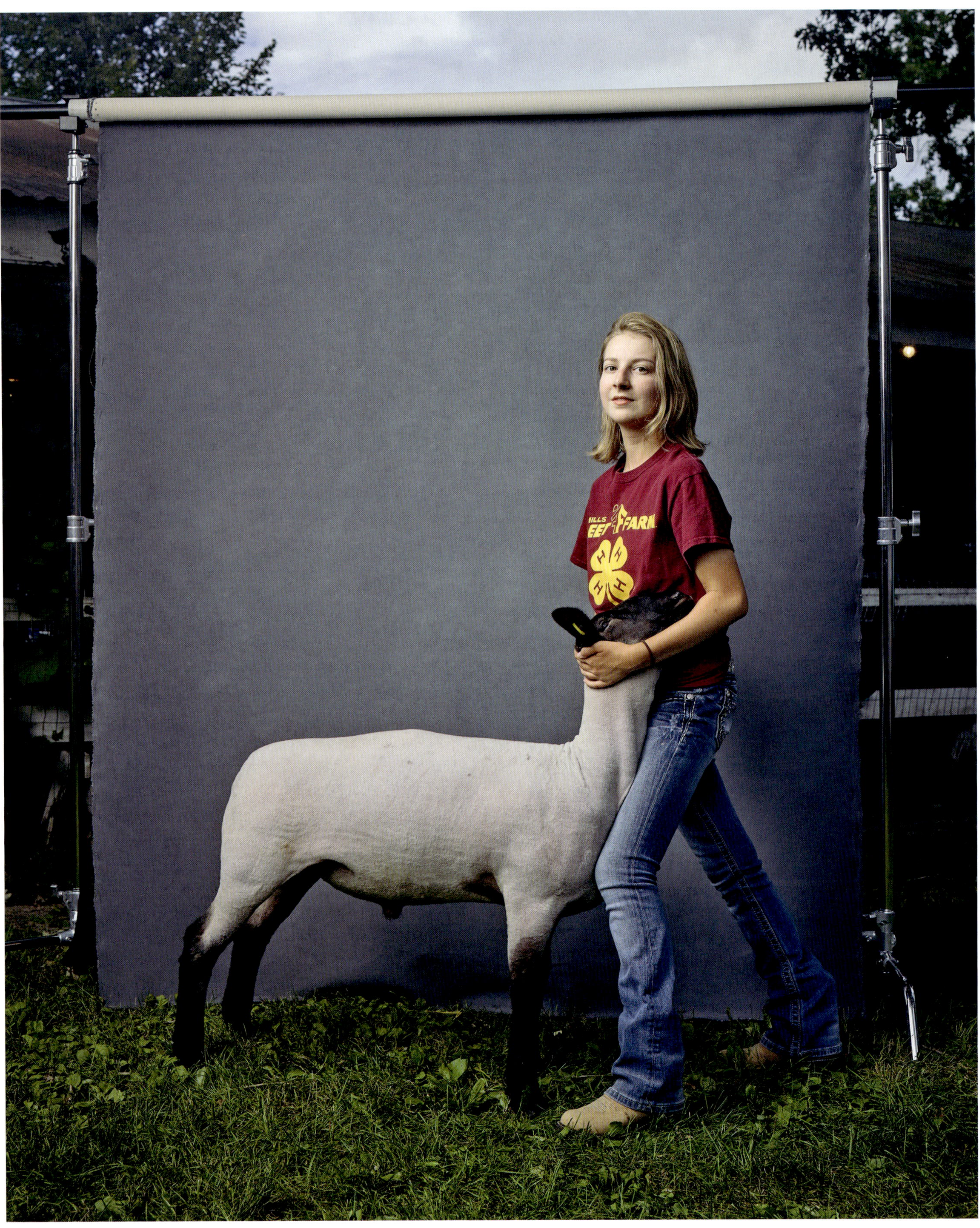

Sara and Sheep, 2016

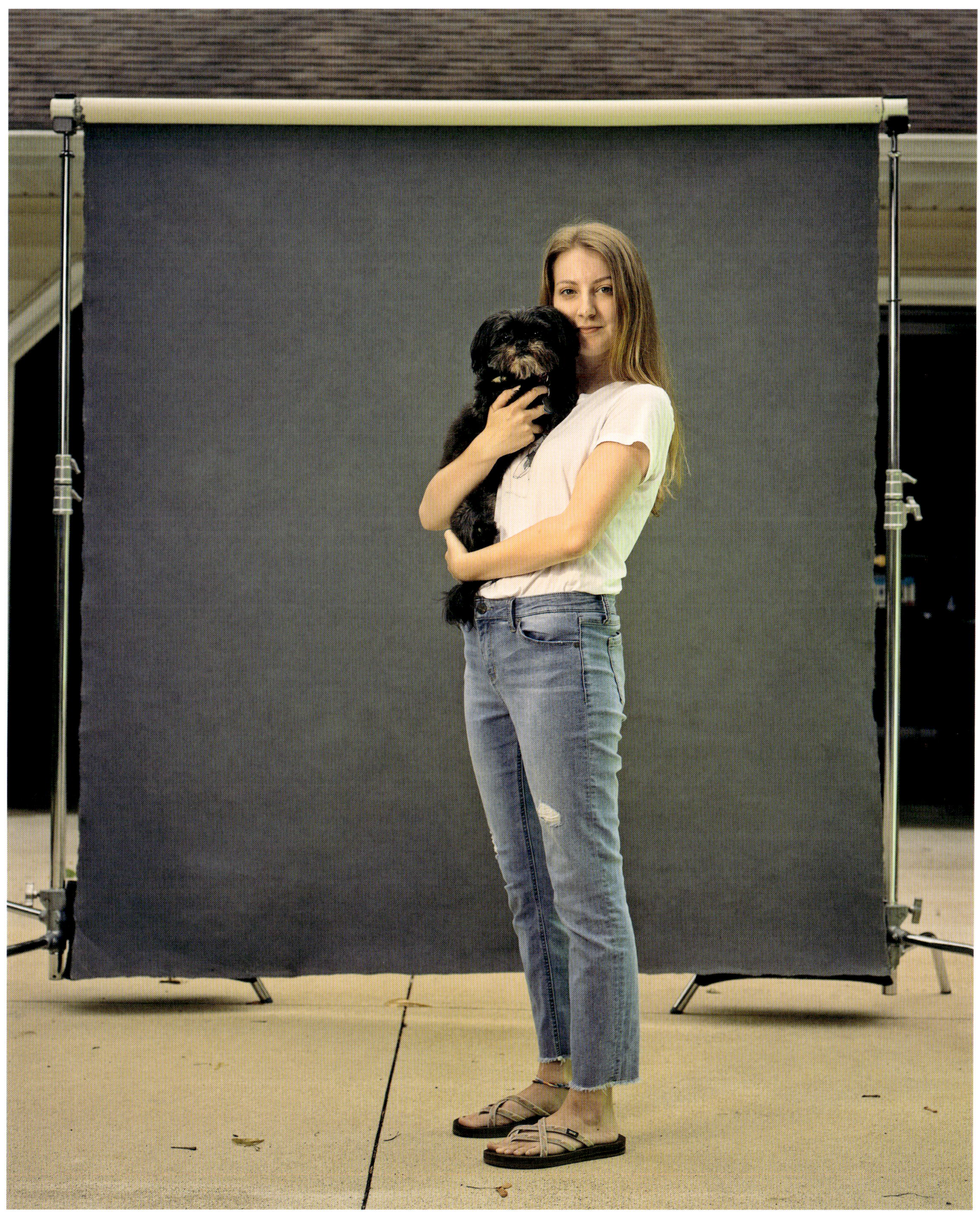

Sara and Lucy, 2020

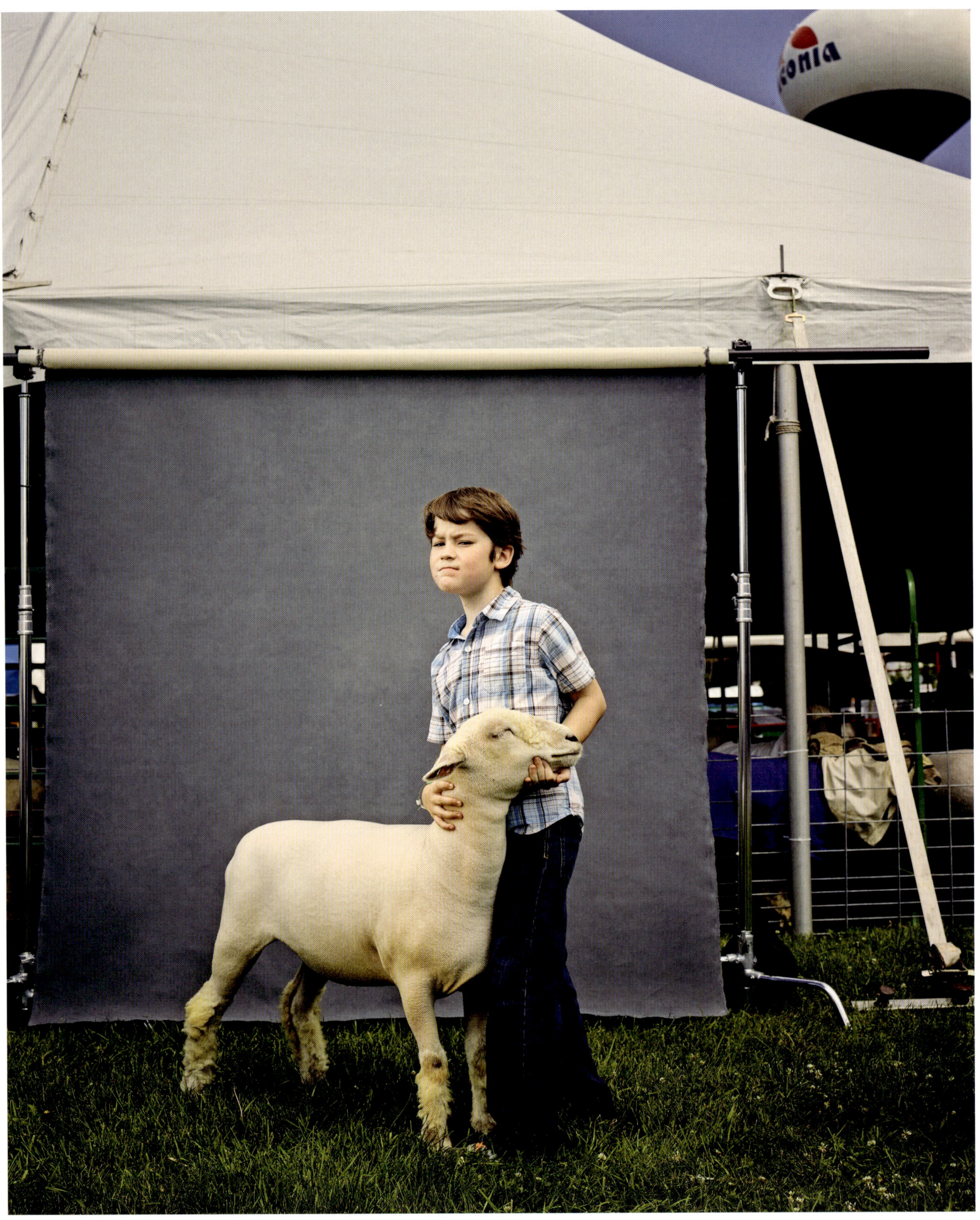

Kael and 317, 2016

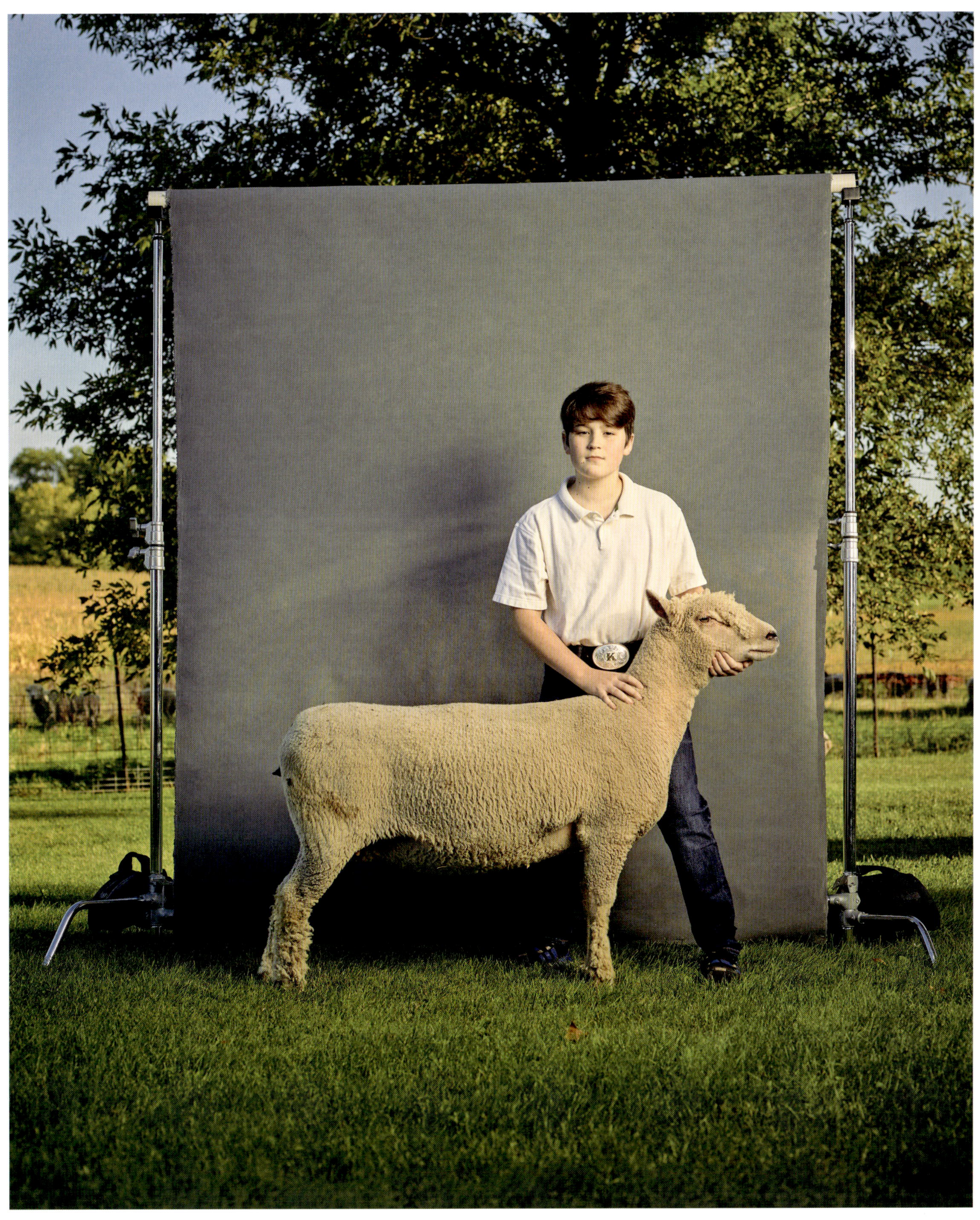

Kael and 317, 2020

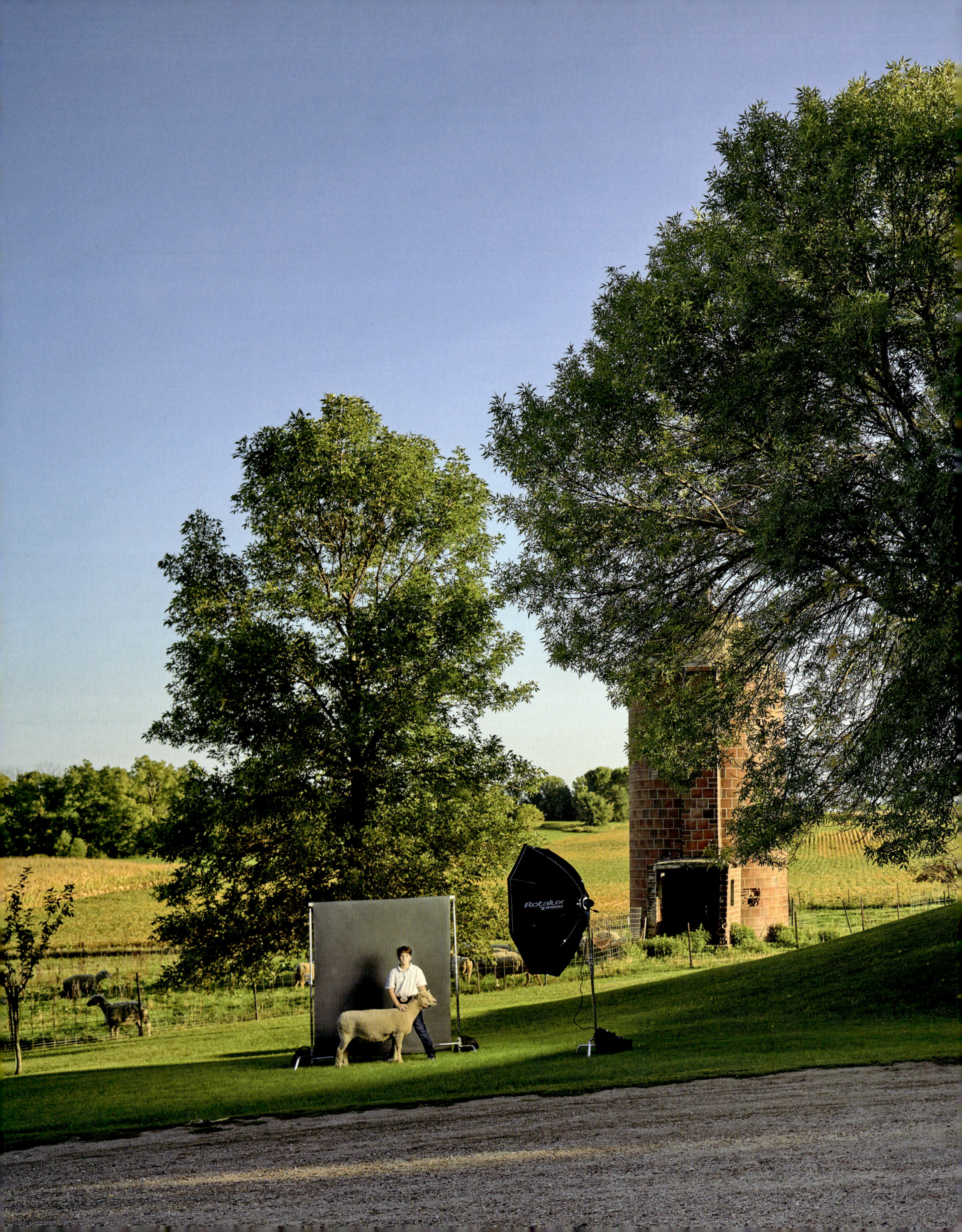

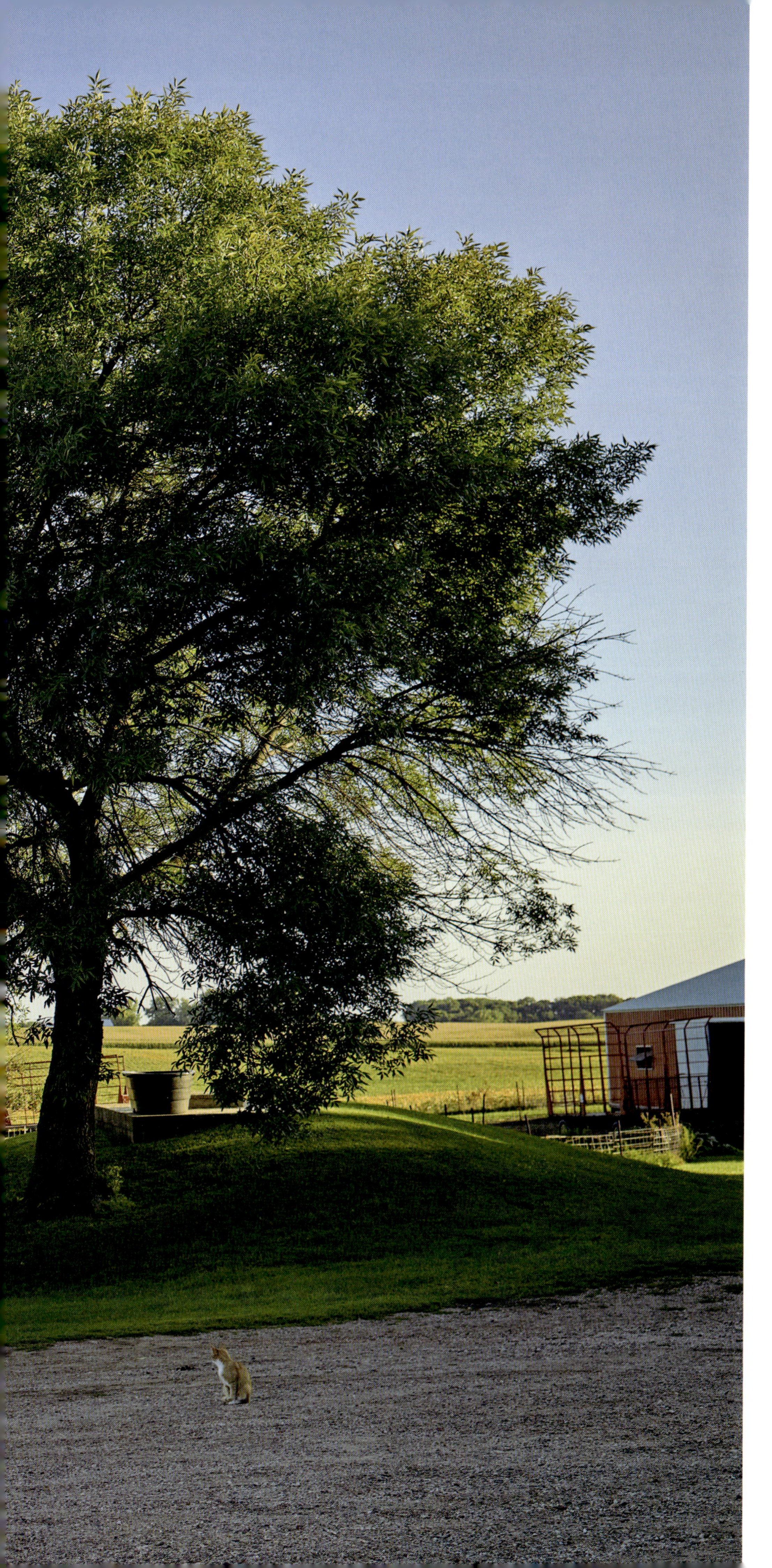

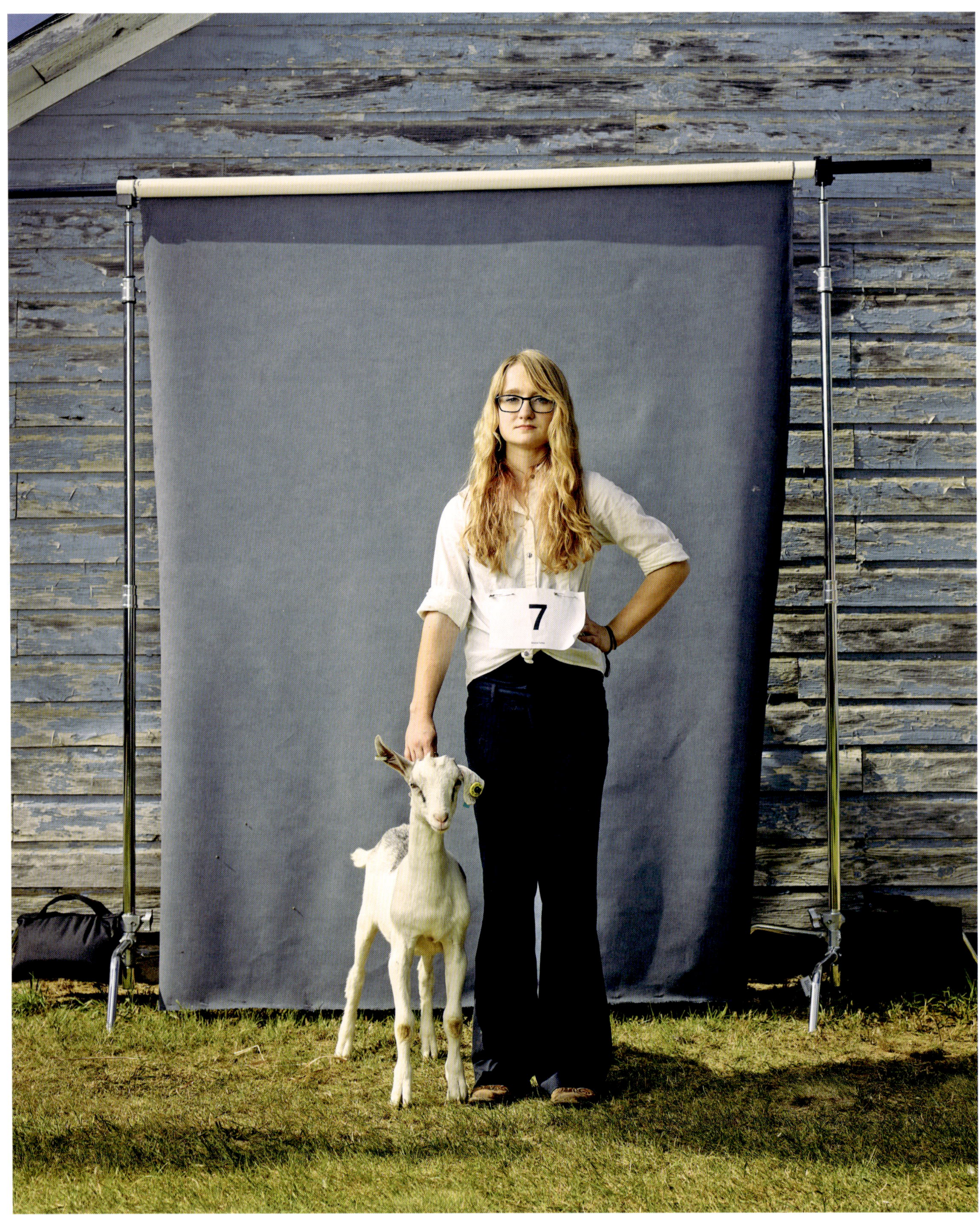

Shania and Greg, 2016

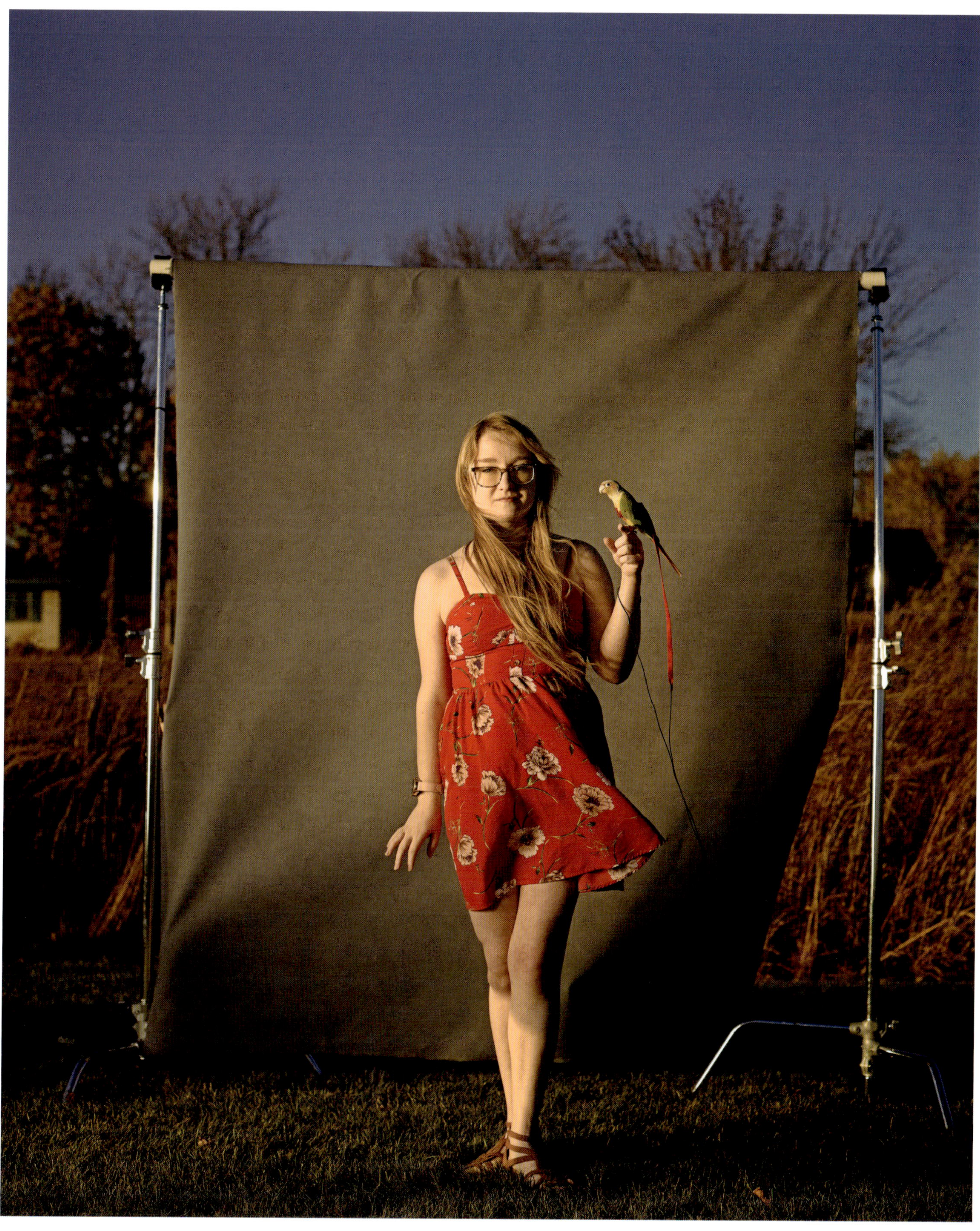

Shania and Pineapple, 2020

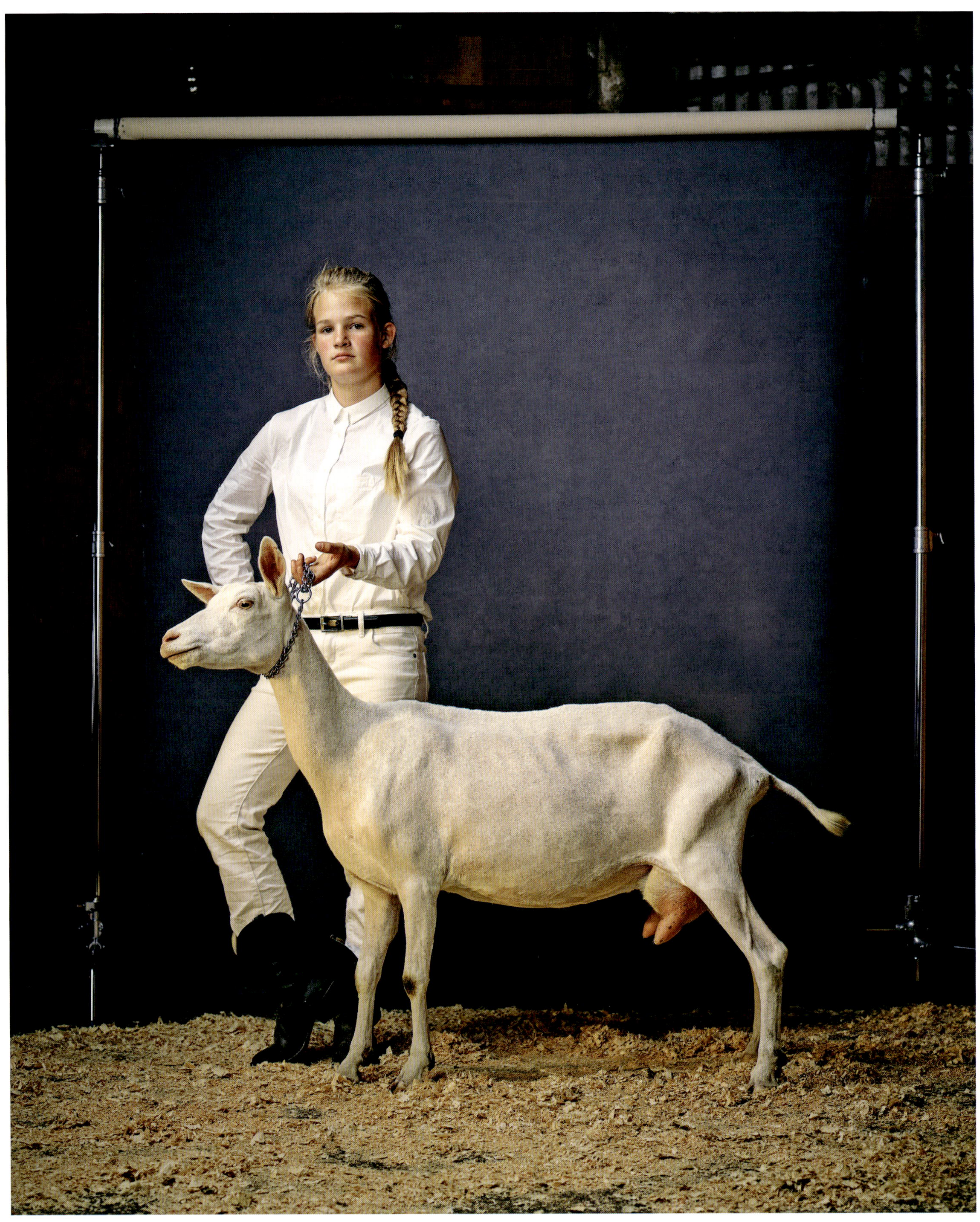

Taite and Evie, 2016

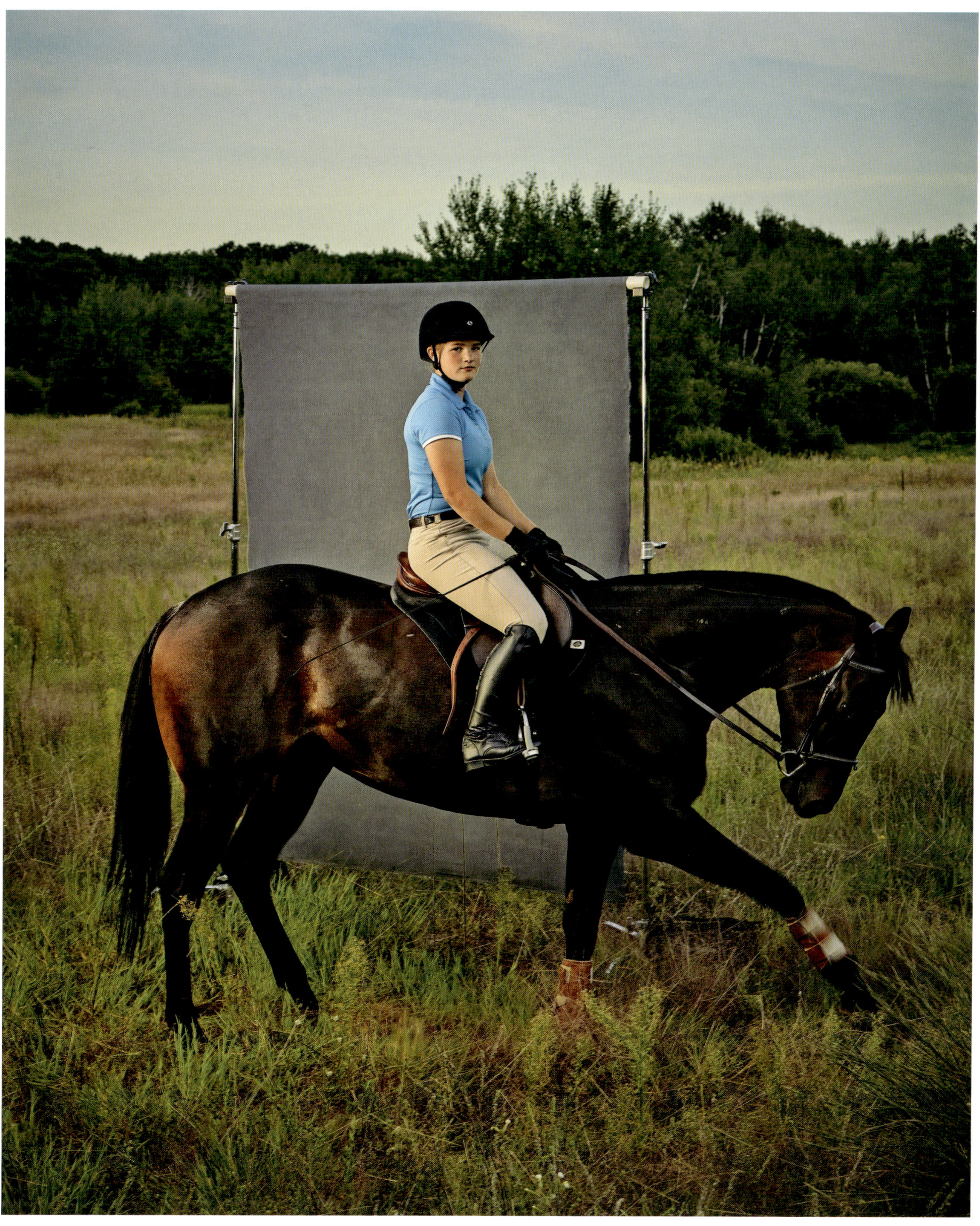

Taite and Beau, 2020

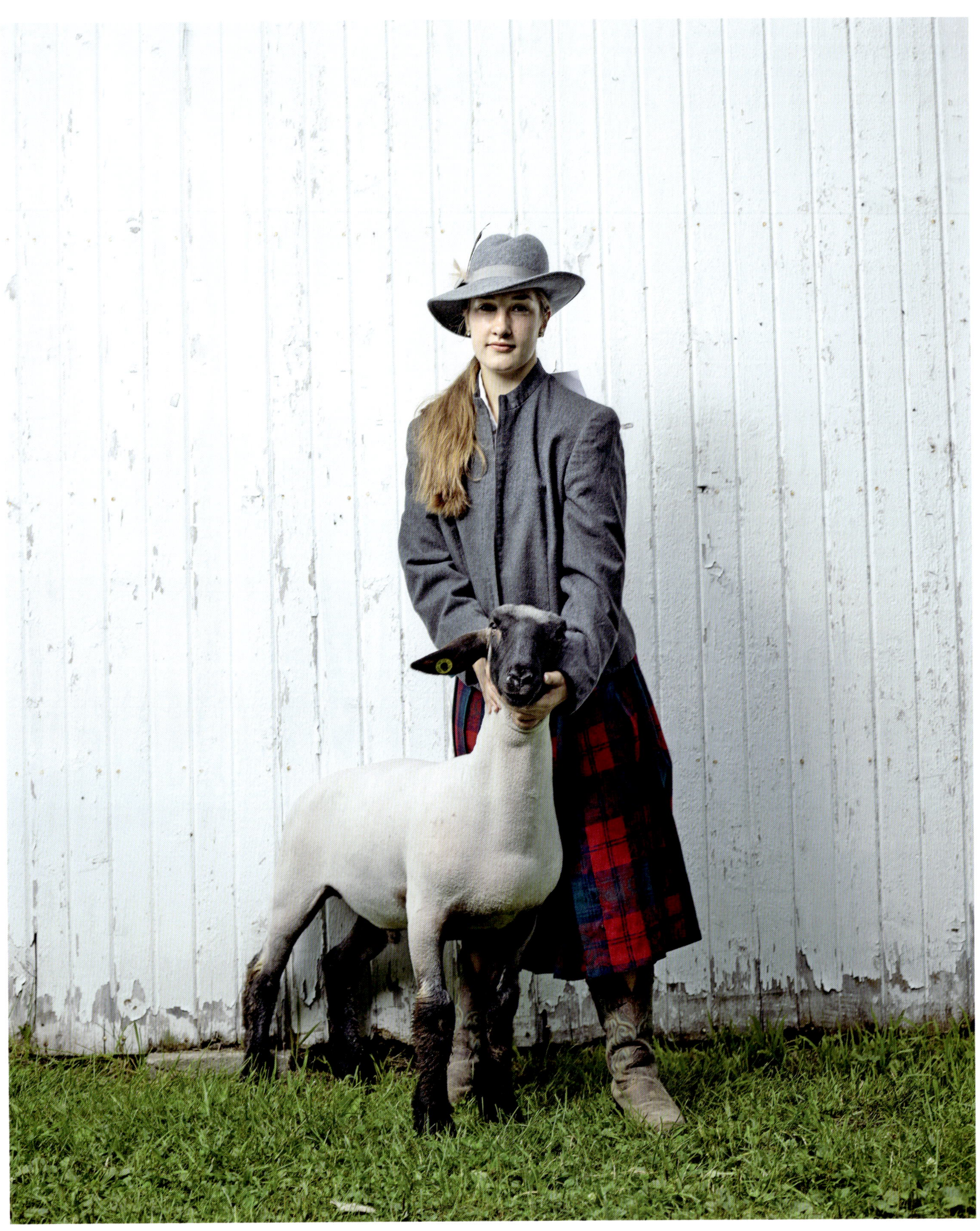

Abigail and Cottonball, 2016

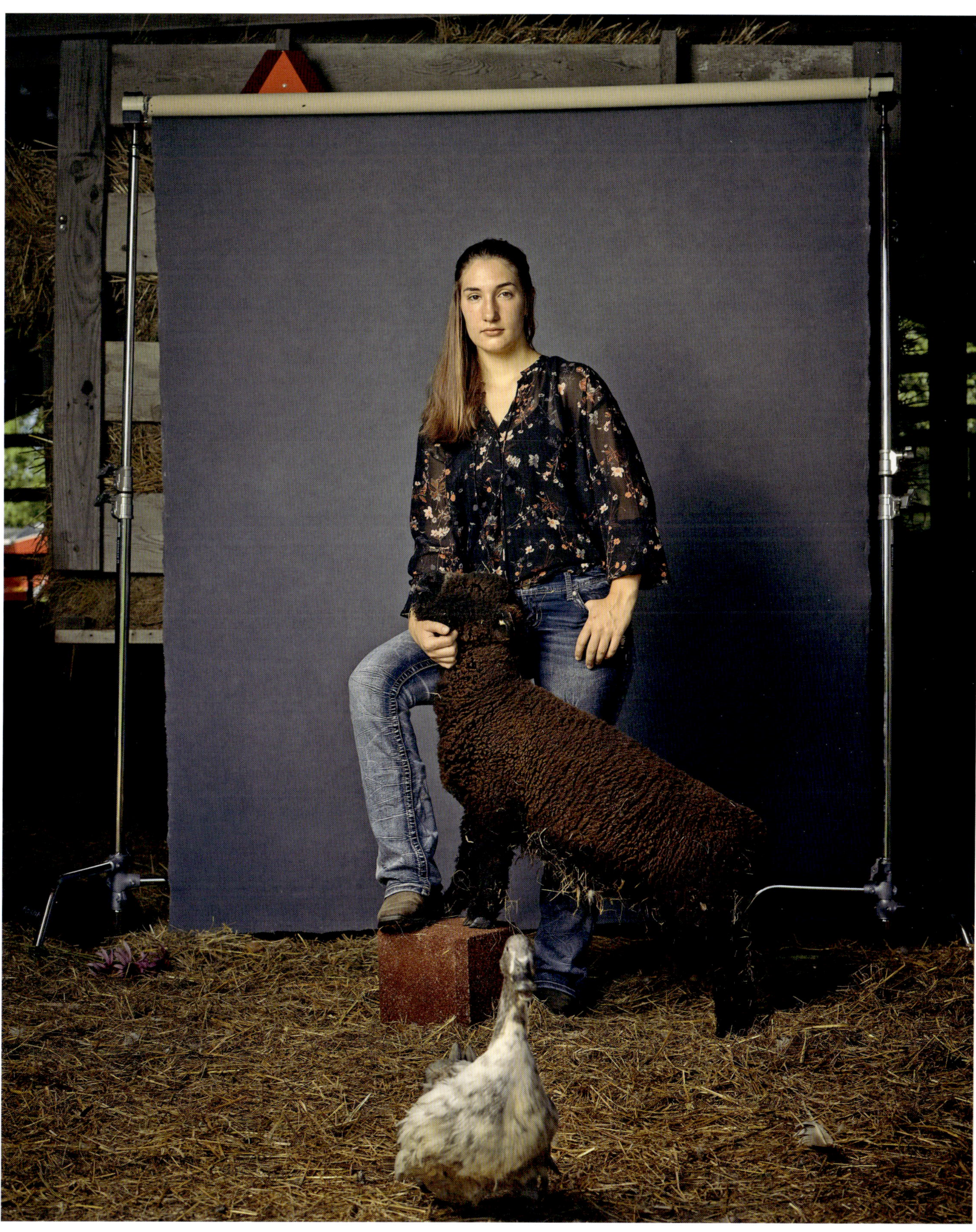

Abigail and Sheep, 2020

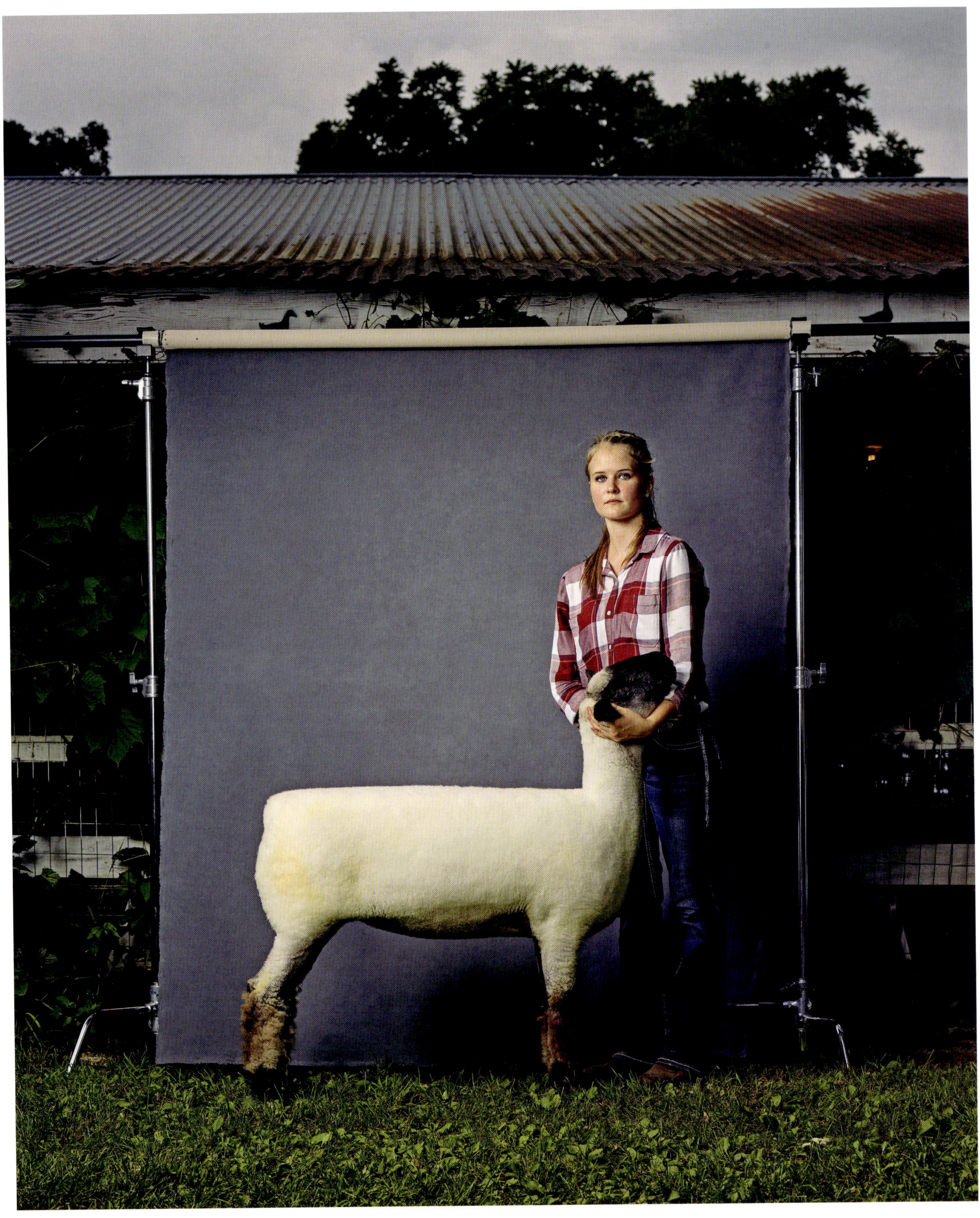

Anna and Helen, 2016

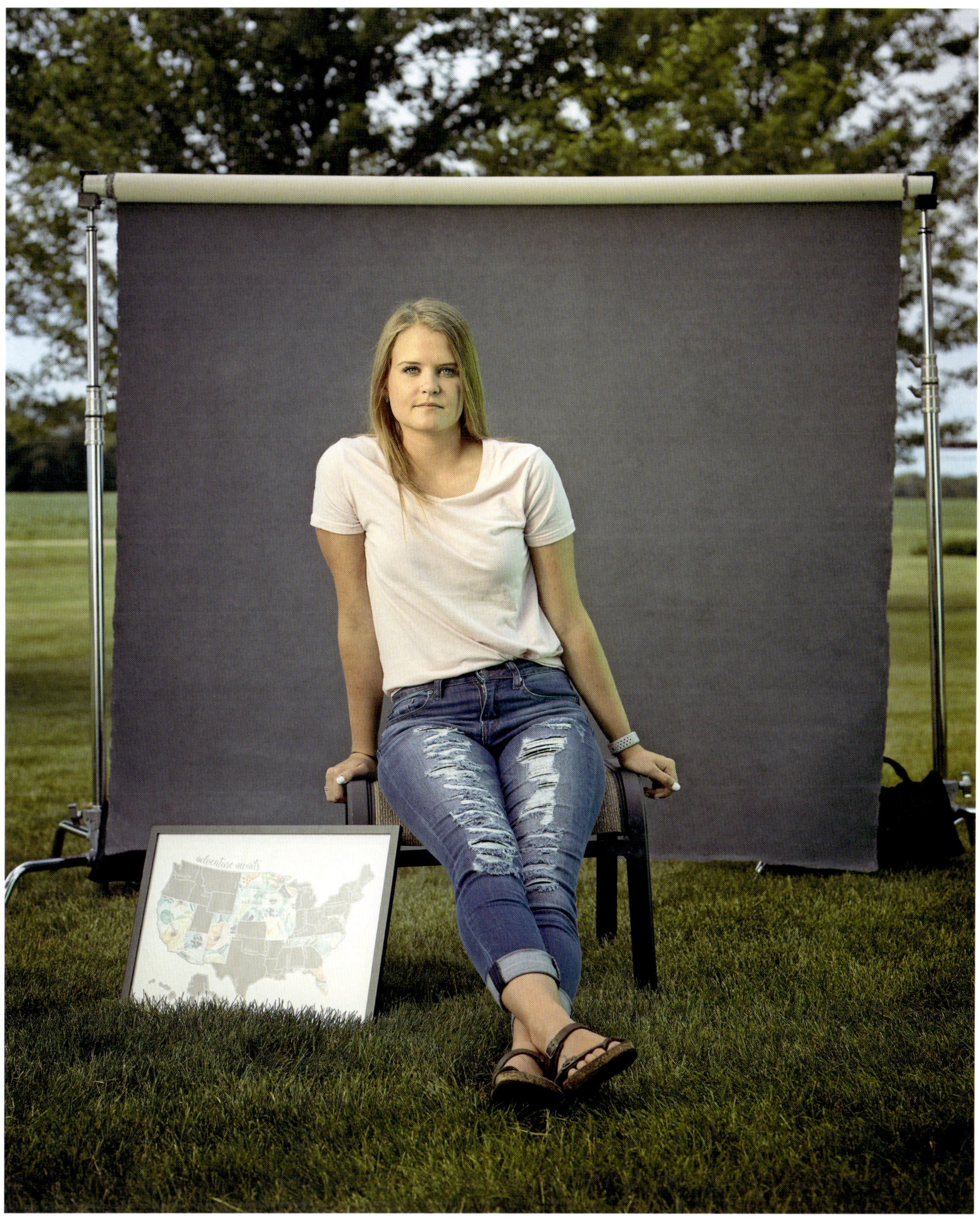

Anna, 2020

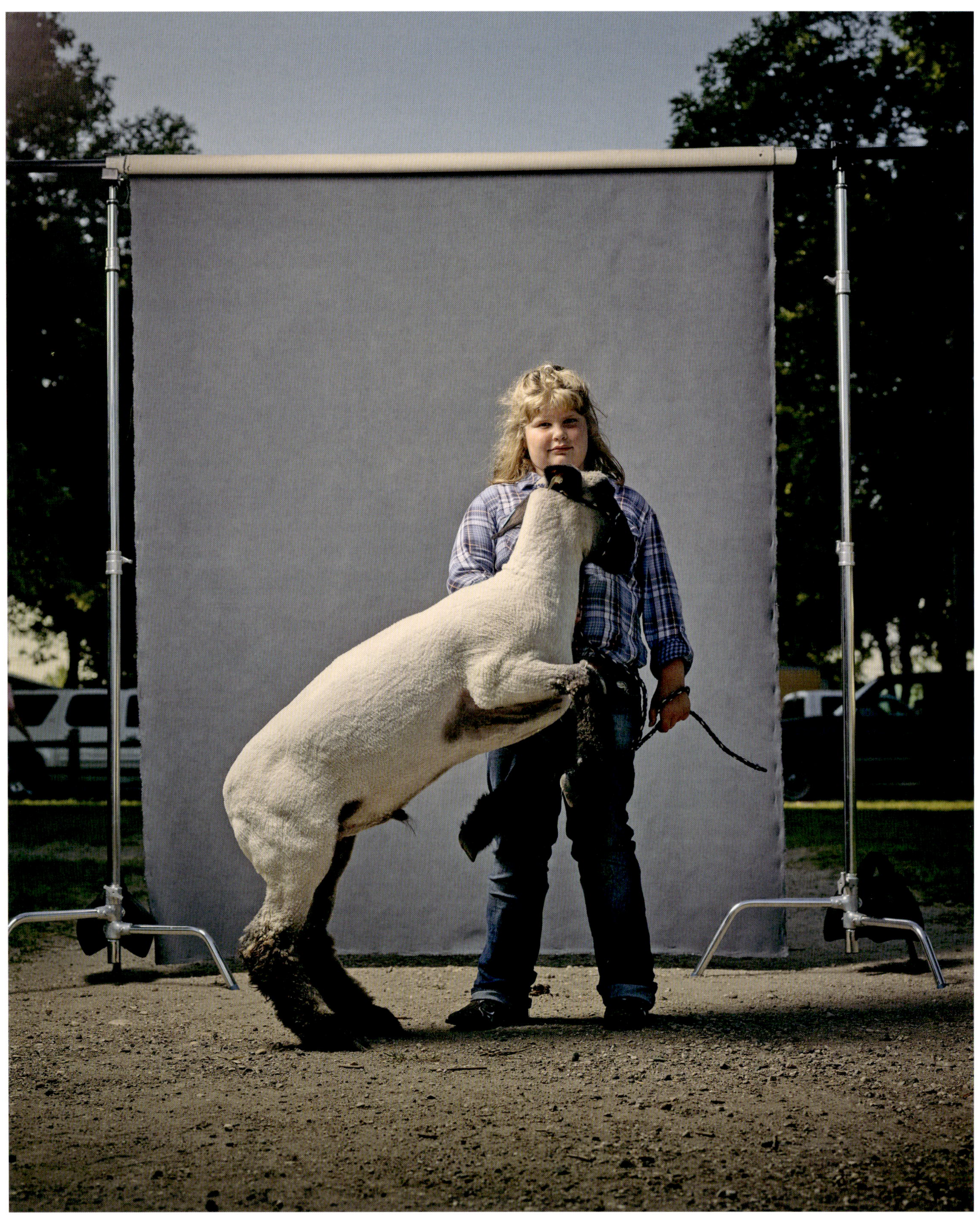

Carlana and Sheep, 2016

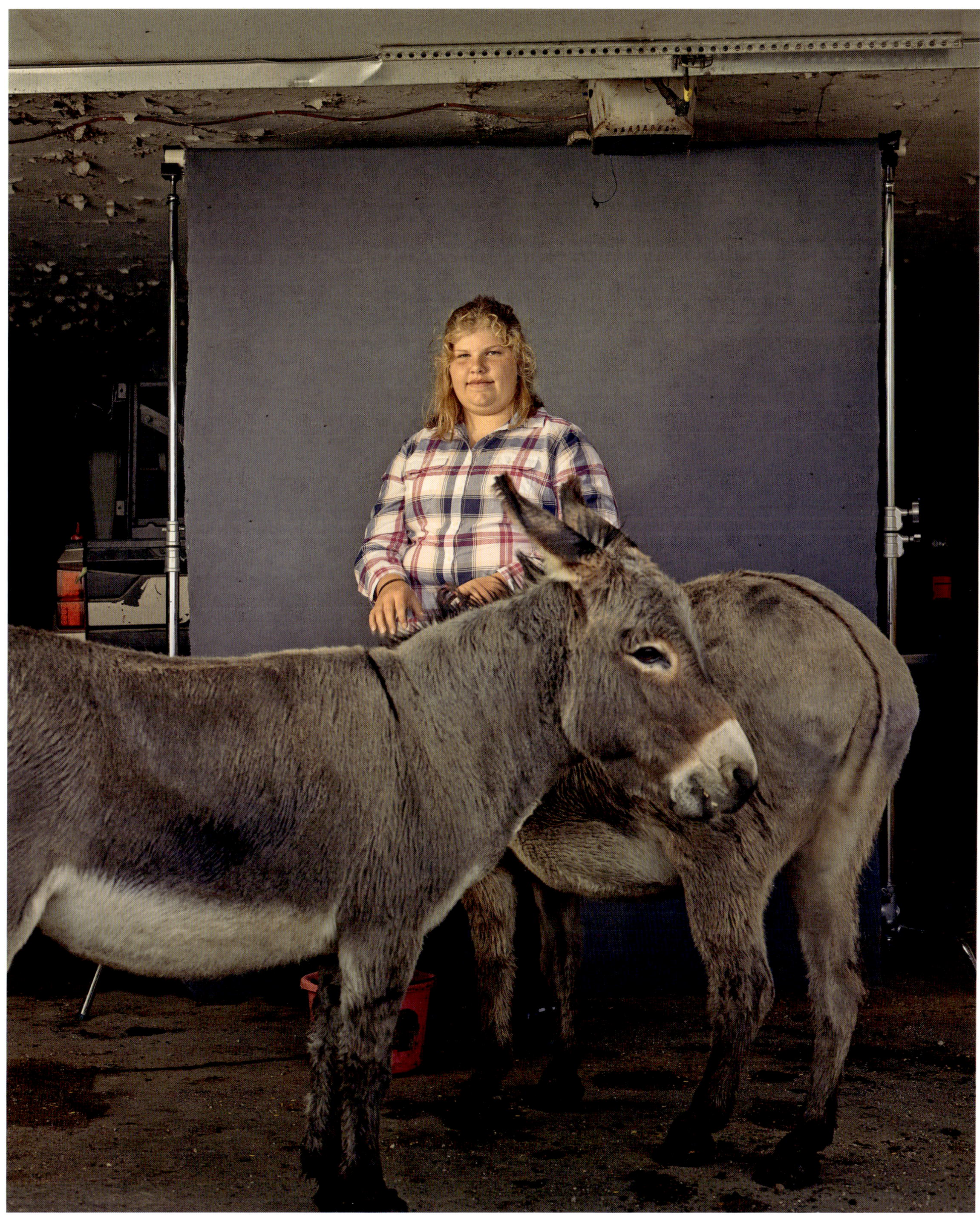

Carlana and Donkeys, 2020

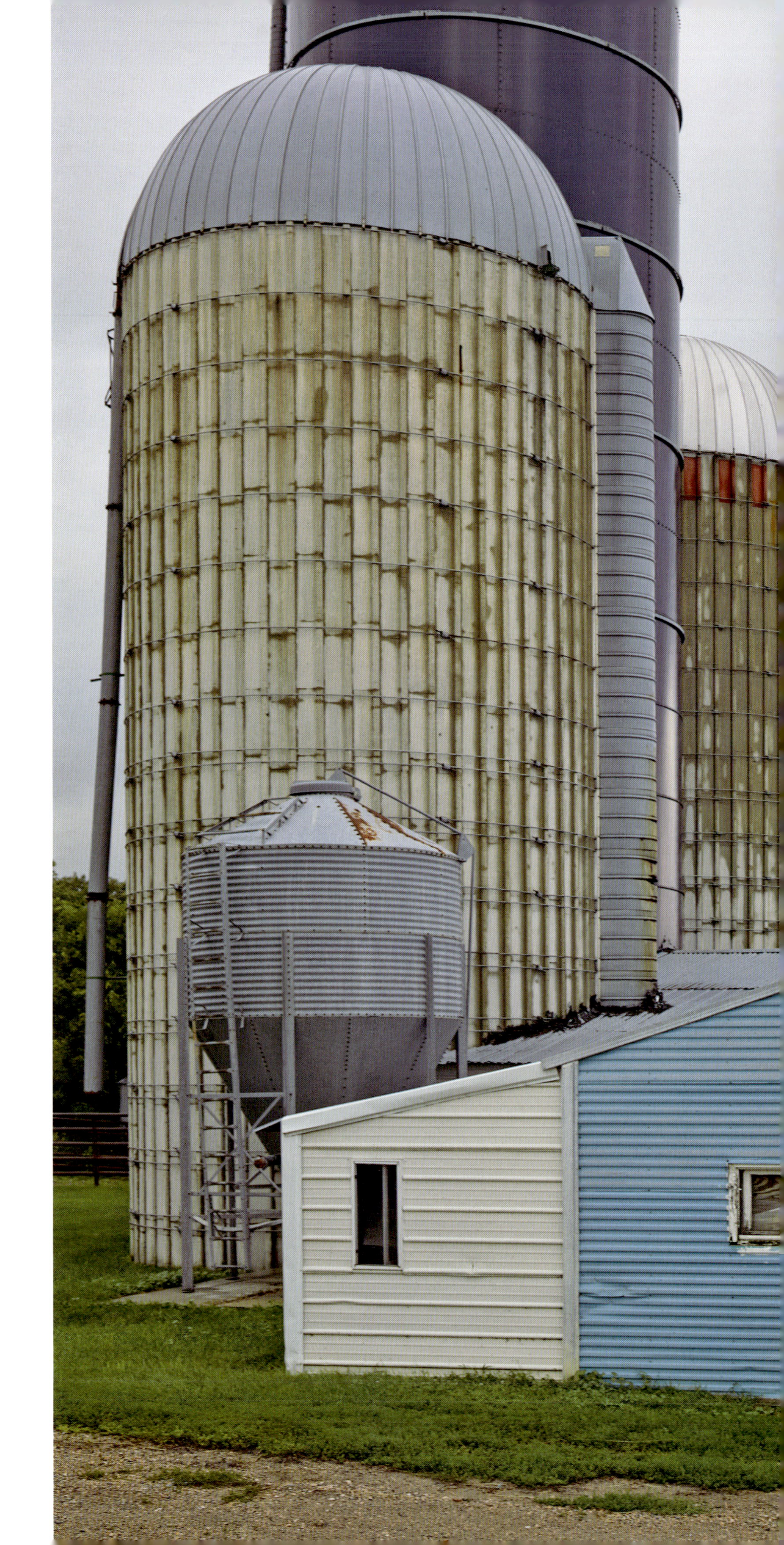

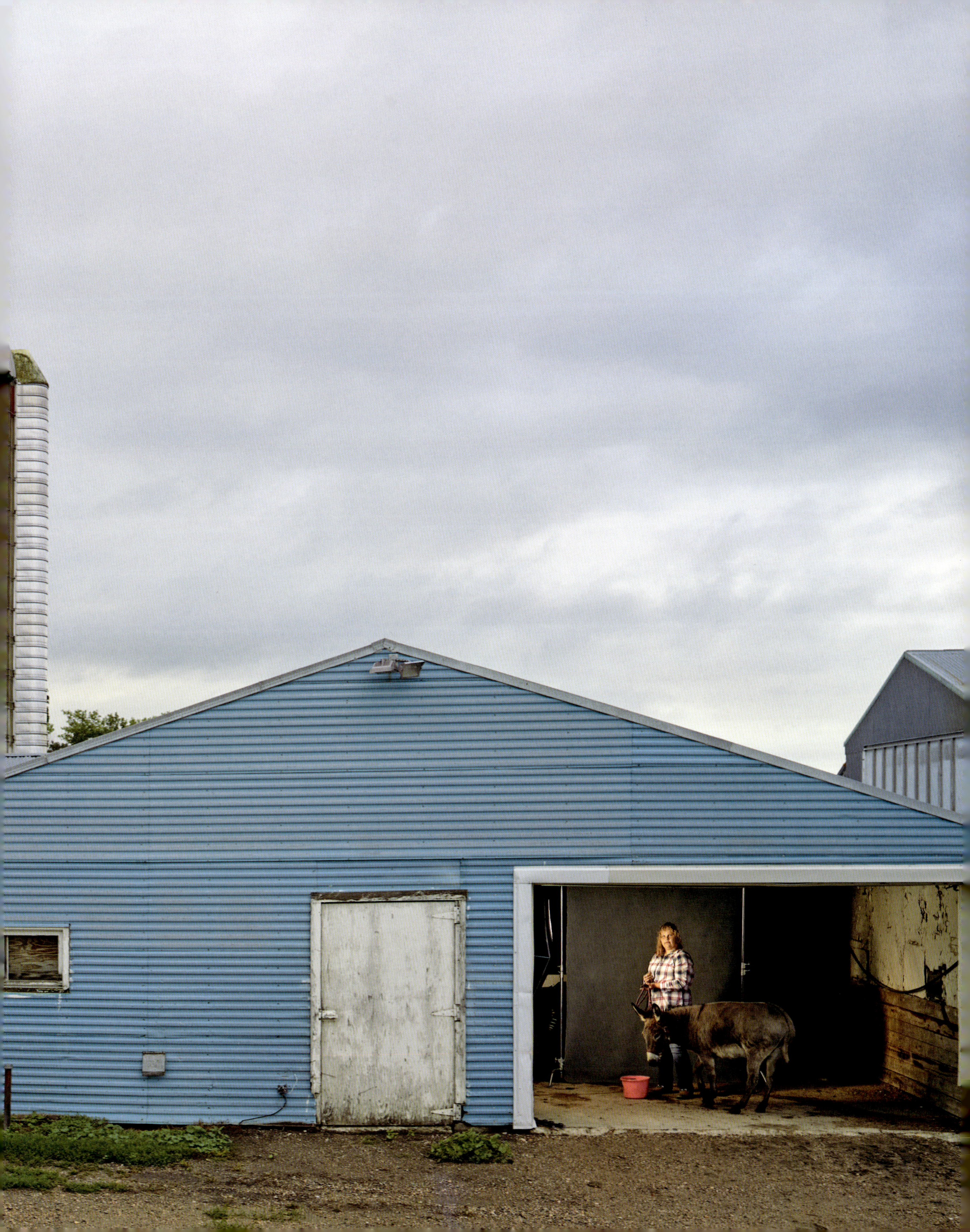

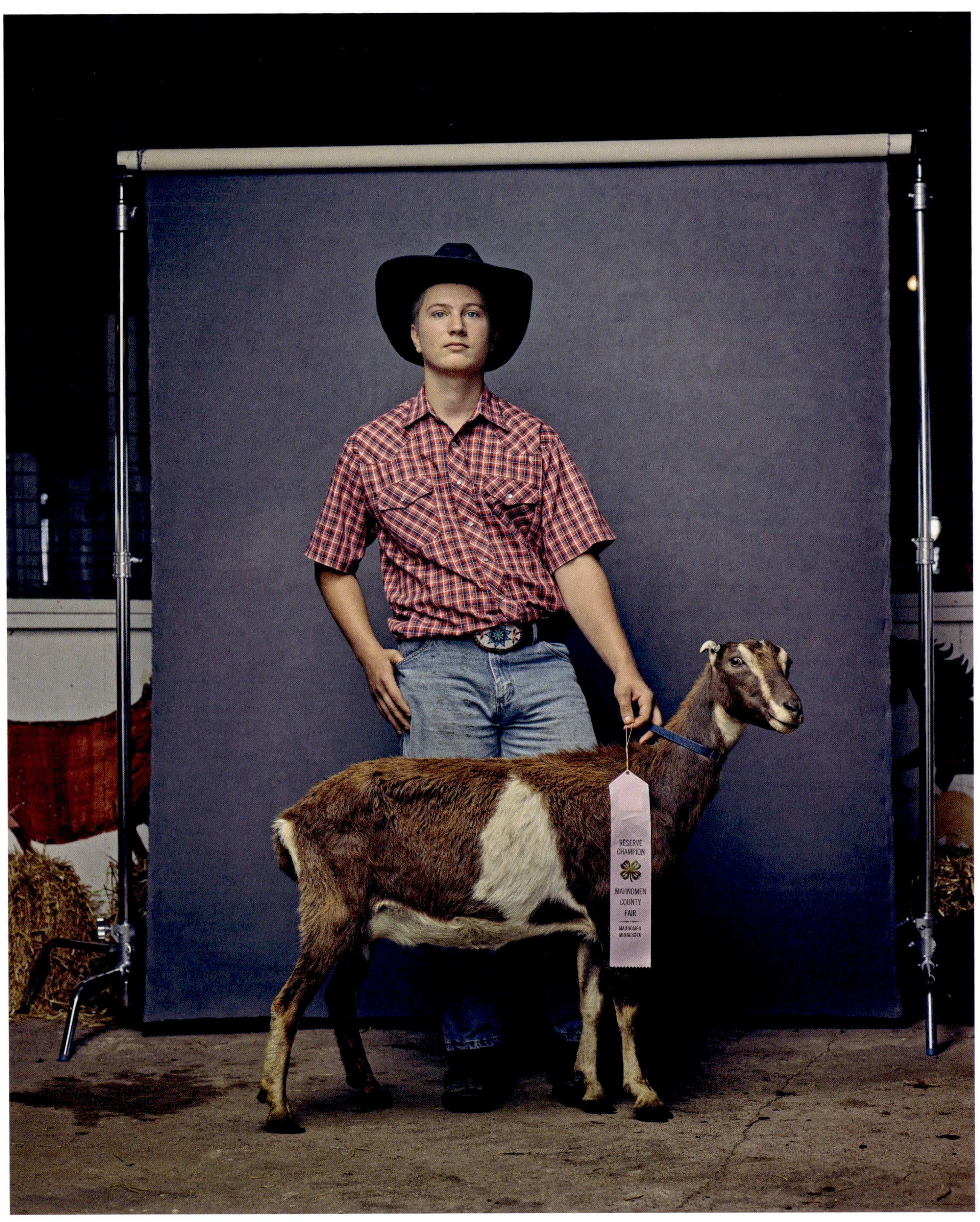

Gus and Doolittle, 2016

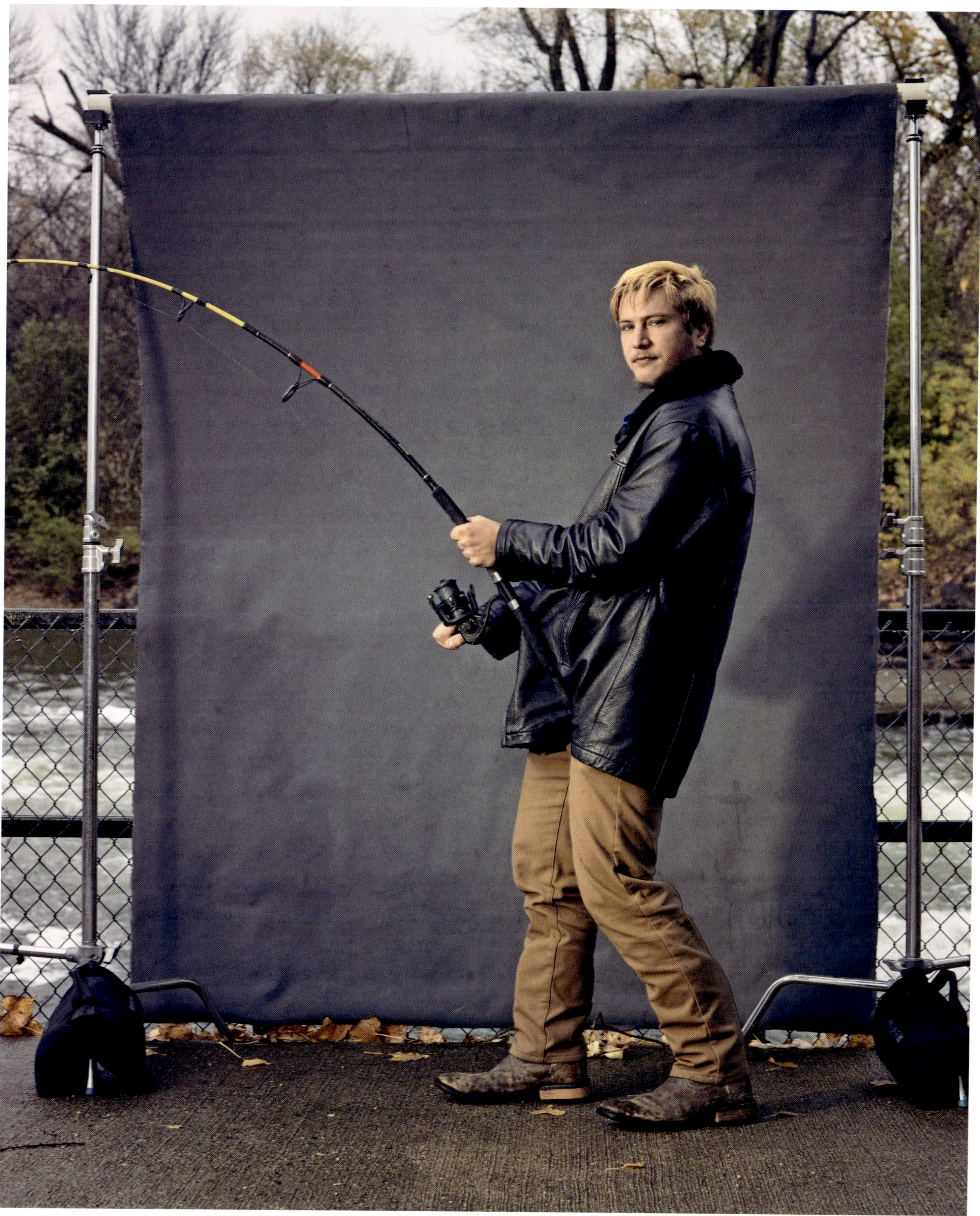

Gus, 2020

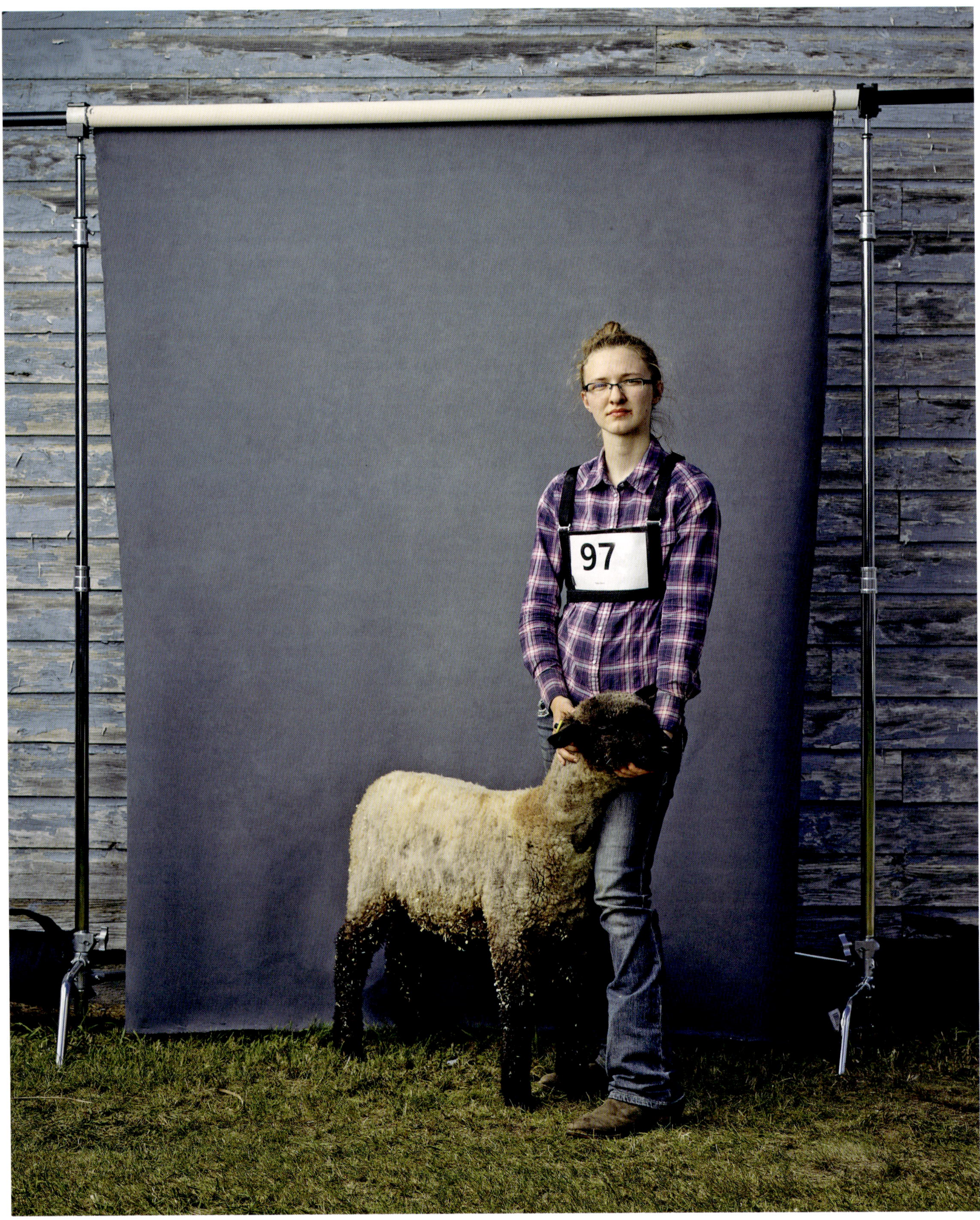

Neka and Sheep, 2016

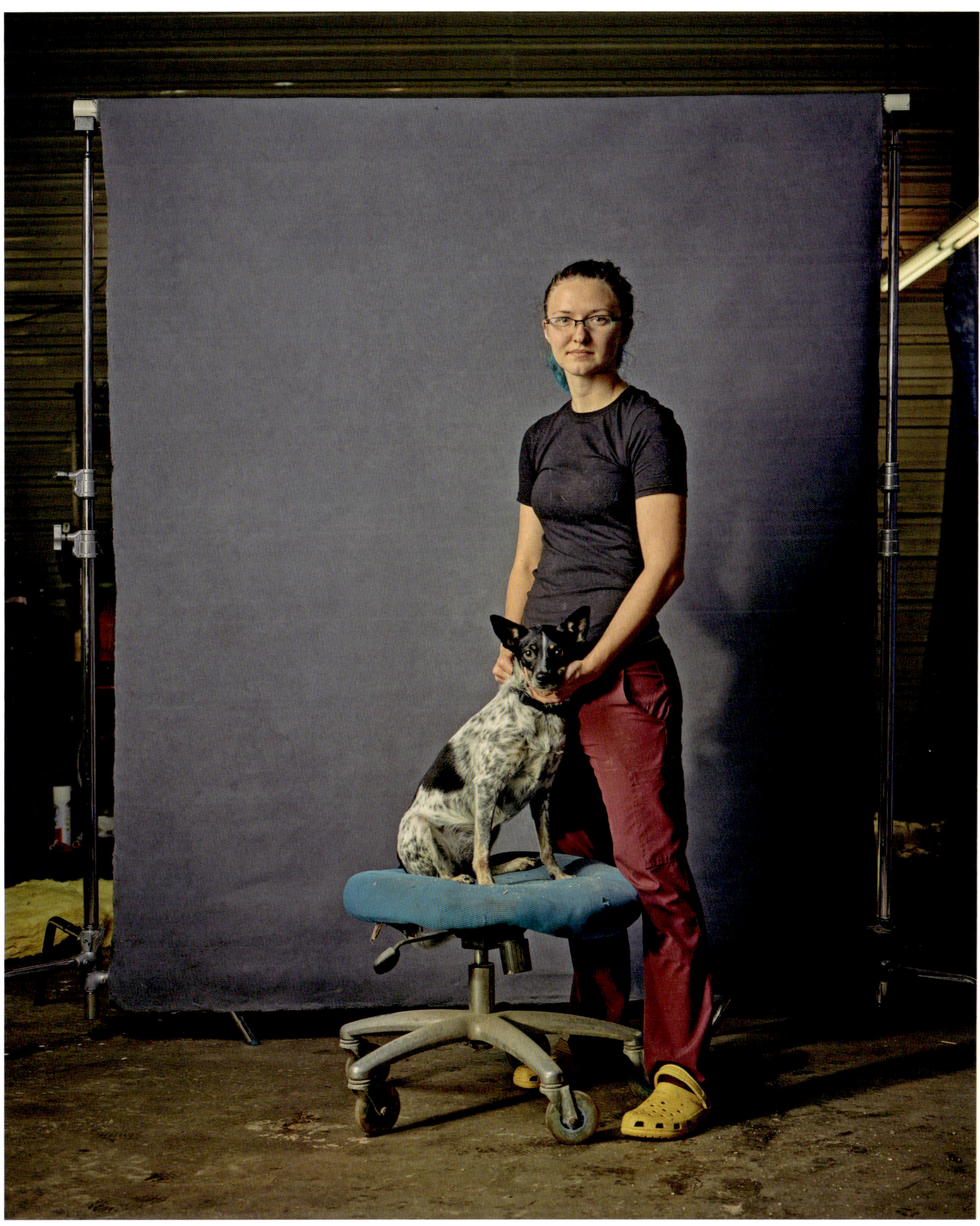

Neka and Bella, 2020

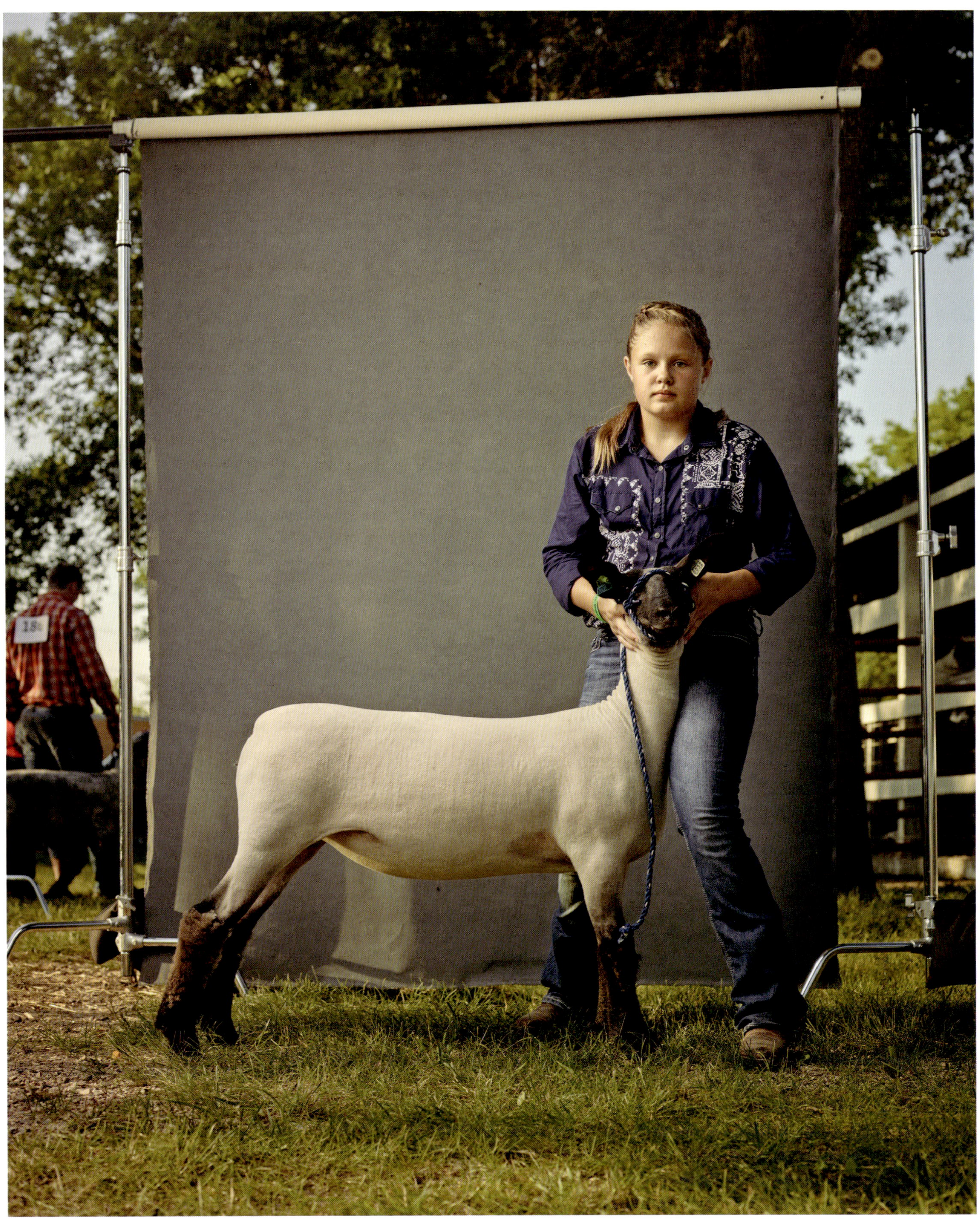

Hannah and B, 2016

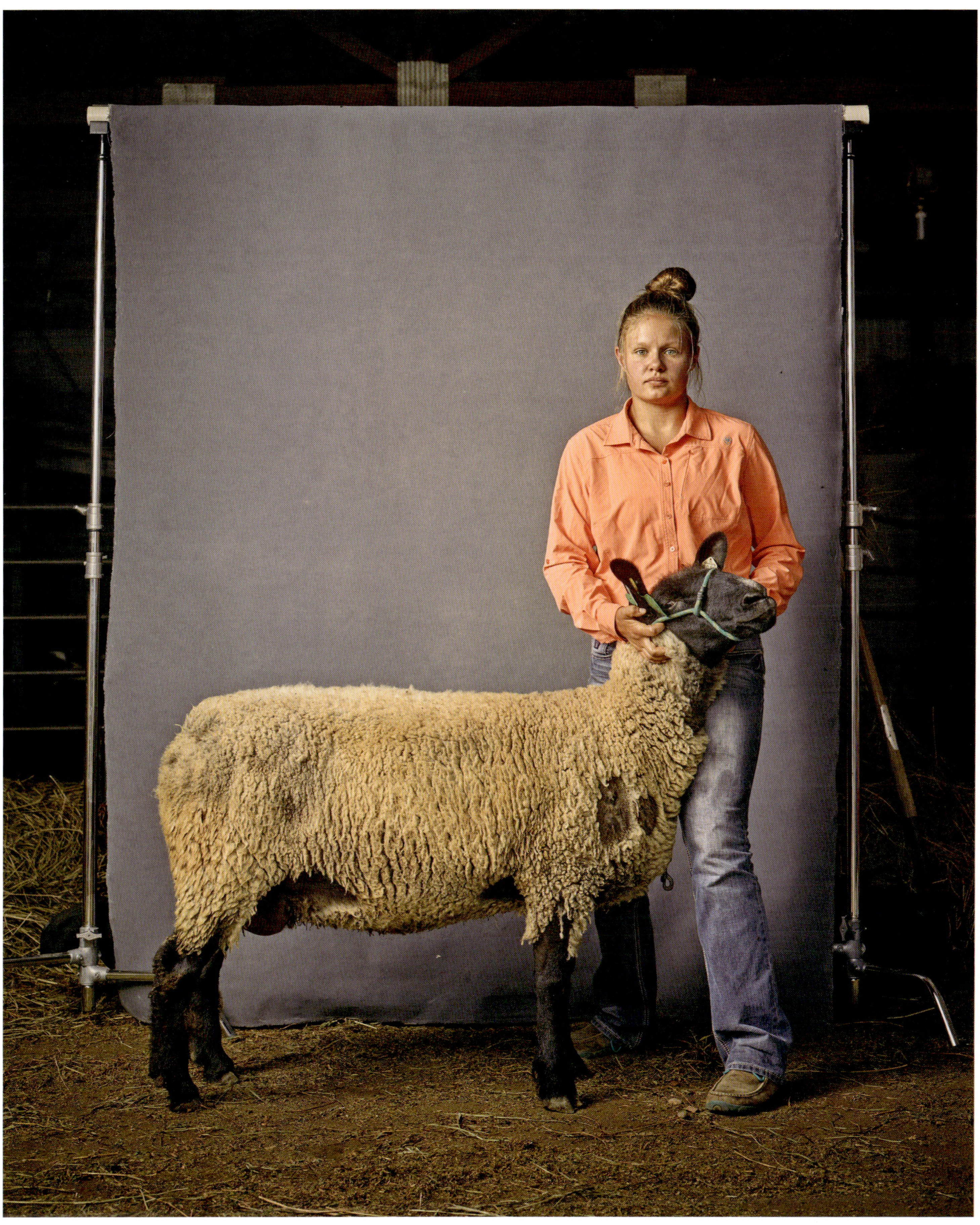

Hannah and B, 2020

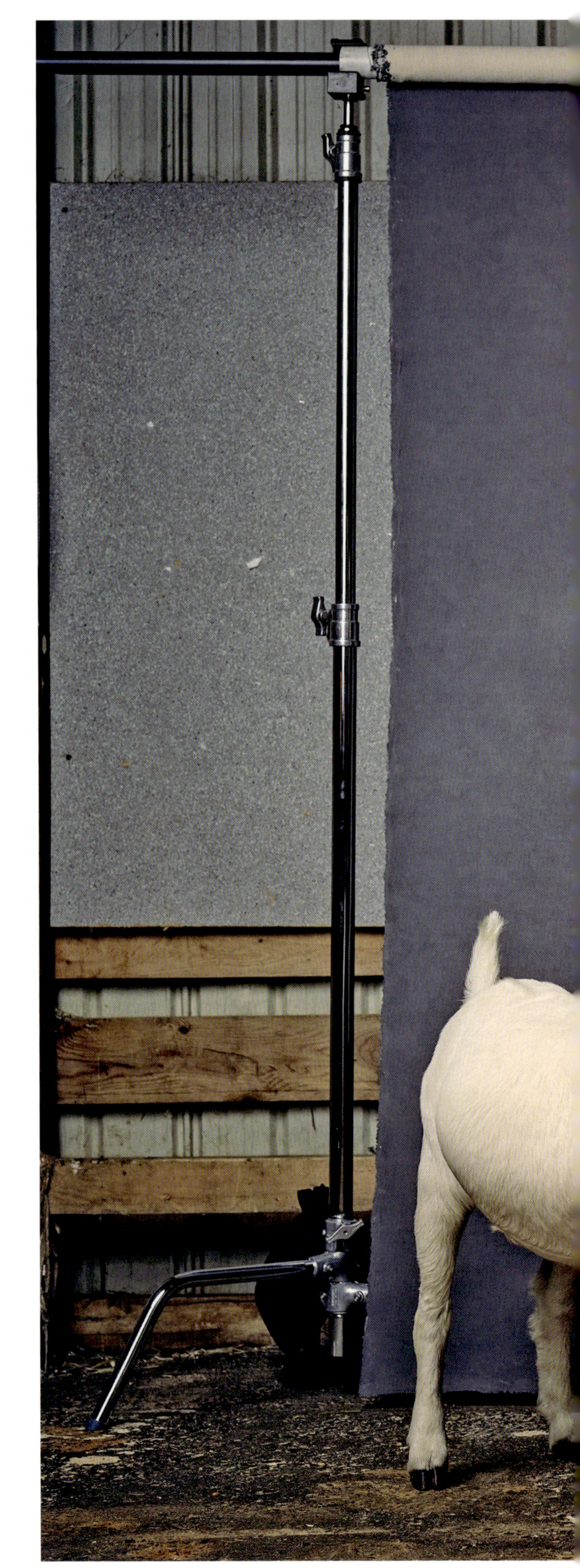

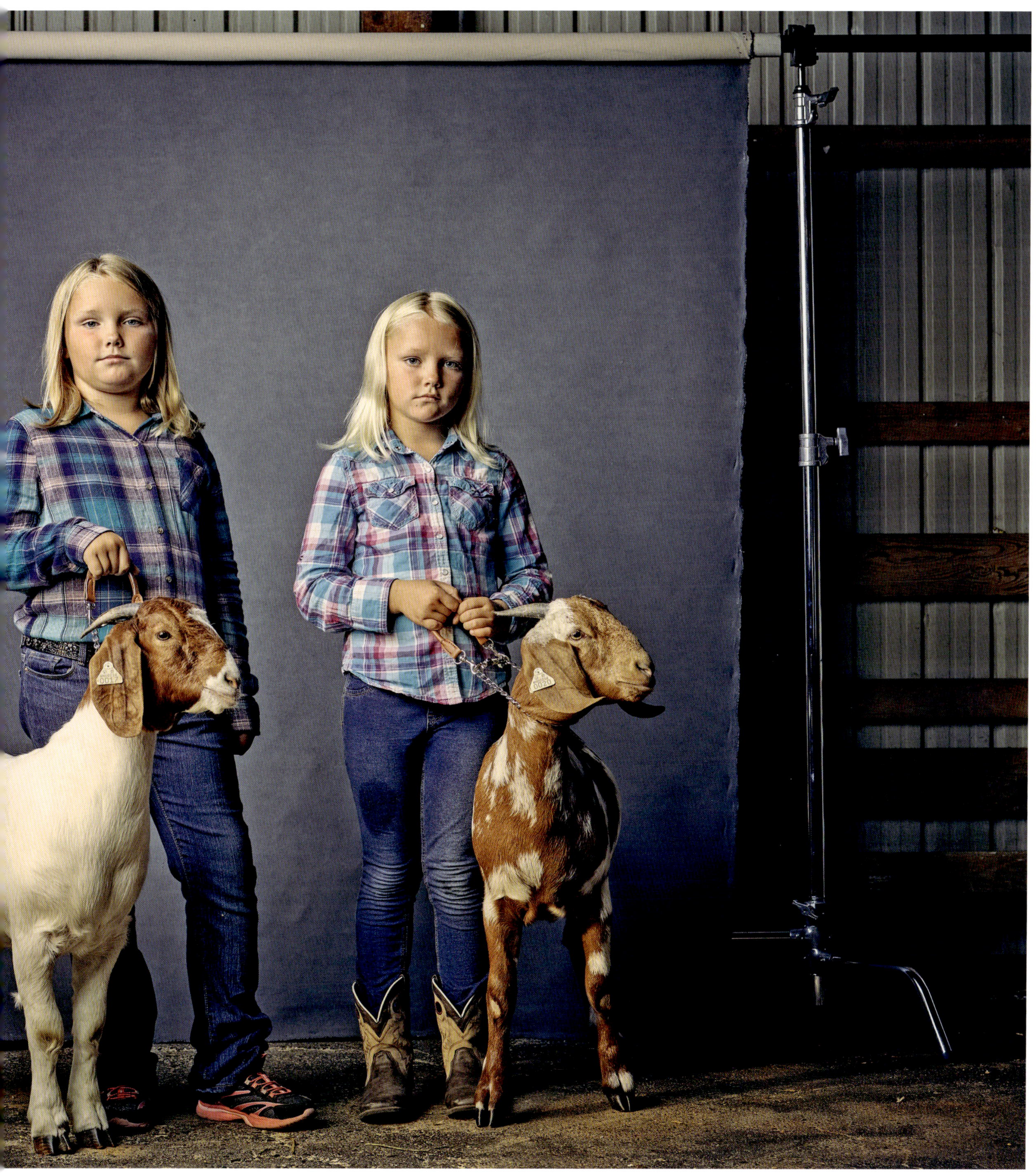

Ava with Sparkle and Ellyana with Dolly, 2016

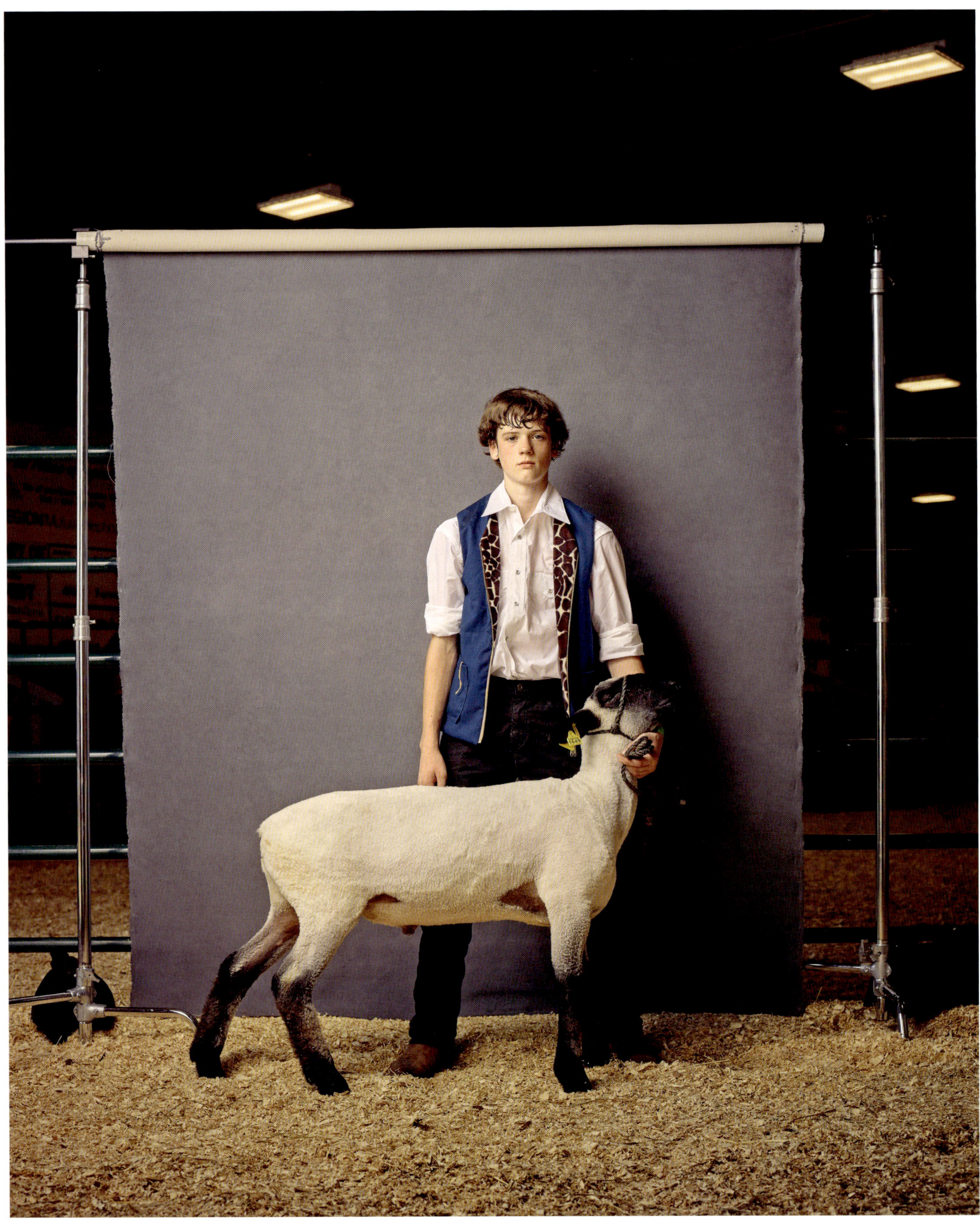

Nick and Sheep, 2016

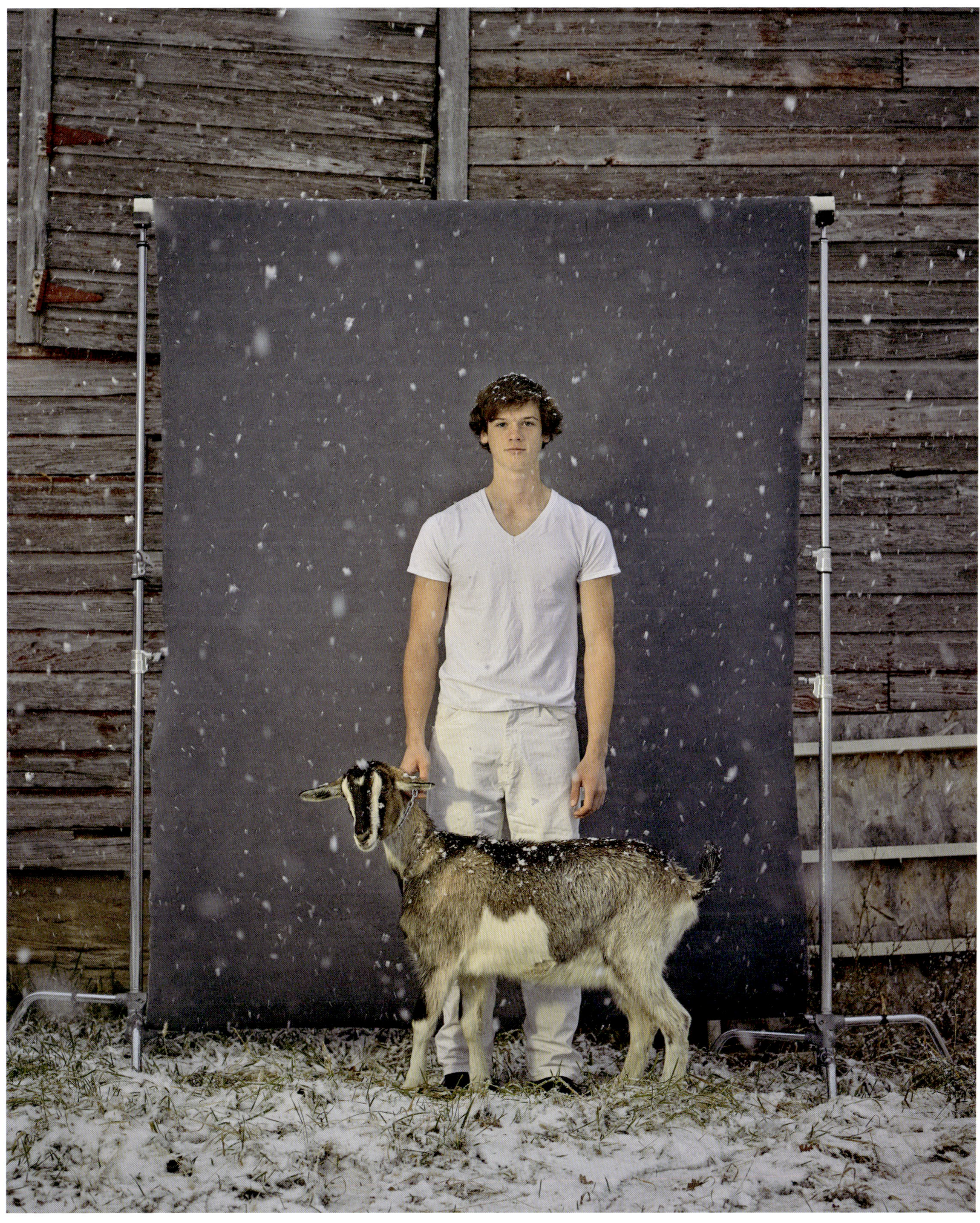

Nick and Fiona, 2020

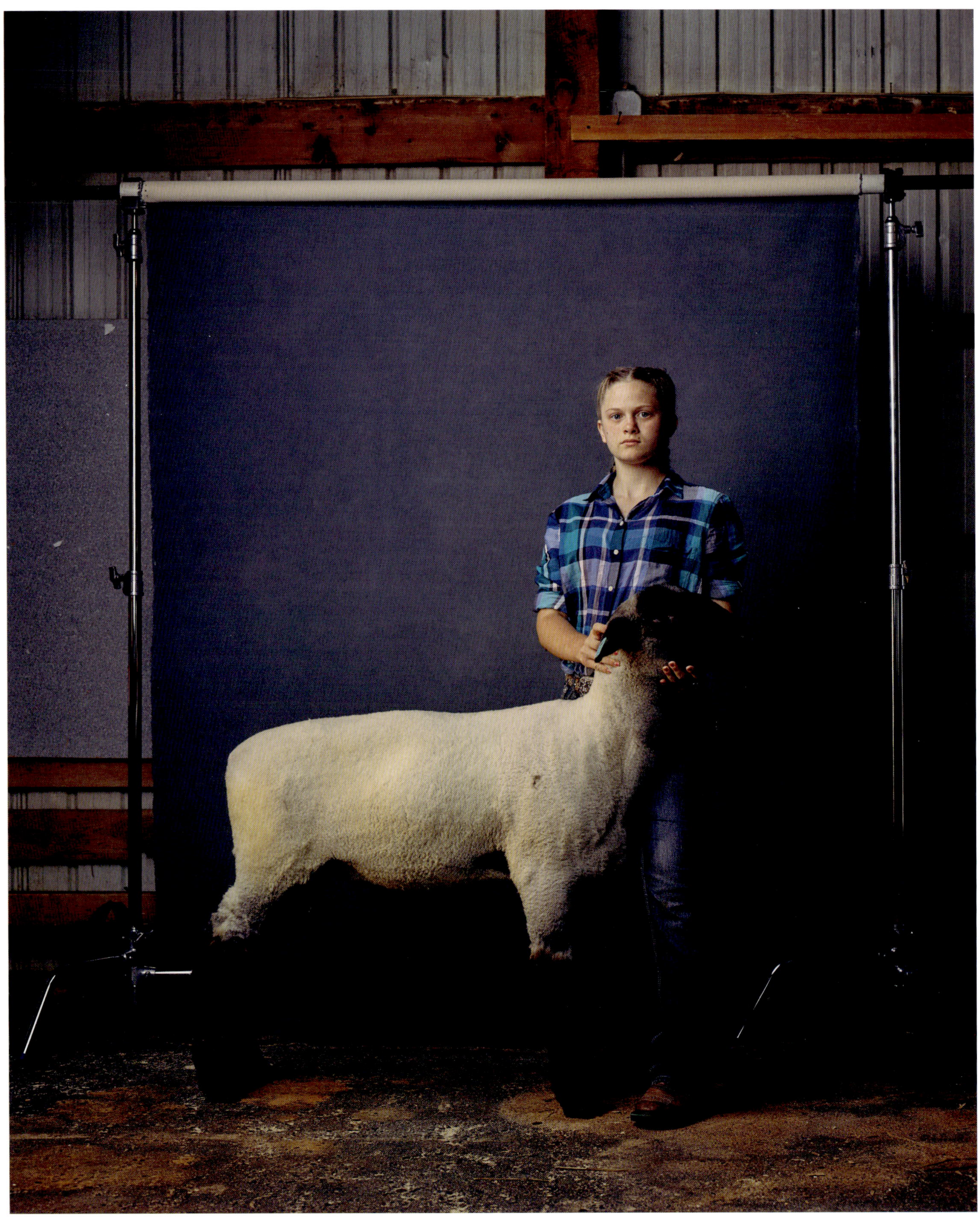

Josilin and Escapé, 2016

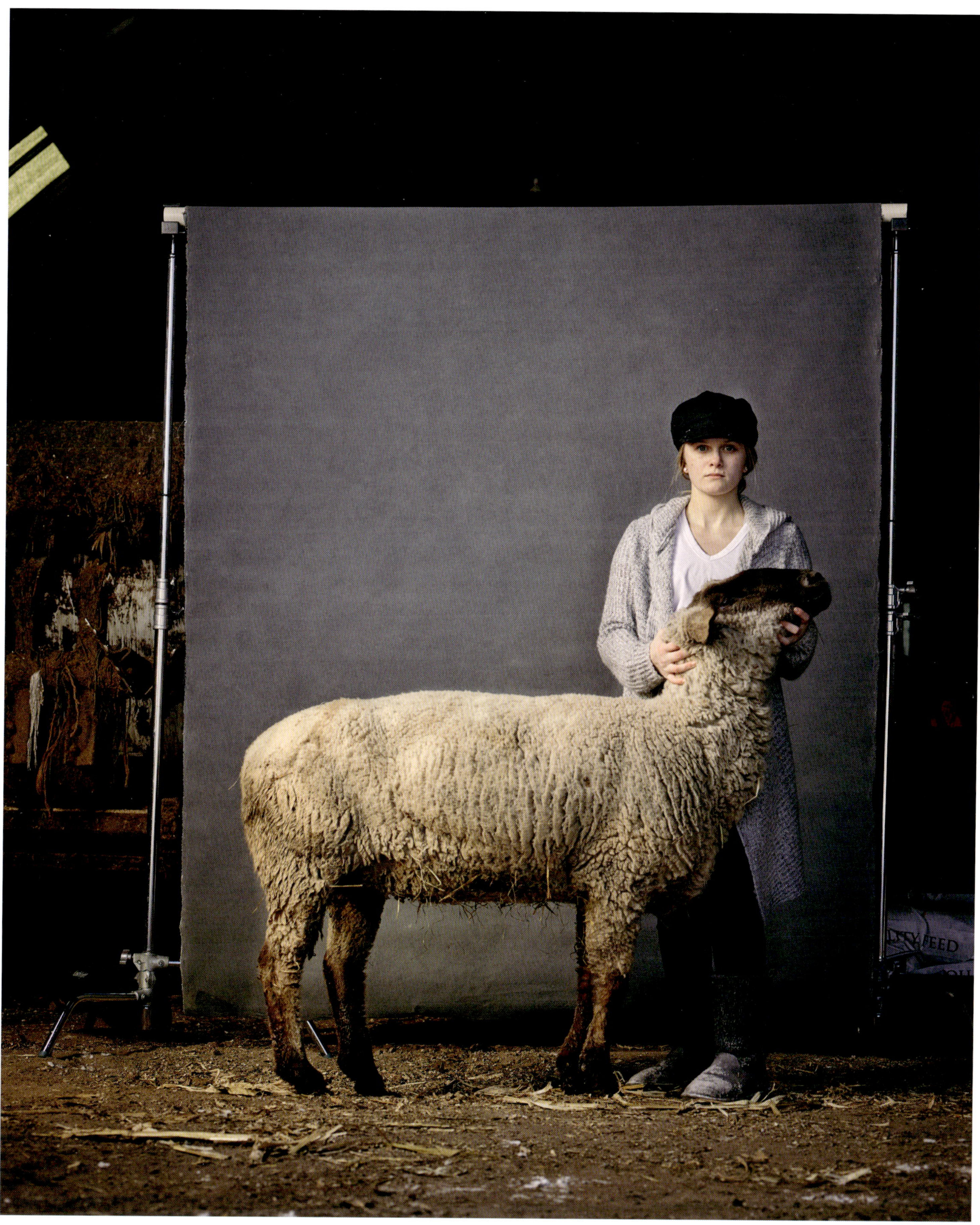

Josilin and Tantor, 2021

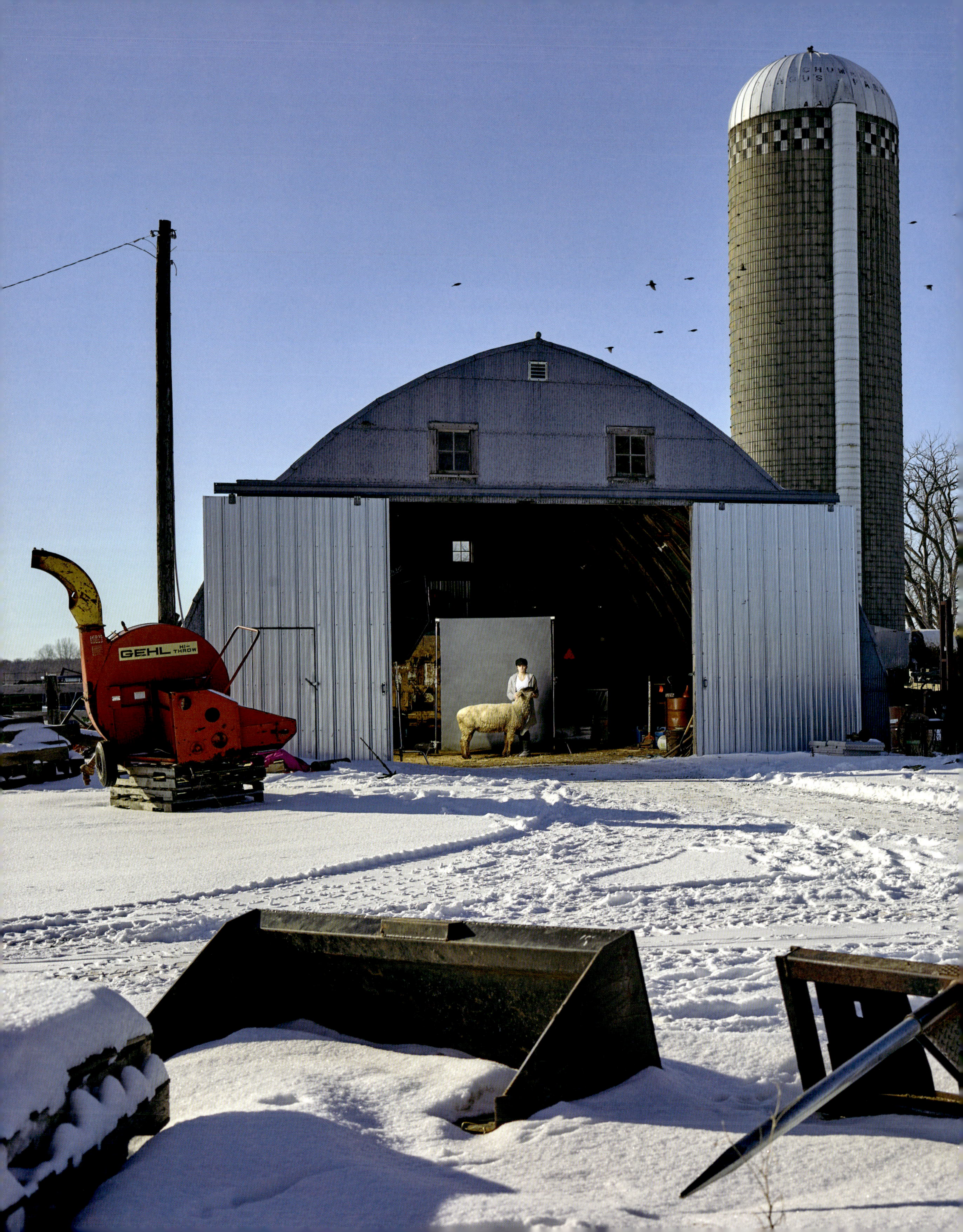

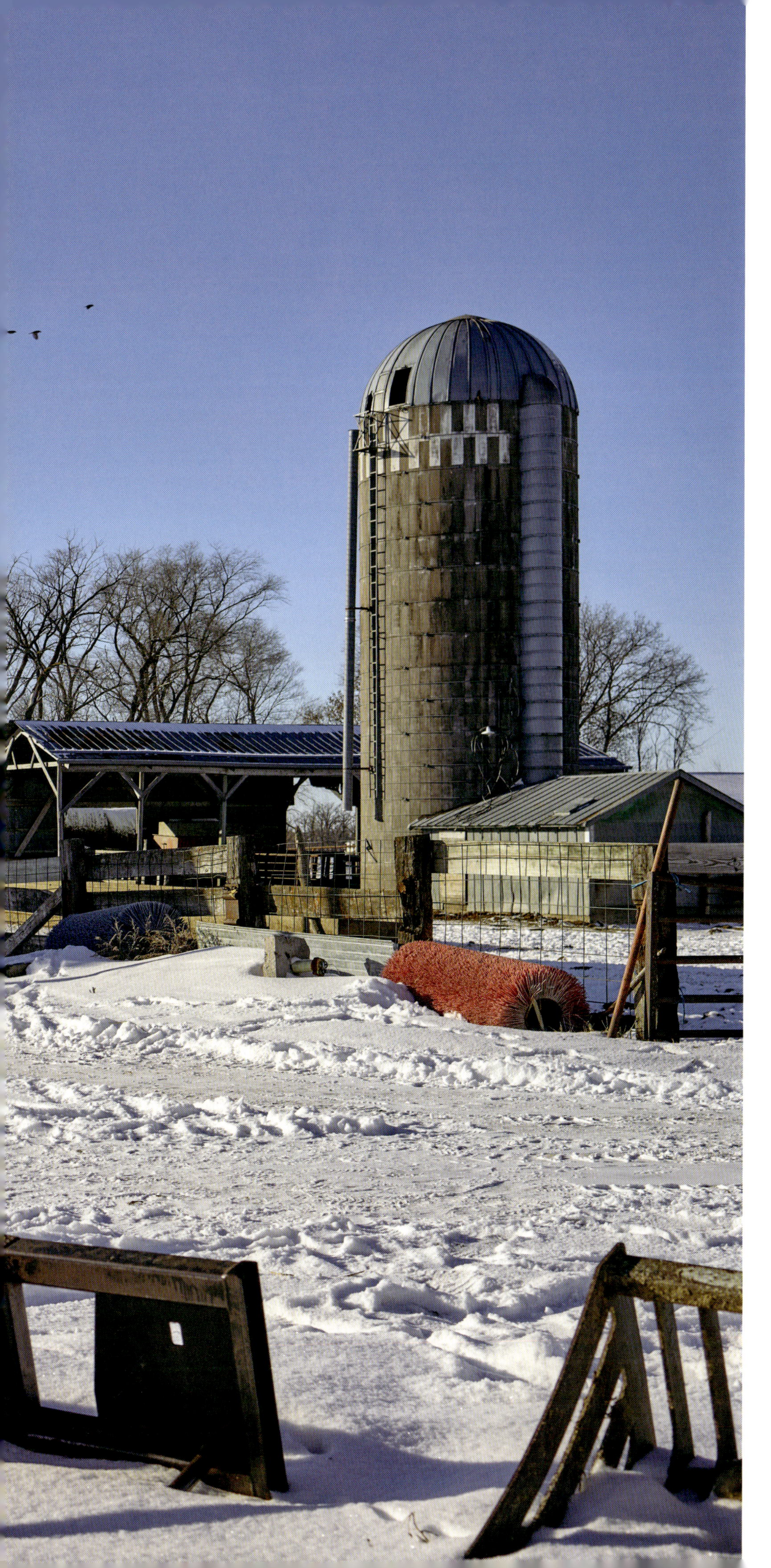

List of Illustrations

All works of art are archival pigment prints, 20 x 24 inches in an edition of 10, 24½ x 32 inches in an edition of 7, and 43 x 53 inches in an edition of 3.

BIOGRAPHY

R. J. Kern was born in 1978 in Peekskill, New York, and lives in Minneapolis with his wife and two children. He studied art, art history, and environmental geography at Colgate University (1996–2000) and completed an MA in geography at the University of Colorado, Boulder (2005).

His work has been included in group exhibitions at the Zurab Tsereteli Museum of Modern Art (Tbilisi), the National Portrait Gallery (London), and the Yixian International Photo Festival (Anhui, China), among others, and in solo exhibitions at the Griffin Museum of Photography (Winchester, MA) and the Plains Art Museum (Fargo). Kern's work has been shown at galleries including Afterimage Gallery (Dallas), Burnet Fine Art & Advisory (Minneapolis), Klompching Gallery (Brooklyn), and Olson-Larsen Galleries (Des Moines).

National Geographic published photos from his series *The Unchosen Ones* and *Out to Pasture* in its November 2017 issue. Kern's first monograph, *The Sheep and the Goats*, was published by Kehrer Verlag in 2018.

Awards and accolades include CENTER 2017 Choice Award Winner (Curator's Choice, First Place), 2017; Taylor Wessing Photographic Portrait Prize (Finalist), 2017; Critical Mass 2018 Top 50, 2018; Royal Photographic Society International Photography Exhibition 160 (Silver Medal), 2017; and three Artist Initiative Grants from the Minnesota State Arts Board (2016, 2018, 2020). Kern was the Commemorative Artist for the 2019 Minnesota State Fair.

Selected Collections
Center for Creative Photography, Tucson
Center for Photography at Woodstock, NY
Fidelity Corporate Art Collection, Boston
General Mills Corporate Collection, Minneapolis
Griffin Museum of Photography, Winchester, MA
Leepa-Rattner Museum of Art, Tarpon Springs, FL
Masur Museum of Art, Monroe, LA
Minneapolis Institute of Art
Minnesota Historical Society, Saint Paul
Museum of Fine Arts, Houston
Museum of Fine Arts, St. Petersburg, FL
Plains Art Museum, Fargo
University of Minnesota Library, Francis V. Gorman Rare Art Book Collection, Minneapolis

ACKNOWLEDGMENTS

The Unchosen Ones wouldn't have been possible without the trust, willingness, and passion of the participants in this project and their families.

Much love to Krista, my wife and best friend, who has supported my work from the beginning. I can't imagine doing any of this without her. My appreciation and love go to my parents, Rob and Marnie Kern, my brother, Sean, and my in-laws, Roger and Carole Olsen, and Trish Wheaton, for their encouragement and support of my artistic career. You have inspired me to grow deep roots in the Midwest and given me a great appreciation for and pride in Minnesota.

The portfolio reviews I have participated in have given me many enriching opportunities, and I have created many friendships through them. These include Alexa Becker, Roy Flukinger, Corey Keller, Robin O'Dell, Christine Renc-Carter, Paula Tognarelli, and Lisa Volpe. I have learned from friends and artists, including Karen Aakre, Mariette Pathy Allen, Eric William Carroll, Tori Gagne, Wayne and Jane Gudmundson, Louise Harris, David Hobby, Stuart Klipper, Eric Kunsman, Felix Kunze, Robert Langham III, Greg MacGregor, Jeanine Michna-Bales, Kyle Olmon, Susan Ressler, Jason Restemayer, Kathleen Richert, Dotan Saguy, Giovanni Savino, Aline Smithson, Herb Snitzer, Keith Taylor, J. P. Terlizzi, and Kelly Thompson.

I'm grateful to David Braun, Philip Brookman, Patrick Coleman, Tasha Kubesh, Casey Riley, Deborah Ultan, and my "technical family," including Dave Gallagher, Ethan Jones, Sarah Oliphant, Jim Ross, Jeff Steaffens, The Photo Touch staff, and assistants Penn Barnes and Anders Olsen.

Many thanks for the support of my galleries: Ralph and Peggy Burnet and the staff at Burnet Fine Art & Advisory, Alex Blaisdell and Jennifer Phelps, as well as Alyss Vernon and Susan Watts at Olson-Larsen Galleries.

Alison Nordström championed this project from the beginning, along with Sarah Leen and Bill Marr, who also shared their keen insights as photo editors. A special thanks to Ewa Monika Zebrowski, my writing buddy extraordinaire, and the Minnesota State Arts Board for their support through Artist Initiative Grants (2016, 2018, 2020) and the Creative Support for Individuals Grant (2021).

Mary Virginia Swanson, you have been a beacon of wisdom, enthusiasm, and encouragement. Joan Brookbank, thank you for believing in this project. I'm grateful to have worked with Amy Wilkins and Robin Brunelle at MW Editions to make this book a reality. Appreciation to Kathy Dowell and Kelly Clark at the Mid-America Arts Alliance for supporting a traveling exhibition of the work.

Thank you to the collectors of my work, including Mark Addicks, Sandy Crary, Nancy and Rolf Engh, Steve Erickson, Tori Gagne, Tom Hoch, Bryn Larsen, Franziska and Bruno Mancia, Sally Miskavige, Joan Morganstern, Susan Opp, Stephanie and Mike Ott, Susie Sproule, and Lynn Stegman.

And finally, thanks to my friends Matt Steaffens, Scott Stebner, and the Scapanski family, whose laughs and talents have shaped this project from the very beginning. We'll never forget, "If you ain't first, you're last."

The Unchosen Ones
By R. J. Kern

Design and layout © 2021 MW Editions, New York
Photography © 2021 R. J. Kern
Essay by Alison Nordström © 2021 Alison Nordström

First published by
MW Editions
www.mweditions.com
info@mweditions.com

Creative Direction: Takaaki Matsumoto, Matsumoto Incorporated, New York
Designer: Robin Brunelle, Matsumoto Incorporated, New York
Editor: Amy Wilkins, Matsumoto Incorporated, New York

Printed and bound by Pristone, Singapore
ISBN: 978-1-7357629-3-7

Library of Congress Control Number: 2021906328

Distribution
D.A.P. / Distributed Art Publishers, Inc.
75 Broad Street, Suite 630
New York, NY 10004
www.artbook.com
orders@dapinc.com

Captions
Jacket, front: *Kenzi and Hootie, Anoka County Fair, Minnesota* (detail), 2016
Front endpaper, recto: *Dustin, Pastoral Study* (detail), 2020
Front endpaper, verso: *Cheyenne, Pastoral Study* (detail), 2020
Frontispiece: *Ava, Pastoral Study* (detail), 2020
Page 4: *Kenzi, Pastoral Study* (detail), 2020
Pages 10–11: *Rylee, Pastoral Study* (detail), 2020
Pages 16–17: *Rylee Walking, Pastoral Study* (detail), 2020
Back endpapers: *Nick, Pastoral Study* (detail), 2020
Jacket, back: *Kenzi and Hootie, Anoka County, Minnesota* (detail), 2020

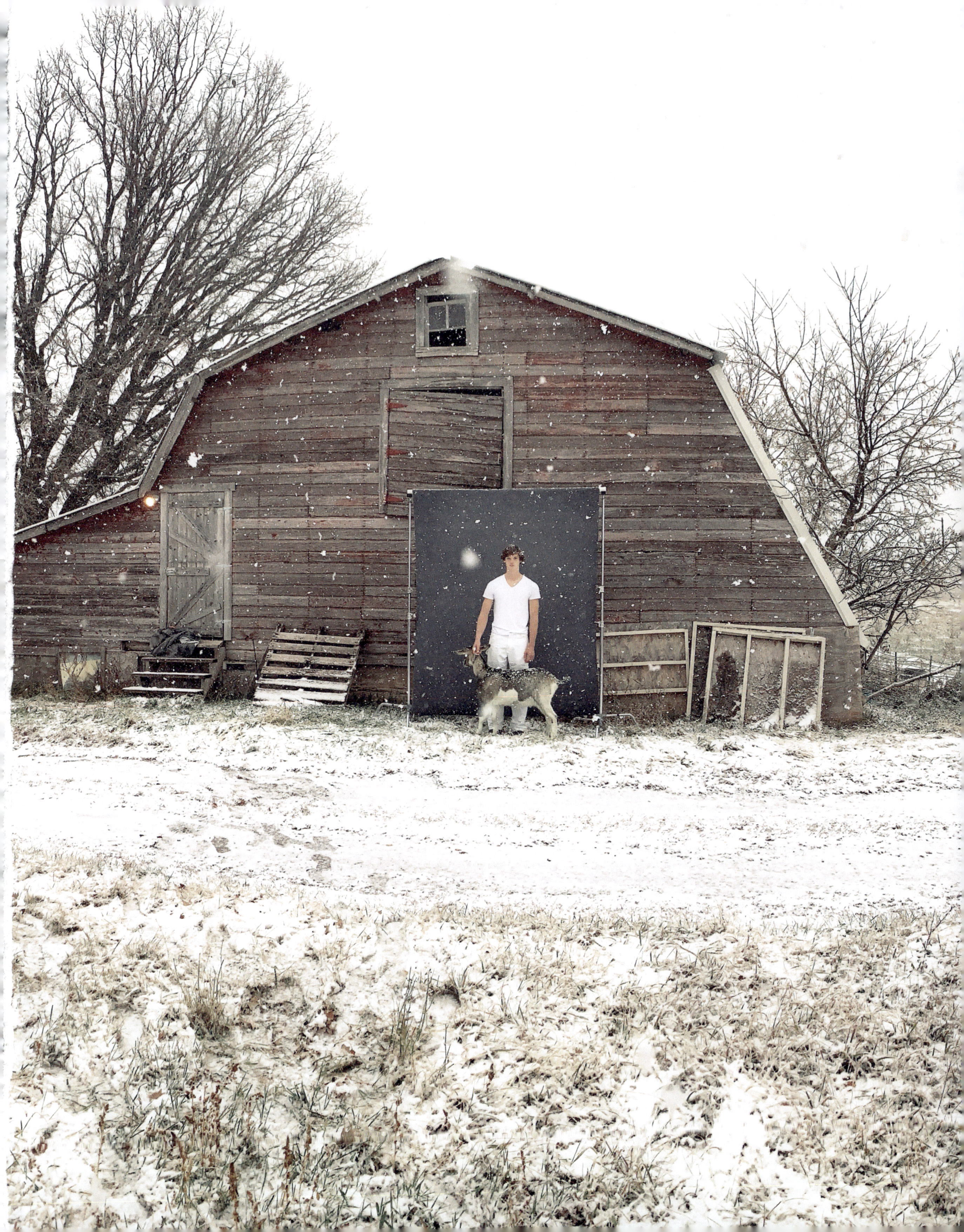

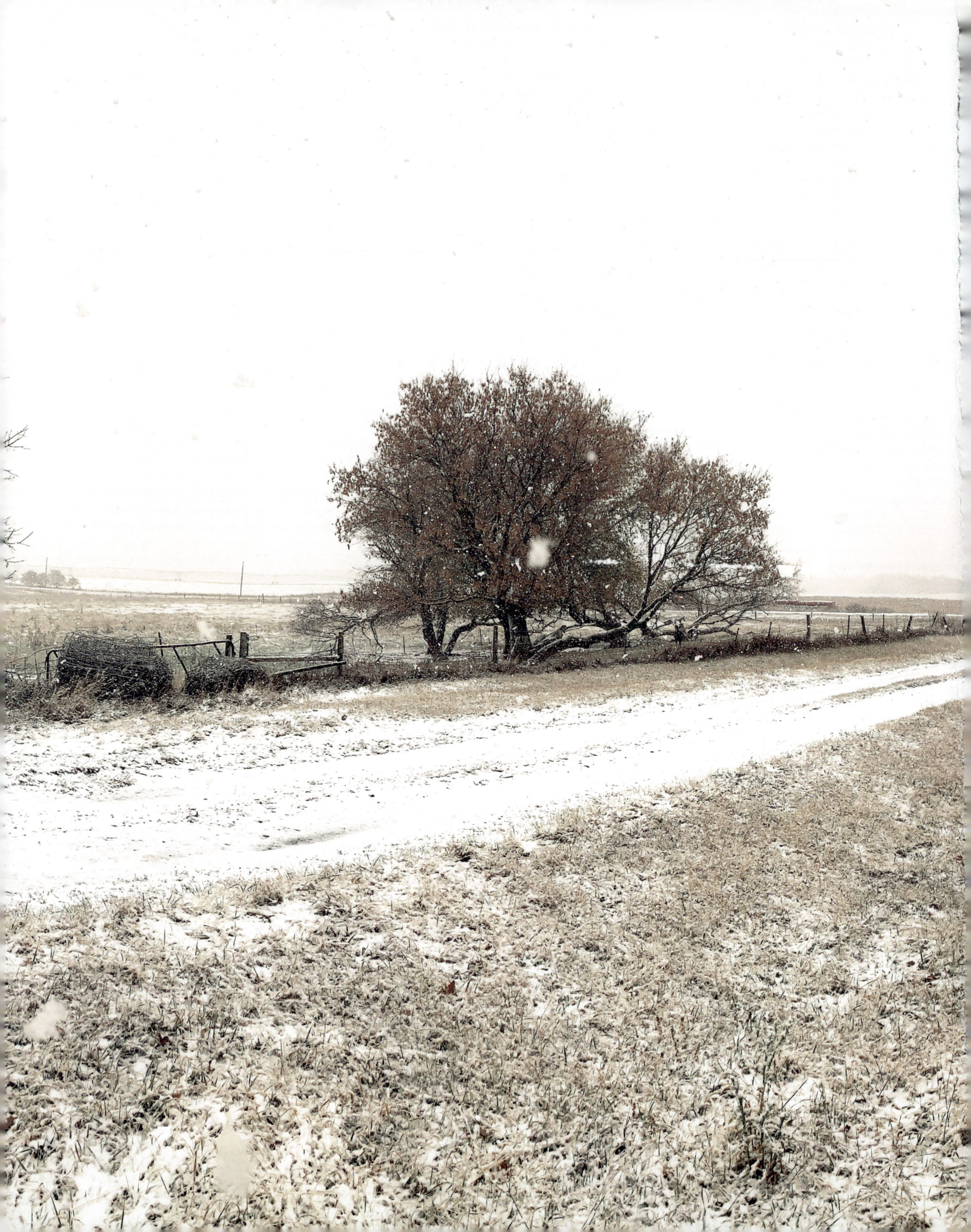